ABSOLUTELY BLEEDING GREEN

THE RAIDERS STORY

First published in 2019

Allen & Unwin
83 Alexander Street
Crows Nest NSW 2065
Australia
Phone: (61 2) 8425 0100
Email: info@allenandunwin.com
Web: www.allenandunwin.com

NATIONAL LIBRARY OF AUSTRALIA

A catalogue record for this book is available from the National Library of Australia

ISBN 978 1 76087 508 4

Index by Puddingburn Publishing Services Pty Ltd
Set in 11/16 pt Minion by Midland Typesetters, Australia
Printed in Australia by McPherson's Printing Group

10 9 8 7 6 5 4 3 2

FSC www.fsc.org MIX Paper from responsible sources FSC® C001695

The paper in this book is FSC® certified. FSC® promotes environmentally responsible, socially beneficial and economically viable management of the world's forests.

ABSOLUTELY BLEEDING GREEN

THE RAIDERS STORY

DAVID HEADON

ALLEN&UNWIN

For three generations of Headons who absolutely bleed green,
and all the loyal family torch-bearers who follow on

CONTENTS

FOREWORD

A few years ago I had a coffee with Dave Headon at a café in Charnwood to discuss the idea of a history of the Canberra Raiders. We were both excited at the prospect. Shortly after, I went to see Raiders Board Chairman, Dr Allan Hawke, putting it to Allan that, with the 30th anniversary of the Raiders' first premiership in 1989 getting close, the time had come to preserve and celebrate the club's story. Of course Allan agreed. The project, a vital addition to the cultural history of the national capital and its surrounds, had begun.

Numerous discussions with Dave since then have rekindled in me all kinds of nostalgic memories. From the time my father Les founded the club—an ambitious organisation from the start, keen to establish its NRL credentials while losing nothing of its country charm—the Raiders have carved out a special place in Rugby League. In the process, the nation's capital gained a genuine identity and, as so many commentators have since observed, a soul. The unbridled crowd scenes in downtown Canberra after the mighty Green Machine's premiership victories in 1989, 1990 and 1994 had to be witnessed to be believed. The club was still a 'family farm', as one writer noted, it was just that the farm had expanded into a whole community and, as the years passed, an entire region.

The attractive way the Raiders played their football was a big part of their lasting appeal, but so too was the quality of the individuals involved. The overwhelming number of boys from the bush recruited in the early years, from New South Wales and Queensland, gave the Raiders a sturdy mix of integrity, humility and spirit of togetherness that we have never lost, despite some testing times.

Through it all, one Raider stands out above the rest. I recall Mal Meninga's enduring impact on our club as if it was yesterday. During our tough inaugural season in 1982 Canterbury Bulldogs Secretary, Peter 'Bullfrog' Moore, sidled up to me with the advice that to be successful the club needed to recruit at least one 'class player'. We embarked on a search-and-locate mission. When I managed to sign Mal in late 1985, the Raiders had secured a future champion. I just didn't anticipate the full extent of his magical influence to come.

The rest, as they say, is history—a history that ranges across a wonderful array of champion players and champion blokes who have put such value into the Raiders name over nearly four decades, building steadily on the foundations of the mostly anonymous footballers throughout the Monaro region who had exhilarated crowds for 100 years before the Raiders began in 1982. This book supplies the essential context of the deeper past, enabling readers to gain a full appreciation of the achievements of the last few decades.

Back in the late 1980s Raider Hall of Famer Dean Lance, at the end of an exemplary career that had produced some of the game's most memorable tackles, commented that the Raiders are more than a football club, they're 'a way of life'. Nothing has changed.

John McIntyre,
Canberra Raiders Patron
and proud Life Member

ACKNOWLEDGEMENTS

When researching and writing this history over the last three years, I have received nothing but encouragement and support from everyone in the Canberra Raiders club. In particular, I would like to thank John McIntyre, Mal Meninga, Ricky Stuart and Chris O'Sullivan, who gave so generously of their time, along with Don Furner, Simon Hawkins, Marian Furner, Anita McIntyre, Allan Hawke, Yvonne Gillett, Tim Sheens and Steve O'Callaghan.

Ros Kelly, Monsignor John Woods, John Mackay and Dennis Richardson provided valuable input, and I was also helped by some sage advice from a number of Raiders players, both past and present. These included Jay Hoffman, Steve Walters, Glenn Lazarus, Steve Jackson, Dave Furner (as player and coach), Andrew McFadden, Brett White, Terry Campese, Sia Soliola and Matt Ford. A discussion I had with the late David Grant's wife, Louise, came at just the right moment to assist me with my work on the club's formative years in the early 1980s.

I did feel the weight of expectation of a few wise spirits, individuals of consequence who are no longer with us but whose inspirational presence was palpable. They are given their due in these pages, though I felt they should also be mentioned separately in my acknowledgments.

I speak of the club's founder, Les McIntyre, genial Fred Daley, first club captain David Grant, the tireless Don Elphick and Meningans' founder, Dr Geoff Caldwell.

I was subtly pushed along by a host of Green Machine enthusiasts such as Wendy Wilson, Gary Dunbar, Dave Rickard, Steve French, Bec Macdonald and the irrepressible Tony 'Victor the Viking' Wood. However, I must give special mention to my wonderful research assistant, Tessa Wooldridge. A Raiders 'tragic', Tessa brought energy, resourcefulness and unfailing good humour to every task I set her. She never let me down. The same can be said about Jason Mathie, the club's commercial and marketing manager, who provided help whenever called upon.

When I was growing up on the northern beaches of Sydney—it seems an age ago now—I spent season after season in the 1950s taking the green double-decker bus to Brookie Oval with my mates to watch the Manly Seagulls in action. Back then, the team comprised mostly locals. It was a different era, many years before the 'Silvertail' Eagles image was created. After living overseas and in Darwin for a number of years, I headed to Seiffert Oval for the first time in mid-1985. Fond memories of my childhood came flooding back. I was hooked, and the expanding Headon clan shared the enthusiasm. We became just another family of ardent fans even before the great Meninga arrived and changed everything.

Finally, I want to thank my wife and best friend, Billie. Writing this book meant that our retirements had to be postponed. I had a million newspaper reports to peruse, and she had to puzzle through my pencil drafts, type the manuscript from go to whoa, correct untidy syntax here and there and gently urge me to ease up on those I was perhaps treating too harshly. Her enjoyment of the unfolding story kept me rolling along.

INTRODUCTION

In their monumental *A Centenary of Rugby League 1908–2008*, Ian Heads and David Middleton describe the Canberra Raiders' first premiership success in 1989 as, quite simply, the code's 'Greatest Grand Final'. Ever. Make no mistake, the Raiders' opponents that day, Warren Ryan's Balmain Tigers, played their part in a game which was one for the ages. But the Raiders' young guns, expertly marshalled by Dean Lance and Mal Meninga, played a brand of football that couldn't, and in the end wouldn't, be denied. Exciting, adventurous, full of precocious ambition and relentless attack.

Older Raider supporters today remember exactly where they were during the late afternoon of 24 September 1989 when John 'Chicka' Ferguson stepped, stepped and stepped again into history, Chris O'Sullivan kicked a crucial extra-time field goal and Steve Jackson bullocked his way over for the match-winning try that ensured him free dining-out rights at any Raider function for the rest of his life.

Renowned Australian novelist Tom Keneally, a Manly Sea Eagles fan, joined a host of ecstatic commentators struggling to find words worthy enough to describe the game they had just watched. Keneally perhaps summed up the euphoria best when he declared it was 'a movie script that came to life', a game destined to be 'a unique memory'. Ricky Stuart's boots (given to him by fellow-Queanbeyan product, rugby legend David Campese) were compared by Keneally to 'fragments of the True Cross'. Too far-fetched? Not for the hordes of Raider true believers.

For the fledgling Raider club (with its wide geographical reach across the Limestone Plains and beyond), this first climax in 1989 was early reward indeed. But the achievement also provided a ringing endorsement for the notable history of Rugby League in southern New South Wales, with its honoured traditions throughout the Monaro and surrounds—traditions and inter-town rivalries virtually as old as anywhere in Australia.

The first European visitors to the Canberra region pitched their tents in 1820 on what is today called Acton Peninsula, a small, fertile area nurtured by the Ngunnawal for many millennia, and now a stone's throw from the Australian National University. Within decades, only a few miles away up a dirt track north in Ginninderra, Canberra's rich sporting history began. First it was wallaby-shooting, horse-racing and cricket. Then Rugby Union in the 1870s. When Rugby League, the professional game, began in Sydney in 1908 it took just over ten years for it to plant lasting roots in the Canberra–Queanbeyan area.

While the 'foundation' Sydney Rugby League teams rightly boast of their longevity, the occasional pundit still persists in labelling the Canberra Raiders as johnny-come-latelys. Such comments are either naïve or ill-informed, or both. For *not only* did the Raiders become the first non-Sydney team (with Illawarra) to play in the Sydney competition; *not only* did the club win a classic Grand Final a mere eight years after its controversial entry into the competition; *not only* did the team go on to win two more premierships in quick succession playing football that arguably re-set the parameters of the modern game; *not only* did they do this by introducing to the code a raft of fresh, new champions, and a few older ones, many of whom have gone on to establish the enlightened coaching patterns of the 21st-century game—*but they did all of this* starting from modest beginnings with a group of players whose character, 1982 right up to the present, has been matched only by their pride in the distinctive lime-green jersey.

When I was considering titles for this history a couple of years ago, the *Canberra Times* newspaper ran a story on the new ACT Australian of the Year, Raider cult hero Alan Tongue. The story featured an old photo of Tonguey training with his (then) ultra–Gen Y teammate, a young, spiky-haired, blond-tipped Jarrod Croker. Asked to recall Tongue as a player years later, captain Croker summed him up perfectly: 'For the size of him, he was one of the toughest blokes I ever played with. Guys like that . . . made you want to come back every week and pull that green jersey on. That's what it's all about. You play for guys like that every week . . . You see guys like Tonguey who absolutely bleed green.'

When present-day coach, club and rugby league legend Ricky Stuart took up his new post in late 2013 he could not conceal his delight in coming home. Stuart soon made it clear that he wanted the Raiders back on their rightful pedestal, after some lean years, as one of rugby league's leading clubs. A product of the powerhouse St Edmund's College in the heart of Canberra, Stuart has many times stated in the media that a crucial part of the pursuit of rugby league excellence involves his players understanding their place in the history of the club.

The pioneer Raider players might not have realised it when they ran onto Queanbeyan's Seiffert Oval for the first time in a competition game against Western Suburbs on a mild March evening in 1982, but they had become overnight ambassadors for a game which had been played with gusto in the region for over 60 years. Stuart strives to ensure that the present-day group is well aware of its responsibilities and connection to the past. When Chicka Ferguson was special guest in the dressing room before a Raiders game a few years ago the coach afterwards noted with satisfaction that his players 'feel the history and . . . respect our past players had for the club. Seeing someone like John come in . . . they see this is more than a football club. It's a lifestyle . . . the players have their teammates as their family, that's what this club is built on.'

Canberra Rugby League, Raiders football. This great club has a wonderful story to tell. The time has come to tell it.

1 ROOTS

FREDERICK CAMPBELL TO 1921

Early newspaper reports confirm that the first games of contact football in the Australian colonies were played by members of the military. In 1829, a journalist for the *Sydney Monitor* newspaper noted for his readers that 'privates in the barracks are in the habit of amusing themselves with the game of football'. What those privates were actually playing we'll never know, but within a few decades in England and in New South Wales the biff and barge of some version of footy acquired rules to create a code that had been developing as part of English folk football for hundreds of years. Some participants insisted on using their feet; others wanted to pick the ball up and run with it. William Webb Ellis is usually cited as the first notable ball carrier, back in 1823.

The renowned Rugby school in England produced a first set of rules in written form for the running game during the 1840s. In colonial Sydney, the Albert Cricket Club published the codified 'Rules of Football as Played at Rugby' in the club's annual reports of 1862 and 1863. Throughout the 1860s in New South Wales scratch matches were regularly organised, with the first well-publicised game taking place in Sydney's Hyde Park on 17 June 1865. It took a few more years, but eventually a pattern of inter-school invitation games paved the way for the formation of the Southern Rugby Football Union (later the New South Wales Rugby Football Union) in 1874. This was the same year that the first two country school rugby teams were established, one in the west at All Saints' College, Bathurst, and the other down south at St Patrick's College, Goulburn. The game was spreading, taking root.

Foundation years

In these formative years, rugby found its home among the middle classes of the 'Mother Colony' of New South Wales, so it was hardly surprising that the sons of the more prosperous citizenry—professional men, landed gentry, merchants and miners who had struck it rich—had established a Sydney University Football Club by the mid-1860s. On 19 August 1865, the students played the Sydney Football Club in 'an exciting struggle' marred, it seems, by 'a misunderstanding with regard to the rules'.

The captain of the University side that day was 21-year-old Frederick Campbell, grandson of the influential founder of Canberra's Duntroon Station, the merchant, Robert Campbell. Born in 1846 and educated at the prestigious Cholmeley School in Highgate on the edge of London (where he was a classmate of renowned Australian novelist, Marcus Clark, best known for the classic convict novel, *For the Term of His Natural Life*), Fred returned to Australia in 1864 following the accidental death of his older brother at Cambridge and, shortly after, the death of his mother. He loved his rugby and played a leading role in the establishment in Sydney of the University's rugby club and the introduction of the game to his fellow-colonists living on the distant Monaro plains.

Campbell purchased Yarralumla homestead in 1882. Within ten years he had made a series of such splendid additions and adornments to the main residence that when Canberra was confirmed as the nation's capital in 1908, and the Commonwealth had acquired all the land it needed, Campbell's fine home became the Governor-General's residence. It still is.

If the rugby game was firmly in the hands of well-to-do colonists in Sydney and country New South Wales in the 1860s and '70s, this situation changed completely in the 1880s and '90s for a few reasons, the most important of them when working men for the first time gained more leisure hours on the weekends. As historian Chris Cunneen points out in *League of a Nation* (1996), by 1888 banks and business houses were closed on Saturdays at twelve o'clock and within twenty years the only workers not getting a half-day holiday on Saturday afternoons were shop employees. The composition of rugby teams altered substantially as a result. Working men revelled in the toughness of the game and many had the physical attributes to succeed. There was only one problem: as the game got rougher, injuries increased. For those working-class players who got badly hurt there was no financial compensation or assistance whatsoever.

It did not take long for the issue of payment of players to be discussed, even within doggedly amateur, middle-class rugby circles. In 1894–95, England's workers with a liking for rugby, virtually all of them located in the industrial cities of the north, took action and created a set of new rules for what they called the Northern Union game—the first version of Rugby League. It would be professional. Players did not get much money, but whatever they got helped.

Australia embraced the new code after a boisterous meeting attracting about 50 men of influence took place at Bateman's Crystal Hotel in George Street, Sydney, on 8 August 1907, to establish the New South Wales Rugby League. Henry 'Harry' Hoyle, a 54-year-old former Labor politician known for his fiery trade union speeches, was elected president; J.J. Giltinan, an entrepreneur and former commercial salesman with a passion for all sport, became honorary secretary; and the legendary cricketer Victor Trumper assumed the treasurer's duties.

It was clear at the outset that the new game (called 'Rugby League' in Australia from the start) had to be taken seriously by rugby's diehards. Those who chose to ignore it initially were forced to recognise the challenge posed when, in August 1909, the 'Great Defection' occurred:

fourteen rugby union Wallaby players changed codes. Considering their day jobs, this should not have surprised anyone. Four were labourers, two painters, two carpenters, a fish seller, storeman, boilermaker, clerk, wharfie, journalist, boat builder, draper, fireman, tailor, compositor, cleaner and two others of vocation unknown.

Here was proof positive of the extraordinary changes that had dramatically altered rugby's playing ranks. Until then, the game's adherents had been confident the code would survive the league threat. The 'Great Defection', together with the vital signing to league of the most celebrated player in either code, Herbert Henry 'Dally' Messenger, gave Rugby League a momentum that—when it continued to be played during the Great War years and rugby was not—it would never lose.

The strength of southern football

From the early 1870s some of the young men of the Limestone Plains decided that they too would like to pick up a footy and run with it. Settlements near and far produced scratch teams, among them Michelago, Williamsdale, Tuggeranong, Gundaroo and Bungendore, and the more distant and populated Goulburn, Yass and Cooma. Records suggest that the first inter-town game of rugby down south, between Queanbeyan and Yass, took place in 1878, in the same decade that the code's fortunes accelerated in Sydney.

The Ginninderra community had a special advantage from the start. In 1864, by coincidence the year that Frederick Campbell returned to Australia, the Cricketers' Arms Hotel at One Tree Hill (a stone's throw from what is now the ACT village of Hall in northern Canberra) opened for business. It became a hub for a range of sporting activities, attracting the locals in droves and many settler sportsmen from further afield. So popular did the Cricketers' Arms become that when Sydney-based politician, committed republican E.W. O'Sullivan, stood for and won the NSW Legislative Assembly seat of Queanbeyan in October 1885, he made it his business at election time over the next twenty years to travel down from Sydney, shout the bar at the hotel and move with dramatic flair into a recitation of his signature poem, *Advance Australia*. Typically, as the *Goulburn Evening Penny Post* recorded in July 1894, O'Sullivan would then treat 'his audience to a couple of excellent songs, after which he took his departure amid cheers'. On other occasions he made good use of the balcony of Queanbeyan's Royal Hotel to deliver his persuasive mix of Federationist, feminist and sporting sentiments. He was an avowed believer in the exciting possibilities ahead for the Australian community, 'a remarkably athletic people'.

Frederick Campbell was patron of the Queanbeyan District Football Club in the mid-1890s while Edward O'Sullivan, for two decades (1885–1904) Queanbeyan's activist Legislative Assembly member, was the patron of the Ginninderra Football Club about the same time.

Points of the Lazarus sundial

In 1860, Nathan Moses Lazarus donated a sundial to his adopted hometown of Queanbeyan. His gift adorns a small square in front of the Visitors' Centre in the town today. A civic-minded, free migrant son of a Jewish couple who had themselves migrated from Holland to Britain, Nathan was well aware that his father, employed in the textile industry, had worked hard to feed and clothe his family in inner-city London. Times were tough. Nathan decided to strike out for the colonies to seek a new life.

Nathan Moses Lazarus's great-great-grandson is Glenn Patrick Lazarus, the 'brick with eyes', an integral part of the Canberra Raiders' machine in the club's first two historic premiership wins in 1989 and 1990. Glenn is a confirmed Raiders and Rugby League legend, but more on that later.

The Lazarus family's involvement in all aspects of early rugby in Queanbeyan was one of the mainstays of the game's popularity in the town in the decades before the Great War. The *Queanbeyan Age* records that a 'Lazarus' played in a game against Cooma in June 1882. This young man was certainly one of the eight sons (and ten children) of Nathan and his wife, Harriet Grogan—an English-born, Roman

Catholic woman for whom Nathan converted to Catholicism. The resilient Harriet had her first child aged 36, her last child aged 52 and lived to be 100! It's all there in the genes, as they say. The Lazarus who played in the Cooma fixture was probably the third son, Isaiah, and the game he played in took place exactly 100 years before the Canberra Raiders' inaugural season in the Sydney Rugby League competition. Members of the Lazarus family regularly assumed administrative positions and team selection responsibilities, but their contribution was just one family expression of many in a thriving, 19th-century rural township intent on growth and, with it, enhanced quality of life.

At the time of Federation in 1901, Queanbeyan fielded teams variously named the Golden Eagles, the Young Men's Football Club (YMFC, organised by the local Presbyterian minister), the Boys' Club and the Seniors. Family members could be pitted against one another, as was the case in July 1906 when a 'Lazarus L.' turned out for the Warrigals against a 'Lazarus A'. The A. Lazarus was Alf, Alfred William, a grand uncle of Glenn who, unlike his grandnephew, was an attacking centre. The *Queanbeyan Age* reported on the July 1906 game that he 'smartly picked up the ball and evading opponents, crossed the line and scored'. A more likely role model in the family tree for the Raiders' Glenn was probably his great grandfather's brother, Isaiah, who was badly injured playing his part in a June 1888 Queanbeyan–Goulburn game that was a particularly willing contest. As the *Queanbeyan Age* reported: 'In one of the scrimmages a Queanbeyan player collared a Goulburn man about the region of the scalp; the man so collared resented this treatment by giving his opponent a gentle shaking, upon which the Queanbeyan player referred to, in a clear and melodious tone, informed several of the visitors that if they "required anything", his address was Royal Hotel, back yard.'

Intense inter-town and inter-settlement rivalries began at this time, with the Queanbeyan teams comprising just some of a number of regional teams vying for local supremacy. These included the Cooma Rovers, Cooma Carltons, Cooma Juniors and Cooma Waratahs, Yass, Goulburn Pioneers, Gunning, Bungendore, Braidwood, Captains Flat,

Numeralla and Hall. In 1905 Queanbeyan hosted a Sydney Tramways team and in 1906 teams from Queanbeyan, Yass, Goulburn and Cooma began competing for the coveted Ryrie Cup. Queanbeyan and Braidwood agreed to do battle for the Mandelson Cup, probably the first time in the region that a well-known hotel owner had sponsored a sporting event. It would not be the last.

Amenable locations for post-match gatherings were an important part of country football's appeal from the start. For many years, the Cricketers' Arms was the best-known spot in the area but as soon as towns (in the region and across the country) began to be more than a few tents, shanties and pockets of itinerants, multi-purpose hotels of all shapes and sizes were built. The Cricketers' Arms became even more popular post-Federation, especially when Morris 'Mon' Lazarus took over as licensee in August 1905. Mon, the oldest son of original patriarch Nathan, made many improvements to the hotel, which thrived until 1908 when Yass/Canberra was announced as the site of the nation's new capital city and Commonwealth priorities took precedence.

Queanbeyan's expanding population in the new century inevitably led to more pubs. Three were popular haunts for sporting clubs of all kinds, particularly the rugby fraternity: Hungerford's Victoria Hotel (favoured by the Golden Eagles team), the Royal Hotel and McPherson's Commercial Hotel. Alex McPherson, born in Dingo Creek, was the first proprietor of McPherson's. For a while this pub was probably the Queanbeyan sportsman's first choice; later, the name became better known locally because of the McPhersons' violin-playing, thespian and footballing son, Alexander 'Barney' McPherson, another talented Queanbeyan youngster who went on to play first grade in Sydney.

When the unimaginatively named 'Queanbeyan Football Club' team was renamed the 'Warrigals' after the native dog, the dingo, it took immediate confidence from the rebranding. On the back of this initiative, the Warrigals designed a new guernsey and, henceforth, their players turned out in a distinctive blue and white horizontal strip. The Warrigals quickly became Queanbeyan's most successful team, a situation that remained basically unchanged through the Great War and for some years after.

A bare three weeks after the Royal Military College (Duntroon) formally opened in 1911, the cadets put a rugby team together to play the best side in the region. It had to be the Warrigals. Over the next decade, the ranks of the college would be decimated, first on the hills of Gallipoli and after that in the mud of the Western Front. While the cadets' team would continue to play rugby post-war, for many years it carried on under the terrible shadow of young lives lost. The game was not the same. Nor was it for their first-ever opponents, but for entirely different reasons. The Warrigals' game quite literally changed completely. Why and how did this happen?

2

A LEAGUE OF THEIR OWN

1921–81

With the formation of the Canberra Raiders still six decades away, Rugby League in the Canberra–Queanbeyan region began in 1921. A pre-season Warrigals Rugby Club meeting in March at Queanbeyan's Triumph Theatre Supper Room, with a 'large attendance', opened in the usual way with no hint of what was to come. Office bearers were elected, Mr E.F. Land donated a football and, not surprisingly for the times given the lively and 'intelligent democracy' of Queanbeyan (as politician Edward O'Sullivan once memorably put it), 'a lot of discussion took place with regard to the entertainment of visiting teams'. Then, according to the *Queanbeyan Age*, a 'reorganisation of the club was decided upon' and on a motion by Messrs F. Hayes and Joe O'Rourke 'it was decided to adopt the League game for the coming season'.

Such bland newspaper reportage conceals a truly momentous occasion. It would change the face of sport and cultural life in southern New South Wales, and also in what had been officially named in 1911 the 'Federal Capital Territory' (in 1938, the Australian Capital Territory). The new secretary-elect, Ancel Kidmore Johnston, was the same man who had been guiding the development of the Warrigals rugby side but he responded to his amended role with relish, in the next 'few happy years' (as he would recall) serving as secretary and president of the League Blue and Whites, as well as a group football delegate, group selector and an official umpire.

Rugby League begins

History was created on 22 May 1921 when the Warrigals team played its opening game of the season against Bungendore, the 'first match under Rugby League rules' as reported in the *Queanbeyan Age*. The journalist penning this story, clearly close to the team and a tough critic of its performances—and apparently unmoved by the club's decision to change codes—went on to write that, with Rugby League:

> Although faster than Union rules, members still go on in the same lackadaisical style and forget that 'nick' is required to give the game their best . . . Girls and pictures and skating are very nice in their place, but when they interfere with the grand old games, cut them out.

In the same *Queanbeyan Age* report, a few of the games ahead were flagged: against Yass, the new (Canberra city) Brickyards team, Captains Flat and Goulburn. Over the next few months, the Warrigals were only moderately successful. While the team was, according to one report, 'defeated but not disgraced' against arch-rivals Yass, the Warrigals' hierarchy felt that a shake-up was needed. An adventurous plan was hatched, a bold endeavour concocted. The club would try to entice down to Queanbeyan one of Australia's best-known sportsmen: Sydney dual international Bob Craig. Someone in the Warrigals camp had probably read a column by 'Tric' in the massively popular *Smith's Weekly* the year before, under the heading 'All-Round Athlete':

> I nominate R.R. (Bob) Craig as one of Australia's most versatile athletes. A one-time champion swimmer of Australia (100 yards), he next turned to Soccer football. Repped Rugby Union and toured Britain with the Wallabies in 1908; next visited the Homeland with Kangaroos under League banner, and for the next ten seasons led Balmain forwards. He is now a delegate

> to the NSW Rugby League executive, and is secretary of Balmain Club. At the Leichhardt baths recently, he stripped for his club team in 100 yards swimming event, and surprised all hands.

Craig was approached. To the delight of the adventurous Warrigals, he accepted their offer.

Bob Craig

The Bob Craig story is a compelling one by any standards of elite achievement. He deserves a biography of his own. Born Robert Robertson Craig on the first day of spring 1881 in suburban Balmain to a working-class mum and dad, he became an apprentice boilermaker at Mort's Dock, the city's ship-building works just down the road from his home. At a young age he was recognised as an extraordinarily gifted athlete in a number of sports but it was in rugby and Rugby League that he really shone. At about five feet nine inches in height and weighing thirteen and a half stone, he was one of the heavier players of his footballing era and he used these physical attributes to telling effect, earning a reputation for his tough, uncompromising defence in both codes. After being a part of the controversial 'Great Defection', Craig joined the Balmain club in 1910 and soon achieved representative honours. In 1912 he was at the peak of a professional career in club and international Rugby League after some outstanding representative years in rugby during which he played for New South Wales against Queensland and Great Britain in 1908, toured with the Wallabies to Britain and North America in 1908–09 (playing fourteen games) and, triumphantly, being a member of the Australian gold medal–winning rugby team at the 1908 London Olympics.

In Sydney club football Craig's Balmain side carved out an enviable record, winning four successive premierships from 1915 to 1918. Craig's reasons for not going to the war in Europe are not known, though it is likely that they had something to do with both his working-class background and family circumstances. At the time, many labour and union newspapers expressed reservations about the Empire 'cause', particularly in 1917 and 1918 when the two conscription referenda aggressively promoted by Prime Minister Billy Hughes opened up such deep divisions in the moral and religious fabric of the Australian community—wounds that would take decades to heal.

As the terrible impact of the Great War finally began to ease in the 1920s, and Craig's playing days came to an end, he set about trying his hand at a number of possible future careers. When he accepted the offer of the Queanbeyan Warrigals to head down south and coach the team for the remaining matches of the 1921 season, his search for a career after his active playing days had tentatively begun.

It was fortunate for the Warrigals that in July 1921, when Craig applied for the job of team manager for the forthcoming Kangaroo tour of Great Britain, he just missed out in the final selection round. Within a fortnight, on 11 August, he had arrived in Queanbeyan to take up a position variously referred to as 'trainer' and 'playing coach' for which he was paid £50. It is not clear from newspaper accounts if he did actually pull on the blue and white strip, but it did not seem to matter. A middling Warrigal season transformed immediately into a successful one. In the words of the *Queanbeyan Age*, Craig 'got to work on the players' with his 'words of wisdom . . . dropped in his epigrammatic way'. The improvement was so dramatic that the two losses to arch-rivals Yass before he arrived were forgotten when the resurgent Warrigals won 11–0 in the first game back in Queanbeyan and followed that up with a 41–0 rout in the second game. Amidst exuberant celebrations, the coveted Moore Cup was back in the Warrigal's trophy cabinet, as the *Queanbeyan Age* recorded:

> What a good football coach can accomplish! Full of hope, Yass footballers went to Queanbeyan last week in quest of the Moore Cup, and received the shock of their lives. They were badly defeated, outclassed, Queanbeyan winning by 41 points to nil. Yass players were surprised at the winner's form, and said it was due to 'Bob' Craig, who had been engaged to coach them.

When Craig was about to head back to Sydney by train on 16 September, a mere 27 days after he had arrived, he was feted by the locals. They met in Mr J. Byrne's refreshment rooms just prior to his departure to reward him with 'a wallet of notes' and an inscribed cigarette case which read: 'Pres. To R.R. Craig by the R.L.F. Queanbeyan 1921'.

Craig was returning to Sydney for a testimonial put on for him at the Balmain Town Hall by his old club. It was a special occasion, but the former boilermaker took the trouble to write a letter to the editors of the two leading Sydney sporting papers of the day, the *Referee* and the *Arrow*, to praise the quality of southern, particularly Queanbeyan Warrigal and Hall village, Rugby League. The *Referee* of 21 September 1921 produced this account, underscoring Rugby League's invaluable community role a century ago:

> Mr. R.R. Craig is back in Sydney after a very delightful time at Queanbeyan, where he coached the local footballers recently. He speaks in glowing terms of the natural ability of the players of the district, of their enthusiasm, and of their power to assimilate knowledge about the game. It is the first season of the League Rugby being played there, and the advance made in picking up the fine points surprised the old Wallaby–Kangaroo forward.
>
> 'People think nothing of travelling fifty miles to either play or witness the game', he remarks. 'And the enthusiasm of the players and the public is nothing less than wonderful. Twice while I was there the Yass team motored across, and though they had previously downed the Queanbeyan boys they were beaten in both games at Queanbeyan.'
>
> Hall, a village close to Queanbeyan, also has its team, men of fine physique. Prior to leaving for Sydney, Mr. Craig was the recipient of two presentations, one from the townspeople and the other from the footballers. He states that the hospitality showered upon him was a most agreeable surprise. It has made him feel that he has not seen the last of Queanbeyan. He thinks that country football is going to make good in the League game. There is not any doubt as to that if it be managed well.

Sadly, the Bob Craig story ended in tragedy. Acknowledged by all his peers as a teammate and coach who possessed an infectious sense of fun, Craig appears to have suffered from depression. Unable to adjust satisfactorily to life after sporting success, he hung himself in a Leichhardt hospital on 5 March 1935, aged 53, after being treated for what was described as a 'nervous breakdown'. Craig was fondly remembered in obituaries in a range of newspapers and magazines.

Between the wars

Was it the Bob Craig impact? An enduring Craig effect that encouraged the spread of Rugby League down south? Possibly, but what is certain is that the year 1921 was the starting point for twenty productive years for the code throughout the region, pre-Second World War—years which embedded it into the identity and social structure of the community. It was not without its setbacks, however. The economic impact of the Great Depression in the 1930s was severe in the cities and in the bush. Many of those playing the game were fathers who needed work, often having to travel considerable distances to earn an income with which to feed the family. Times were tough and football was never the top priority.

In Canberra, the game's progress reflected the evolution of the capital city itself. From the mid-1920s, as the opening of the Commonwealth Government's 'provisional' Parliament House in 1927 got closer, the fortunes of Rugby League in the infant capital and Queanbeyan became intertwined. It was so strong in the Monaro region, and so widely respected, that by the end of the 1922 season when a representative Sydney team was selected to play two games in late September (against the Warrigals, who lost 15–3, and then a combined Queanbeyan side, who won 13–11), one Sydney sporting journalist stated that it was 'one of the best that could have been selected', such was the expectation of the challenging encounters ahead of them. The team included players from the Western Suburbs club, St George, Newtown, North Sydney, Eastern Suburbs, South Sydney, University, Glebe and Balmain.

The games drew large crowds and, as the *Queanbeyan Age* pointed out, the visitors received a civic reception as well as 'a big banquet followed by a dance in the Protestant Hall'.

New teams started up in the Federal Capital Territory (FCT) with apt and descriptive names that left little doubt as to their origins—names such as the Sewers (made up of men who laid the pipes necessary for every community!), the Powerhouse and the Brickyard. Workplace camaraderie usually led to the formation of the first Canberra teams. By 1927, the year when Parliament House was opened by the Duke (later King George VI, 'Bertie', Queen Elizabeth II's father) and Duchess of York (the 'Queen Mother'), the league competition in the FCT had broadened its base to include a 'Canberra' team, alongside Duntroon, Westridge, Hall, Molonglo and West Queanbeyan.

The years from the middle to late 1920s belonged to football-hardened Hall village, population not many. In March 1928 a *Canberra Times* reporter admitted to 'surprise' at just how good the Hall team had become, with its playing core made up of individuals 'who had to travel from their farms and other outlying places to play'. Since their inception, the column continued, 'they have lost very few matches. They hold three cups and are the winners of the Federal Territory Competition Season of 1927.'

What a dazzling season it was for Hall in 1927. The side went undefeated in twenty games, playing the likes of Gunning, Yass, Braidwood, Queanbeyan and a number of the Federal Capital teams. They scored twice as many points as their opponents, won both the Walsh and Resch Cups, and played a rugged style of football admired by all local lovers of the new code. Like the Warrigals in 1921, the Hall club also went in search of a quality coach who could take their game to another level. And they found him in an individual fleetingly recorded in the papers of the time as 'L. Sheeley'—almost certainly Lionel Sheeley, who pops up as a 'painstaking and impartial' referee in a few local games and who went on to play for Western Suburbs in Sydney. Sheeley gets a mention some years later in Melbourne's *Herald* newspaper as 'a dinkum Australian', skilled in a variety of football codes including soccer and Australian Rules.

The upstart 'professional' code was blossoming in communities both big and small.

A homegrown nursery

When Ian Heads delivered the sixteenth annual Tom Brock Lecture in 2000, the prolific rugby league historian and journalist observed that:

> Over the seasons Rugby League has constructed a tradition of great characters and notable stories—a body of colourful deeds, tales of courage and famous contests so deserving of respect to be strong enough to underpin any sport.

In the formative period between the wars, Rugby League in southern New South Wales certainly played its part in the founding of that tradition, producing a steady stream of some of the game's most talented players, 'great characters' all. Some individuals can be singled out as trail-blazers.

Steve 'Tracker' Darmody, 'something of a wild man'

Steve Darmody (1890–1969) was the first of the genuine stars of the southern football nursery. Born at the beginning of the decade that ultimately produced a Federation of the colonies, he was a representative product of the Australian 'native-born' of the 19th century, a burgeoning group whose self-confidence and determination caught the attention of a number of overseas visitors including renowned English novelist Anthony Trollope and historian J.A. Froude.

A deserving Queanbeyan Hall of Famer in recent times, Darmody grew up in Sutton. He was a natural in a number of sports at school, but footy was his first love. With two of his brothers, William and Frank, he first played Rugby League for South Sydney in 1910. In recognition of his strong performances in one of the Sydney competition's leading clubs, Tracker was selected as a member of the second Kangaroo Rugby League team to tour Great Britain, in 1911–12, aged 21, playing alongside Bob Craig among others. The one photo we still have of Steve in his Kangaroo uniform and soft velvet cap is a cracker. He looks like a male model.

On tour, Darmody played in six matches, though no Tests, and he kicked nine goals. Another photo of him on tour, published in the Sydney *Daily Telegraph* under the headline 'Fighting Kangaroo', has him crouching theatrically for the cameras with two teammates and a live kangaroo. The 'fighting' caption was relevant beyond the furry marsupial on site for the shoot. During the tour, the English press reacted with hostility to the tackling of the Australians, alleging that it was too aggressive. They were critical as well of the language used by the visitors, one journalist describing it as 'vile', language that might have come out of the mouths of 'aborigines, rather than men claiming the honoured name of Colonials'.

The accusations would not have lessened in their fury after the tour match against the Widnes side (won by the Australians 23–0) in what was described in one English paper as an 'unparalleled scene of roughness and foul play' which featured a series of 'disgraceful incidents'. Two players from each team were given their marching orders, one of them Tracker Darmody. A contemporary account called him 'something of a wild man'.

Was it the physicality of his game? Probably. Tracker certainly attracted the interest of the Northern Union game's most respected scouts because he signed a contract with the Hull Football Club. Between 1912 and 1914 he made 89 appearances for Hull as a loose forward/lock, scoring a total of sixteen tries and kicking seventeen goals. The fervent Hull supporters loved his approach to the game. Tracker always gave his all, especially in a terrific 1914 Challenge Cup Final at Thrum Hall, Halifax, in front of a capacity crowd of 19,000. Hull defeated Wakefield Trinity 6–0.

At the outbreak of the Great War, Darmody enlisted in the British Army and saw active service in Flanders as a despatch rider for the

Service Corps. On 12 January 1917, the *Queanbeyan Age* reported that 'after some heroic fighting [he] was severely wounded'. In fact, his foot had been severed in a machinery accident and the leg had to be amputated. Undeterred, Tracker got himself fitted with an artificial limb and re-enlisted, determined as he said 'to tickle the Fritzes'. The Hull club organised a benefit for him which raised £300, a large sum in those days. He married and had one daughter, eventually settling his family in Scotland where he died, aged 80, in 1969.

Clarence 'Clarrie' Edwin Hincksman, a 'dinkum' hometown hero

Clarrie Hincksman (1898–1974) was one of twelve children born to Annie Lough and Joseph Hincksman. Joseph's parents migrated to Australia from Liverpool, England, in 1863, and by the time young Clarrie was born 35 years later in Queanbeyan, his father had become one of the town's most respected citizens. Town clerk from 1892 to 1926, Joseph played an active role in Queanbeyan's bold attempt to become 'the treasure house of the nation's heart', Australia's capital city.

Clarrie had the good fortune to grow up in a big family in a bustling country town and he had quite a story. While he was one of 12 kids fathered by Joseph, Clarrie's mother Annie had four additional children from an earlier marriage. Individual members of the Hincksman hordes had plenty of scope to do their own thing unencumbered, and this suited Clarrie down to the ground. When the Great War began, two of his older brothers, Clem and Percy, enlisted in the AIF. Clem was killed in action on the Somme on 25 July 1916 and Percy was wounded in action. Having joined up in November 1915, aged seventeen, Clarrie was charged with desertion in September 1917, eight weeks after Clem's death. There must be a story behind this alarming turn of events but we have, unfortunately, few details. A court-martial followed and Clarrie was given a five-year gaol sentence. 'On account of his youth' he received a reprieve soon after and was sent back to the front, where he was wounded in action in October 1917. It must have been a traumatic few weeks for a 19-year-old, Presbyterian boy from the Limestone Plains.

Clarrie survived the horrific conflict. Like many of his countrymen who felt lucky to have somehow got through alive, he was held up in London post-war until a suitable ship could take him home. During the year he spent in limbo, he met and married an English woman in September 1919. The couple returned to Queanbeyan, where a handful of returning veterans of the town, including the promoted Corporal Hincksman, were accorded a civic reception. The *Queanbeyan Age* covered the joyful event:

> Queanbeyan folk turned up in large numbers to welcome 'Back again to dear old Aussie' the final batch of our brave boys who, having 'fought the good fight' for liberty and justice on Gallipoli's heights and in Flanders' mud, are returning to their native shores literally staggering under the load of glory they have heaped upon themselves . . . the Town Band rendered appropriate airs and as the digger guests (Cpls. Clarrie Hincksman and J. Cartwright, and Munition-worker W. Banyard) marched up the hall they received a great reception.
>
> The Chairman remarked that one of the 'dinkums' on the platform that night had taken unto himself a wife while on the other side. He referred to Corporal Hincksman and at his instigation, three hearty cheers were given for Mrs Hincksman.

The coming months must have been a culture shock for young 'Mrs C. Hincksman', Marie Hincksman, particularly when her husband, possibly in reaction to his recent war experiences, threw himself so energetically into the Queanbeyan sporting scene. The *Queanbeyan Age* happily reported in May 1920 that 'Digger Clarrie Hincksman is a "livewire" and indefatigable Secretary for the Warrigals and it will not be his fault if the Club does not have a successful season'. Rugby League played a big part in Clarrie's convalescence. The Warrigals' best player in 1920, 'the idol of barrackers and spectators alike', he was the first man picked for the team that played Bungendore in

1921 in the first-ever game played under the rules of the league code. Like Tracker Darmody, he adapted with ease to the thirteen-a-side game.

In February 1924, Clarrie accepted an offer to play with the powerful Eastern Suburbs club in Sydney, a move that Sydney's *Labor Daily* felt was 'well-received by all followers of the League code in Sydney'. The *Labor Daily* was keen to acknowledge his sporting versatility: 'Besides being a splendid footballer, he is a first-class cricketer, billiardist and rifle shot. His friends say that everything in the way of sport is second nature to him'.

When Clarrie died, he was accorded a fitting tribute in the *Queanbeyan Age*. Later he was inducted into the Queanbeyan Hall of Fame, which has three invaluable pieces of Hincksman memorabilia, his 1924 NSW cap and pocket, and a later blazer. Treasures indeed.

Alan Ridley, 'a giant speed merchant', an 'Adonis'

Of all the players between the wars associated with the Canberra–Queanbeyan region, Alan Ridley (1910–93) was arguably the best. Born in Gulargambone, in the central western plains of New South Wales, his family moved to Queanbeyan when Alan was a child. A member of a fine sporting family (one brother was a tennis star, another reputed to be the best footballer ever turned out by Goulburn High School), as a youngster Alan attended Queanbeyan Public School. He was noticed on a few occasions for his various sporting talents, winning numerous sprint races and other athletic events.

Aged seventeen, he played league for the local Acton Rovers, the 'Knickerbocker Club', with whom he won the Federal Capital Territory (FCT) competition in 1928, and the following year he switched clubs, turning out for the Queanbeyan Blues. The *Goulburn Evening Penny Post* described him as a 'promising football colt', which was a fair assessment. In 1929 he won the FCT 100-yards championship foot race. He had electric speed.

Ridley was also a very big unit, six foot tall and nearly fifteen stone, and he played on the wing virtually his entire career. Built like Eric

Grothe in an era of small, nippy flankers, he must have been a terrifying sight for any opposition would-be tackler, much less his direct wing opponent. In his first full league season in 1928 as an 18-year-old, he represented Group 8, Southern Districts and NSW Country, playing so well that despite his inexperience he was picked in the Kangaroo party to tour England in 1929–30. Ridley's astonishing rise to the top echelon came at the precise time when Sir John Butters and his Federal Capital Commission (FCC) were in the midst of constructing the nation's capital. Those tasked with administering and promoting the new city took advantage of any good news stories, Canberra community stories, which came their way. Alan Ridley fitted the bill perfectly.

He was given no less than three farewells as he prepared for the Kangaroo tour: one was organised by the FCC and held at the new Capital Theatre in Manuka, where Ridley received 'a wallet of notes on behalf of the sporting bodies and citizens of Canberra'; a second was a dinner at the Hotel Canberra hosted by the FCT Rugby Football League; and a third was held by his old Knickerbocker Acton teammates at the South City Football Club's dance at the Causeway Hall, the special guest presented with a 'Reflex Camera'. The club was keen to have him return 'the same clean sportsman he was before he left'.

Ridley was the 'baby' of the Kangaroo tour but it did not take him long to make a lasting impression on the league-mad crowds in the north of England. At Castleford, in a 53–2 massacre inflicted by the tourists, the former Acton Rovers and Blues winger, described as the 'Adonis' of the squad, scored five tries, an achievement not equalled until Terry 'Baa Baa' Lamb managed it in 1986. Unfortunately, it was on this first tour that Ridley suffered a serious injury and missed the later matches. He made up for it on his second Kangaroo tour to England in 1933–34 when he played two Tests, and overall was the squad's leading try-scorer with 25 tries. He played for Australia against England in Australia for the first time in 1936, appearing in all three Tests.

Domestically, Ridley's reputation as a true try-scoring winger went from strength to strength. Western Suburbs coaxed him to Sydney in

1931 and in his six years with the club he scored 64 tries. He was the NSWRFL's top try-scorer with eighteen in 1932, scored a record six tries for Wests in a 1934 grade match during a season when his team won the competition, and he was honoured—rightly honoured—when only recently voted as a member of the Wests Tigers Team of the Century and the Western Suburbs Magpies Team of the Century.

A 'giant speed machine', as he was once described, Ridley even had the good sense to leave the game while he was, as the Sydney *Sun* put it, 'at the peak of his prime'. He accepted a job with Country Broadcasting Services Ltd, based in Orange, and eventually became a popular mayor of the town in 1956–57. A selection of items representing Ridley's international career—his Kangaroo caps, jerseys and boots—are showcased in the Orange Hall of Fame. Queanbeyan's Hall of Fame claims him as well.

War years and after

During the Great War years, broad divisions of class and religion within the Australian community had a marked effect on soldier recruitment and this indirectly led to the consolidation of the Rugby League code in New South Wales and Queensland. The Second World War, however, was a different proposition altogether. After the collapse of Singapore and the Japanese bombing of Darwin in 1941, divisive domestic issues evaporated. Australia itself was under direct attack. In the midst of this crisis, various sports tried to continue as best they could in order to maintain morale at home. Prime Minister Robert Menzies spoke for many when he said that we 'will still have exercise and recreation at a time of testing like this'.

Rugby League did continue in its strongholds, Sydney and Brisbane, but at greatly reduced levels. The situation in most country centres was different, primarily because of the tyranny of distance. With petrol rationing strictly enforced, town teams simply could not manage to travel to distant opponents to get a game of footy. The Canberra–Queanbeyan region, like so many areas of New South Wales and

Queensland, had to shut down its competitions. Between 1941 and 1945 there were no inter-town matches, nor indeed area competitions of any kind.

When the European theatre of conflict neared its conclusion in the early months of 1945, and Germany's surrender appeared imminent, a Rugby League club was re-formed in Queanbeyan in March 1945. The new team played its first game at the Queanbeyan Showground on 6 May, one day before the German surrender. Over the next ten years, as community life returned to normal, almost all of the league competitions commenced once again.

Yet for the national capital region, it was a case of revisiting some of the more controversial aspects of the past. The same problems that had plagued the code between the wars re-emerged. With the return of inter-town Cup games, town competitions once again suffered, especially when a little bit more money became available to pay for imported players. Improved economic conditions in Sydney and Brisbane encouraged many country footballers to head off to the city in search of financial security. Despite this migration, the great game did not disappear in the bush. In fact, in the midst of some testing post-war years, many country footballers across New South Wales and Queensland determined to take their code into a more prosperous era. Country life was too good to give up. In their endeavours, they were ably supported by the sport-loving citizens of their hometowns.

International glamour

In the Canberra region, Rugby League was given a timely boost by a number of international fixtures, games that brought some of the world's best players to the backblocks. The youngsters of a new generation were excited by what they saw.

It did not take long, post-war, for the first representative games to take place. In May 1946, a match pitting an inexperienced team from the Canberra district against Queensland was won by the visitors 40–7, in the process emptying the small number of Commonwealth offices of public servants, who were all given a day off. This was followed just two weeks later by a game against the might of England no less, at Manuka Oval.

Its economy static since the onset of the Great Depression in the late 1920s, the national capital was desperate for signs of recovery. Fortunately, popular Labor Party Prime Minister Ben Chifley recognised that getting Canberra back on its feet was not only a matter of attending to economic matters. In his younger days 'Chif' played both union and league, and he understood sport's galvanising qualities. He made a point of welcoming the English Rugby League team at Parliament House. The visitors won the football easily, 45–12, in a game watched by a crowd of about 5,000, one of whom was another celebrity local resident, an appreciative Governor-General, the Duke of Gloucester. The Monaro team, a Group 8 representative squad, turned out in the blue and gold colours of Canberra and, in the tradition of days gone by, the visitors were entertained after the game at a dinner in their headquarters at the Hotel Kingston.

The *Canberra Times* captured the prevailing mood when it declared that the 'stirring' football on show was 'the greatest exhibition of Rugby League ever played in Canberra'. All parties were better off financially, the locals played 'excellent football' and Canberra's federal politicians were provided with a cultural template for electoral appeal in the future.

The next important milestone for local league was another visit by the English team four years later. This tour by Australia's traditional rival, occurring in mid-1950, has been cause for celebration in all Australian histories of Rugby League ever since. Why? The Australian team, after going down narrowly in the First Test at the Sydney Cricket Ground, 6–4, bounced back to win the second in Brisbane 15–3 (the first Test win over the English in 30 years) and then returned to the hallowed turf of the SCG for the decider. A game of tenacious defence and at times ferocity was won by the green-and-golds 5–2 after two of the visitors were sent off for 'back chatting' the referee. James Giltinan (generally regarded as the founder of the league code in Australia and given a permanent place in league's pantheon with the J.J. Giltinan Shield awarded to the competition premiers) went into the sheds of the victors and said to one of the game's stars, the 'Little Master', captain Clive Churchill: 'Thanks a lot, Clive. I've waited all my life for this day.' Tears flowed. Five weeks later, Giltinan died—a contented man—having witnessed Australia's first Ashes series win in three decades. He was 84.

The first game the English played on their 1950 tour took place in Canberra during the first year of Robert Menzies' second prime ministership. Expectation and anticipation were high, reflected in the advertising that preceded the fixture. The nation's capital was now firmly located on Rugby League's map. Spectators travelled vast distances to be there—from Sydney, yes, but also from a number of league areas near and far such as Wollongong, Cootamundra, Braidwood and Goulburn. Those lucky enough to be living closer were not going to miss out on being the first Australian league fans that year to assess the 'Chooms', as they were then called. The fan base of nearby Sutton, Captains Flat and Hall was also well represented at the game. Special carriages were added to the Federal Capital City Express train to handle the crowd, which included NSW Rugby League heavyweights such as the legendary former Board Chairman Mr H. 'Jersey' Flegg and Mr S.G. Ball.

The English approached their opening tour game with caution, choosing 'one of their strongest teams'. It proved much too good, winning 37–10 in front of a crowd so big that officials at short notice decided to trial an 'innovation': 'free admission of truck drivers and trucks ... [to be] used as miniature grandstands to allow the spectators ... an uninterrupted view of the play'. Clearly, more attention needed to be given to the standard of Canberra's footballing amenities, and more money spent to get Manuka Oval up to international scratch.

One of a number of diplomatic and political VIPs in attendance was Great Britain's paymaster general, Lord Macdonald. He was no token invite, nor was it a case of the NSW Rugby League simply following protocol to have him take the symbolic kick-off. At an earlier point in his life, Lord Macdonald played for the famous Wigan club and the 1950 squad of English footballers had no less than eight Wigan players. Further recognition was accorded the match when Prime Minister Menzies, a Victorian and avid follower of Australian Rules, delivered a welcoming speech at a formal function containing elements of the dry wit for which he would soon acquire a reputation at many a Prime Minister's XI cricket match in the years to come. For his league audience, Menzies jokingly noted that he had just left a 'scrum', a Liberal Party meeting. The footballers lapped it up.

There is no doubt that the first English team visits to Canberra were a valid measure of the respect held by those in authority for the high standard of league in southern New South Wales. Other league-playing nations followed suit, the French playing a string of games against representative Monaro teams in 1951, 1955, 1960, 1964 and 1975. A real mixed bag, the contests did have one common element: they were always fiercely contested.

The renowned 1951 squad, with names such as eccentric but brilliant fullback and captain, Puig-Aubert, halfback Jean Dop and the intimidating, unpredictable forward Elie Brousse, won the inaugural encounter against the locals 37–12. If the home team was initially disappointed at the result, the next couple of months showed that they had no reason to be. Puig-Albert's Frenchmen, parading for their Australian audiences a new symbol on their jerseys of the Coq Gaulois (the tri-coloured rooster), were a major surprise. Expected to be beaten easily by the Australians, especially after losing the First Test by a comfortable 26–15 margin, the Tri-colours regrouped to win the Second Test 23–11 and the Third Test 35–14. Australian Rugby League went into shock. Canberra followers of the game, on the other hand, probably felt in hindsight that their squad had performed pretty well against an outstanding international football team.

When a second French team played Monaro in May 1955, the home side went into the game with an ever-improving squad of players who were not prepared to take a backward step. The French had a similar resolve and the match, described as 'wild' by the *Canberra Times*, did degenerate at one point into an all-in brawl. There was more, as fists flew and the fight escalated:

> Police and officials surged toward the fight but not before spectators were over the fence. The combatants were soon lost among the hundreds of spectators who crowded onto the ground. When the teams were finally separated and sent back to the middle of the field to cool down, both captains Dop and Bennett required ambulance attention.

The governor-general was there and he must have left the match appalled by the brutal spectacle. Fortunately, none of the three games between France and Monaro's representative teams over the next twenty years into the mid-1970s was as controversial—or violent—as the 1955 encounter. But the rivalry continued. France won 25–17 in 1960; 38–16 in 1964; and, after the heavens opened with a downpour that rendered Manuka Oval unplayable, the 1975 fixture was switched to Seiffert Oval where the Monaro team this time won easily, 26–0. It was a scoreline that confronted NSWRL officials with the quality of southern Rugby League.

Could the door of the elite Sydney competition be prised open at last?

One more international match played through the years of post-war reconstruction in Canberra must be mentioned. It took place at Manuka Oval on 27 May 1953. 'Southern Districts' played a team describing itself with characteristic brash confidence as the 'American All Stars'. All Stars they were not, as curious Australian audiences and Rugby League officials soon discovered. The team played eighteen games in Australia, winning three, losing thirteen and drawing two. When they faced good local sides, they were thrashed. The novelty value soon wore off.

In the squad's opening two games, and probably to accentuate their extroverted points of difference for the camera, the 'All Stars' turned out in grid-iron's standard long trousers. The first of the matches was against the Monaro Southern Districts team, all in shorts. The contrast made for good publicity.

Many stories have circulated since about this bizarre game played 65 years ago—some reported, others not. We know a few things for sure: the 'All Stars' were behind 20–8 at half-time and somehow recovered to win 34–25; easily the 'All Stars' best player was Alvin Kirkland, a 'one-man team' according to the *Goulburn Evening Post*; and the team included Bill Albans, an American Olympic hop, step and jumper whose athletic expertise failed to help him on the day. Albans was injured and triple-jumped into Canberra Hospital.

As the first fixture on the Americans' itinerary, the Canberra game received considerable attention in Sydney and Melbourne, pushed hard by local league administrators and the diligent efforts of the squad's manager, Mike Dimitro—you guessed it, a wrestling promoter! Dimitro had been an outstanding professional footballer in America but neither he nor those he brought out had a clue about the rules of Rugby League. The *Canberra Times* diplomatically observed that a 'liberal interpretation of the rules allowed the game to be played at a rattling pace'. The upbeat report of the *Goulburn Evening Post* was probably as good as it got for the Americans on the entire tour. 'On the field the Americans show a strong sense of the theatrical. In their dazzling neck to ankle royal blue nylon suits they look like musical comedy chorus boys.'

The only puzzle about the Canberra game needing an explanation was how the outclassed Americans managed to turn the game around from its half-time score. Raiders stalwart and former CEO John McIntyre has an explanation. He attended the game as a 10-year-old with his dad, Les—Canberra Raiders godfather in the making—and he tells the story that at half-time, with the locals comfortably ahead, their dressing room was visited by some of NSW Rugby League's leading officials in a state of panic. If the Americans were beaten first-up in the bush, then thrashed in the next game against a strong Sydney outfit, the entire tour would effectively be consigned to the dustbin of history. The officials put it to Les McIntyre that 'for the good of the game'

Southern Districts had better run dead in the second half. They did. Les apparently paid a monetary price for the greater cause. Having backed the local boys to win, he was invited to persuade them to tank. And they did.

A record Canberra crowd of over 6,000 watched the Manuka match and a sell-out 65,453 headed out to the SCG for the NSW game, lost by the Americans 52–25. The tour and the crowds went into freefall. The Uncle Sam All-Star experiment had run its course.

Johnny 'Feathers' Hawke

In the same year that the American bulldust and razzamatazz came and went, Norman John 'Johnny' Hawke (1925–92), Queanbeyan footballer born and bred, drove up to the northern NSW town of Kyogle to reassess his options after injury had curtailed an outstanding if all too brief football career at the St George club. Like the Queanbeyan Warrigals when they approached Bob Craig in 1921, more in hope than confidence, the Kyogle club in 1953 was acutely aware of Hawke's brilliant past few years in both domestic and international football, and the difficulties experienced in 1952 when a slipped disc resulted in him being put in a plaster cast from neck to thigh. But Kyogle knew who they were recruiting—someone whose character, football intellect and experience could turn around their club's ailing fortunes.

In his only season with Kyogle, Hawke did coach as expected, even pulling on the boots in a few games as he shuffled around the paddock calling out instructions. Kyogle duly won the comp. After one more season coaching, this time with the Woy Woy club on the NSW central coast, Hawke retired while still in his twenties as the result of injuries sustained over several years of tough Sydney football when his star status made him a target for every opposition enforcer looking to make a name for himself. It was the right decision for sure, but one that brought to a premature close a career that in only seven short years, 1946–52, took Hawke from bush footy to a Sydney premiership and six Tests for his country along the way—international games that produced his nickname

'Feathers' and booked his placed securely in Queanbeyan's Sport Hall of Fame and the ACT's Sport Hall of Fame in later years.

Like so many products of the fertile Queanbeyan nursery of footballers, Johnny Hawke stood out as a youngster for the sheer variety of his footballing skills. By the accounts of a number of astute Australian Rules observers, he could have been anything in their game, but he eventually chose league as his main sport. Whether at five-eighth or centre, his handling, speed and perfect tackling technique gave Hawke's Queanbeyan Public School obvious on-field advantage in all of the inter-school matches he played in.

As the linchpin of undefeated school teams for several years, Johnny graduated into the Queanbeyan Blues team in 1946 as a 20-year-old. He was accustomed to winning. The Blues that year boasted established footballers such as captain Terry Freebody, Ron Williams, Roy Savage, Harold 'Skinny' Williams, George Sherd, Teddy Rowley, Roy Harman, Steve Mauger, Alan Pooley, Ron McInnes, Johnny Reid and Tommy Gibbs. The baby-faced Hawke was the icing on the cake for a team that was so good, so dominant, that the *Sydney Morning Herald* on 18 September 1946 featured a large box of seventeen caricatured heads of the Blues players and officials under the heading 'Queanbeyan League Personalities'. In the first full season post-war, the Blues went through a demanding game schedule undefeated and, in the process, the gifted Johnny Hawke became valuable Rugby League property. So valuable that in the following year, 1947, Canberra snapped up his services, a move which enabled the national capital team to go through its season undefeated. Johnny's reputation grew. The region's league fans knew that this special talent was destined to play footy in the city. It was only a case of when. In the 1948 season when he stayed on in Canberra to play for £6 a week, representative honours rightly came his way—first group selection, then Combined Country Firsts, followed by a game for Country against New Zealand and finally, after a series of stand-out representative performances, selection for New South Wales against Queensland. He scored the game's first try.

By the time Hawke's name was read out in the Kangaroo squad to tour England in 1948–49, he was widely regarded as the best five-eighth or centre in the world. The England tour confirmed it when the young man (dubbed 'Feathers' by his tour roommate and league tough man Doug McRitchie) played in 24 of the 33 games including four Tests. The Queanbeyan product had barely got his feet back on the ground in Australia when he was snapped up by the St George club for the coming 1949 season. His teammates included Dragons greats such as Matt McCoy, Noel Pidding, Noel Hill, Jack 'Dutchy' Holland and McRitchie—whose close friendship with Hawke was probably the main reason he signed with the Red V.

It is now part of St George's legendary history that young captain Johnny Hawke led his team to the 1949 premiership after a first semi-final when, like the more publicised John Sattler for South Sydney some years later, he played on with a broken jaw and loose teeth that caused him to leave the field. When Souths surged back to take the lead in the game 12–10, Hawke returned to set up winger Ron Roberts for a try that effectively sealed a gallant Saints win. Hawke was chaired from the field by exultant teammates, then shortly after he was rushed to a dentist to have the two loose teeth removed. When the needle's anaesthetic failed, he was evidently given a bottle of brandy to drink to deaden the pain for oral surgery, which went for four hours. Only then did he get taken to a doctor to have the jaw set. Just three weeks later, he led St George to premiership victory.

No wonder he was chosen the following year, 1950, to captain New South Wales against the English in a game which drew a record crowd of 70,419. It was an honour that would almost certainly have seen him captain Australia in the forthcoming Test series except that he sustained a knee injury in the NSW game that was so serious it ruled him out of all further representative games that year, including the Tests.

Hawke later played in one of the three Tests against France in 1951 (his sixth for Australia) but that game brought his international career to an end. In the same year, as captain–coach of St George, it was reported that he got £1,000 for the season, an enormous sum at that time.

Johnny turned out again for the Saints in 1952 but it was clear that injuries and the general wear and tear of Sydney football were taking their toll. This was after all the era of enforcers like 'Bumper' Farrell, a time when no prisoners were taken, the 'stiff-arm' tackle came into vogue, and what happened on the field stayed on the field. Attacking players, especially smaller halves with a reputation, were targets. Players today get far more protection, from referees, commentators, journalists and TV replays. Not so 70 years ago. League followers mid-century were robbed of seeing Johnny Hawke play for at least five or ten more years.

When Hawke died in 1992, his great mate Doug McRitchie attended his funeral along with a large number of league fans who wished to remember his contribution to the game. The Canberra Raiders by then had already won two premierships for the southern region where he had grown up. Kids from Queanbeyan and Canberra no longer had to head to the Big Smoke to gain recognition. Opportunity was right on their doorstep. It must have brought a big smile to Johnny's face in his last years.

Blues, Roos and a blur named Larry

When the Massey and Carr Cup inter-town matches wound up as the game re-shaped itself in country areas post-war, the Group 8 and ACT District Rugby League competitions eventually came to dominate southern region football in the 35 years leading up to the Canberra Raiders' first Sydney season. Of the two neighbouring competitions it was Group 8, with its wider geographical and social reach, which generated the most community interest.

Premierships in Group 8 were shared around in the 1950s between Queanbeyan, Captains Flat, Yass and Crookwell but at the beginning of the 1960s Goulburn's two teams—Goulburn Workers and Goulburn United—made a powerful statement of intent to their rivals. Between them, the Goulburn sides went on to win all five premierships from

The sundial donated to the town of Queanbeyan in 1860 by Nathan Moses Lazarus, Glenn Lazarus's great-great-grandfather. *(Mariana Rollgejser)*

Nathan Morris 'Mo' Lazarus and his wife, with their horses, outside the renowned Cricketers' Arms Hotel near Hall, in the early years of Federation. *(Lyall Gillespie collection/Hall School Museum)*

A young Frederick Campbell, about the time he introduced rugby to the sport-loving citizens of the Limestone Plains. *(Mariana Rollgejser)*

A caricature of Bob Craig, dual international and 1908 Olympic gold-medal winner for rugby, the man who introduced Rugby League to Queanbeyan and the region. *(Gillespie collection)*

The NSW representative cap and pocket (1924) of star Queanbeyan footballer Clarrie Hincksman. Clarrie remained involved in League for several decades, as his 1947 blazer indicates. *(Mariana Rollgejser)*

The Sutton rugby team circa 1900, inspiration for a young Steve Darmody, the region's first rugby league international (1911–12). *(Gillespie collection)*

The all-conquering Hall rugby league team, at the peak of its dominance in 1927, the year the Parliament House opened just down the road. *(Gillespie collection)*

Arch-rivals Queanbeyan and Yass clash in 1922, the second year the League code was played in the region. *(Queanbeyan Leagues Club)*

The Queanbeyan Warrigals team, 1922. *(Queanbeyan Leagues Club)*

The Queanbeyan Blues team, 1946, unbeaten during a year when they played teams from both the region and from Sydney. Johnny Hawke (back row, second right) was one of many fine players.

Champion Queanbeyan footballer Johnny Hawke resplendent in his 1948 NSW uniform. The blazer, treasured by his family, was given to Johnny to recognise his captaincy of the 1949 premiership-winning St George Dragons team.

The inaugural meeting of the provisional Board of Canberra and District Rugby League Football Club, 21 August 1981, at Queanbeyan Leagues Club. L–R: Dr Geoff Caldwell, Allan Crawley, Gordon McLucas, Jonathon Bell, Chairman Les McIntyre OAM, Secretary John McIntyre, Gerry Edwards, Hank Inderwisch, Kevin Thorn and Development Manager Don Elphick. *(Canberra Raiders)*

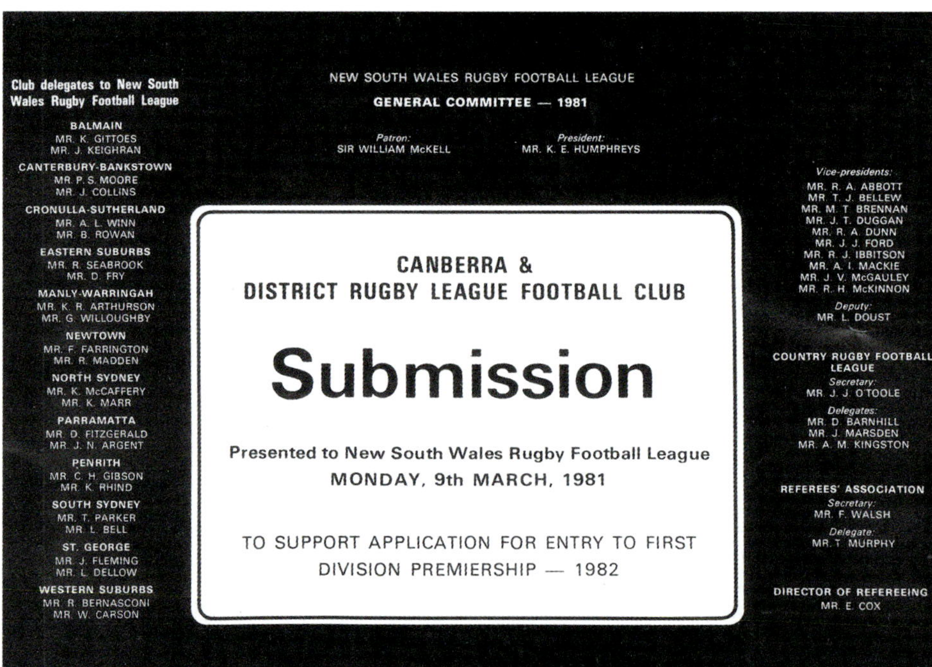

NEW SOUTH WALES RUGBY FOOTBALL LEAGUE

GENERAL COMMITTEE — 1981

Patron: SIR WILLIAM McKELL

President: MR. K. E. HUMPHREYS

Club delegates to New South Wales Rugby Football League

BALMAIN
MR. K. GITTOES
MR. J. KEIGHRAN

CANTERBURY-BANKSTOWN
MR. P. S. MOORE
MR. J. COLLINS

CRONULLA-SUTHERLAND
MR. A. L. WINN
MR. B. ROWAN

EASTERN SUBURBS
MR. R. SEABROOK
MR. D. FRY

MANLY-WARRINGAH
MR. K. R. ARTHURSON
MR. G. WILLOUGHBY

NEWTOWN
MR. F. FARRINGTON
MR. R. MADDEN

NORTH SYDNEY
MR. K. McCAFFERY
MR. K. MARR

PARRAMATTA
MR. D. FITZGERALD
MR. J. N. ARGENT

PENRITH
MR. C. H. GIBSON
MR. K. RHIND

SOUTH SYDNEY
MR. T. PARKER
MR. L. BELL

ST. GEORGE
MR. J. FLEMING
MR. L. DELLOW

WESTERN SUBURBS
MR. R. BERNASCONI
MR. W. CARSON

CANBERRA & DISTRICT RUGBY LEAGUE FOOTBALL CLUB

Submission

Presented to New South Wales Rugby Football League
MONDAY, 9th MARCH, 1981

TO SUPPORT APPLICATION FOR ENTRY TO FIRST DIVISION PREMIERSHIP — 1982

Vice-presidents:
MR. R. A. ABBOTT
MR. T. J. BELLEW
MR. M. T. BRENNAN
MR. J. T. DUGGAN
MR. R. A. DUNN
MR. J. J. FORD
MR. R. J. IBBITSON
MR. A. I. MACKIE
MR. J. V. McGAULEY
MR. R. H. McKINNON
Deputy:
MR. L. DOUST

COUNTRY RUGBY FOOTBALL LEAGUE
Secretary:
MR. J. J. O'TOOLE
Delegates:
MR. D. BARNHILL
MR. J. MARSDEN
MR. A. M. KINGSTON

REFEREES' ASSOCIATION
Secretary:
MR. F. WALSH
Delegate:
MR. T. MURPHY

DIRECTOR OF REFEREEING
MR. E. COX

The original submission bid by the Canberra and District Rugby League Football Club to enter the 1982 NSWRL competition. *(Canberra Raiders)*

The Raiders' 'founding father' Les McIntyre, pictured at the Raiders' original home ground, Seiffert Oval. *(Canberra Times)*

One of Les McIntyre's favourite pastimes was watching replays of Raiders matches. Here he is with Raiders Group CEO Simon Hawkins in 2006, watching a game at his Queanbeyan home. *(Canberra Raiders)*

The program cover from the Raiders' official launch, at the Queanbeyan Leagues Club, 19 February 1982. *(Canberra Raiders)*

The cover of the program from the Raiders' first official trial match, against the Illawarra Steelers, 13 February 1982. The Steelers were also admitted into the NSWRL for the 1982 season. *(Canberra Raiders)*

Queanbeyan United's dominance of Country Rugby League in the late 1970s, through their Queanbeyan Blues team, was the catalyst for the birth of the Raiders. This 1979 team photo includes inaugural Raiders' head coach Don Furner (Senior), as well as foundation players and support staff including Peter McGrath, Jon Hardy, Mark Brennan, David Reid, Graham Waugh, Richard Cooke and Brian Burke—with Don Furner (Junior) and David Furner the two ballboys. *(Queanbeyan Leagues Club)*

The official team photo and poster of the 1982 Canberra Raiders, the 'Pioneers'. *(Canberra Raiders)*

Inaugural head coach Don Furner gives a thumbs up during a vintage car cavalcade in Monaro Street, Queanbeyan. *(Canberra Times)*

Raiders coach Don Furner alongside inaugural captain David Grant (Raider #2) and David Reid (Raider #22). *(Canberra Times)*

Don Furner in deep concentration as he watches from the sideline. Furner was instrumental in developing the Pioneer Raiders into a premiership-challenging team in 1987 with co-coach Wayne Bennett. *(Canberra Times)*

Les McIntyre pictured with Jim Woodger at the announcement of the club's first major sponsor, Woodgers. *(Canberra Times)*

A fearsome sight. Raiders first captain, David Grant, in full flight. 'Nana' always led from the front. *(Canberra Times)*

A pivotal individual in the Raiders push into the NSWRL was popular Labor politician Fred Daly. In the vital foundation years he was club patron. *(Canberra Times)*

A colossus on the field but a gentle giant off it, David Grant was a real family man. Here he is with his son, Matt, the team's ball boy. *(Canberra Times)*

David Grant evading a tackle against Manly in 1983. *(NRL Imagery)*

The club's first major signing, Jay Hoffman (Raider #6). Hoffman is a two-time winner of the Raiders Clubman of the Year. *(NRL Imagery)*

Craig Bellamy (Raider #26), a Pioneer, played 148 games for the Raiders. He has since gone on to forge a hugely successful coaching career with the Melbourne Storm. *(NRL Imagery)*

A local junior from nearby Crookwell, Ashley Gilbert (Raider #32) played 135 matches for the club in a career which spanned nine seasons. He is a member of the Raiders Hall of Fame. *(NRL Imagery)*

Two-time Player of the Year and two-time premiership winner Chris O'Sullivan (Raider #24) was an instrumental part of the club's early success. He is a member of the Raiders Hall of Fame. *(NRL Imagery)*

The occasion was a dinner in the Blue Room Restaurant for wives and girlfriends of Raider players and officials. Guest of honour was co-patron Ros Kelly, Member for Canberra.

Pictured back row (l to r): Anita McIntyre, Trish Bennett, Ros Kelly, Vivian O'Sullivan, Debbie Meninga, Wendy Bellamy. Front row: Jenny Hoffman, Jayne Backo, Sheryl Ferguson, Beth Fahey and Debbie Lance.

Pictured back row (l to r): Sandy Crawford, Allison Cousins, Ros Kelly, Jo-Ann Dodd. Front row: Tania McInnes, Vicki Innaimo, Jodie McInnes, Bev McInnes.

Pictured back row (l to r): Anita McIntyre, Margaret Watson, Ros Kelly, Marian Furner, Pam Petherbridge. Front row: Lorraine Bradley, Judy Edwards, Elsie McIntyre, Elaine Lowe, Catherine Williams.

20—Queanbeyan Leagues' Club Journal, April 1987

The Raiders have always been a proud family club. These photos from the *Queanbeyan Leagues Club Journal* show the wives and partners socialising during the 1987 season. *(Queanbeyan Leagues Club)*

Steve O'Callaghan (Raider #10) played 53 matches for the Raiders from 1982 to 1987. *(NRL Imagery)*

Ivan Henjak (Raider #55) played 118 matches for the Raiders, including the club's first grand final in 1987, when he played halfback. *(NRL Imagery)*

Ron Giteau (Raider #38) played 78 matches for the club and captained the side in 1984 and 1985. *(NRL Imagery)*

A club cult figure, Sam Backo (Raider #43) played 115 matches for the Raiders, including the 1987 Grand Final, at prop. *(NRL Imagery)*

The most significant signing in club history, Mal Meninga (Raider #76) here puts his name on a crucial contract extension in 1987, to the delight of Club Secretary John McIntyre. *(Canberra Times)*

1960 to 1964. While both continued to be competitive in the late 1960s, another change in the pecking order occurred. Queanbeyan, with a wealth of football history behind it, took Group 8's centre stage. While it was a resurgence based on smart team recruitment, there was another influential factor at play—or more accurately, several factors, off-field factors, all of them significant signposts on the road to the Canberra Raiders.

At the inaugural meeting of the Queanbeyan District Rugby League Football Club (QDRLFC) at Walsh's Hotel on 3 March 1959, strategic decisions were taken to more aggressively promote the code in the area and, importantly, secure adequate financial support in pursuit of a new vision for the future. Firsts, reserves and junior teams were formed and the Queanbeyan Showground confirmed as the QDRLFC home ground. Eighteen months later, steps were taken to open a club house that would make fundraising that much easier.

Les McIntyre, well-known citizen of the town and QDRLFC president, had for some time watched other towns advance the fortunes of their sporting teams on the basis of a licensed club to raise revenue through poker machines and the sale of alcohol. For years, McIntyre had pushed the idea of a licensed club and, on 28 July 1961, Queanbeyan Leagues Club Ltd was incorporated as a company. It started unobtrusively as a small shop on Monaro Street, though plans were hatched almost immediately for a substantial stand-alone facility. Built in three stages on the corner of Monaro and Collett Streets, the imposing Queanbeyan Leagues Club as we know it today had its official opening on 19 September 1965. Re-built after a fire in 1972, it remains Queanbeyan's most influential club with easily the biggest turnover. An initial membership of 250 quickly grew to 4,000-plus. One in three residents of the town became members.

It surprised no-one that the leagues club's rapid development coincided with success on the football field. What wasn't anticipated, however, was the extent of the good fortune. From the time the Queanbeyan United Club won the Group 8 competition in 1965, snapping Goulburn's momentum and starting its own run of three competitions in a row, a period of dominance for the town began. This lasted for fifteen years and in effect anchored the region's eventual bid to put a team into the Sydney competition.

All those involved in the realisation of the Queanbeyan Leagues Club (and they included individuals whose forebears had established union and then league in the town the best part of a century earlier) refused to rest on their laurels. Before the completed club opened its doors for the first time, the search had begun to find a more suitable home ground for the league-playing 'Blues' (the 'Whites' of the town played union). During 1964 the leagues club, prospering well beyond expectations, loaned most of the $700,000 required by the J.W. Seiffert Trust to develop the NSW government-owned Seiffert Oval to the standard sought by the QDRLFC. Three years later, in 1967, the refurbished ground was christened with a game played between the Queanbeyan Blues and the Canberra Tigers. This first match, played 'in the wet', had no effect on the ground's vastly improved playing surface, which was generally acclaimed as first class. The quality of the pitch was matched by the expanded facilities available to the paying public: a grandstand able to seat nearly 3,000, ample parking facilities, and a designated area for those wanting to watch the game from the comfort of their cars—a long tradition in bush footy.

The prolonged success of the Queanbeyan Blues, the Queanbeyan United Club's team, played an important part in the town's social and economic progress at the time. There were some interesting spin-offs. One developed when two dyed-in-the-wool locals, passionate league men brothers Terry and John Matthews, felt that it was time to start a second rugby league club. Whether they were aware of Queanbeyan's notable league history between the wars when the town hosted several competitive teams, we don't know. Regardless, they went about their work so effectively that in February 1966 a meeting at Walsh's Hotel passed a motion to found a second rugby league team, to be called the 'Queanbeyan Kangaroos' (the Roos). The twenty-odd attendees at the inaugural meeting were motivated by a desire to give those local players regarded as not good enough to pull on the Blues jersey the chance to get a game without having to leave the area. The Roos' founders settled on maroon and white as the new club's colours.

Blues Secretary Les McIntyre acknowledged that the creation of the cross-town rival Kangaroos would impact on his club, yet he supported the new venture confident that the town's pool of talent was sufficient to accommodate two competitive squads of players. In the first years of Blues *and* Roos, the shrewd McIntyre was proven to be both right and wrong. Yes, the town did adapt with enthusiasm to the new era, but neither McIntyre nor his band of Blues supporters could have foreseen just how smooth the transition would be. The Roos developed so rapidly that the team won the Group 8 competition three years in a row, 1969–71, beating the Blues on each occasion. The Blues in turn responded to this furious challenge from within, going on to win the coveted Group 8 premiership no less than six times in the eight years up to 1981.

There were many reasons for this extraordinary run of success, but the main one was the role played by Blues coach Don Furner. Born in Condobolin in country New South Wales, Furner played much of his own football in Queensland as a hard-working second rower. He was rewarded for consistent performance when he toured England with the Kangaroos in 1956 after representing Queensland nine times. When serious injury prematurely ended his playing career, the unfussed Furner moved into coaching, initially with North Queensland's Mackay club in 1957. For the next three decades he coached every year but one, half of them with the Queanbeyan Blues. His record with the team was remarkable: 13 grand finals, 10 premierships.

During the years from the mid-1960s to 1981, and excluding a three-year stint in Sydney with Eastern Suburbs from 1970 to 1972 (with one grand final appearance), Furner made an unmatched contribution to the progress of the code in country New South Wales. This was duly recognised with his appointment to the coaching position of a number of Southern Divisional teams, the highlight being his Monaro team's country championship in 1977, in the same year that the side crushed the touring Great Britain side 33–12.

Judging by the number of people you talk to today who remember the epic victory over Great Britain as if it was yesterday, half of country New South Wales was there. Memories abound but for most of those who attended, or imagine they attended, the flashback moments inevitably focus on Larry Corowa's five spectacular tries. The papers wrote the game up as an outstanding team effort but none could disagree with Corowa receiving the $150 Caltex Man of the Match Award. Some have said that when Larry went to bed in those days he could turn off the light switch and be in bed before it got dark.

Don Furner's Group 8 coaching dynasty, with its St George–like statistics full of Blues–Roos local derbies and representative team triumphs, was undoubtedly the catalyst for Queanbeyan and Canberra league followers to contemplate a larger dream: placement of a team from southern New South Wales in the blue-ribbon Sydney Rugby League competition.

Changing the game

When Bill Buckley died in 1973, he left an indelible impression as president of the New South Wales Rugby League (NSWRL) and chairman of the Australian Rugby League (ARL). Having learned his football as a youngster growing up in Queanbeyan, he gained a reputation for the same kind of 'autocratic leadership' (as league historian Gary Lester has colourfully described it) that typified the famed Harry 'Jersey' Flegg's 32 unbending years in the job before Buckley. The winds of change were blowing in the 1970s, however, with many lovers of the game feeling that Rugby League had to reinvent itself in order to stay competitive with its rival codes. The volume *A Centenary of Rugby League 1908–2008* accurately observes that in 1970 the game was 'as raw and bloody' as it had ever been. There were also fears at league headquarters about a possible power vacuum at the top after Buckley's death.

It was in this unsettling environment that Kevin Humphreys assumed the presidency of the NSWRL unopposed and he immediately set about putting his own stamp on the important position he had attained.

Humphreys was no mug in the boardroom, but more than that he had a progressive set of ideas about where the league code had been, where it stood in 1973 and the path it should embark on in the future. It is well documented that he would experience a dramatic alteration in his personal fortunes that triggered his resignation in 1983, amid allegations of misappropriation of money, perverting the course of justice and government interference. All this was in the future. At the beginning of the 1980s, he was the commanding figure within Rugby League's hierarchy of power and influence.

Humphreys was determined to see the code on his watch expand its premier competition beyond Sydney's stifling geographical borders. For Rugby League to survive and thrive, he asserted, new teams had to be introduced—teams that hailed from locations beyond Sydney. And he went further: the number of Sydney teams had to be reduced. While this was heresy for many of league's diehards, facts and figures were firmly on the new president's side. The game was in trouble. In Humphreys' first year, the 'Pioneer' South Sydney club was forced to admit that it was in serious financial difficulties. A couple of years later Cronulla stated that its single-minded pursuit of a premiership had landed it in the same predicament. By 1982, the year of the Raiders' entry, no less than half of Sydney's rugby league teams had admitted that they too were in debt.

Just as disturbing for administrators with the long view was the parlous state of Sydney's suburban grounds. A number of the ovals had hardly been improved since the end of the Second World War. Amenities were run down, and with them crowds. The future of the game itself was in doubt. Naysayers said it was already too late.

For those outside Sydney, by contrast, such a precarious situation smacked of opportunity. The volatility of the 1970s decade encouraged ambition in both the Wollongong and Monaro regions. Maybe, just maybe, there was a chance for a non-Sydney team or two to make it into the big time. Then it happened! First, Illawarra gained entry, its place in the elite competition for season 1982 as the thirteenth team formally announced on 13 December 1980. At the same event, the NSWRL stated that there would be fourteen teams playing in that historic year. One spot was still up for grabs.

Kevin Humphreys' commitment to the idea of fewer Sydney teams and new non-Sydney teams did not waiver at this time. In the eighteen months prior to the vote for the fourteenth team, to be taken on 30 March 1981, he manoeuvred skilfully to maximise the chance of getting the result he wanted. So when the NSWRL placed advertisements in the media inviting those 'interested Rugby League bodies in New South Wales to submit applications for admission to the NSW Rugby Football League Sydney Premiership Competition in 1982', the notice stated that all submissions were to be sent directly to 'Mr. K. Humphreys, Executive Director'. He personally would oversee the process. For league fans in the Canberra–Queanbeyan region, this was no bad thing at all.

Three candidates soon emerged for the one remaining spot in the historic 1982 competition: Canberra–Queanbeyan, Campbelltown and the NSW Central Coast/Newcastle. Curiously, several months before applications even closed, on 27 October 1980, the NSWRL's general committee voted overwhelmingly (36–5) for Canberra to host the 1981 City–Country match at Bruce Stadium—and acted on this decision despite criticism in the media from Secretary of the Country League Rugby John O'Toole. ACT Rugby League (ACTRL) President Don Elphick worked tirelessly to get the game for the national capital and he was heartened in the coming months when Humphreys and his committee refused to budge as O'Toole increased the pressure to veto Canberra.

All the Canberra bid's advocates were emboldened, and they were handed some invaluable tactical advice off the record. Les McIntyre wanted his Queanbeyan Blues team in the Sydney competition; Humphreys thought otherwise and he made his position known. McIntyre later acknowledged the ground he had to concede or suffer the consequences. The NSWRL, he said, 'didn't want a club side, they wanted a district team'. Get the message or get prepared for disappointment. A district team it would be.

At this point developments unfolded rapidly: on 15 December 1980 the Queanbeyan United Club held its annual general meeting and the main item for discussion was whether the Canberra–Queanbeyan region should seek entry into the Sydney competition; a week later Humphreys personally inspected Bruce Stadium's facilities in order to assess its capacity to host the City–Country game the following year; Humphreys' endorsement encouraged Les McIntyre to convene a meeting (held on 4 January 1981) of the sixteen clubs in the Canberra–Queanbeyan area in order to gauge support for an application to the NSWRL; at this meeting the clubs unanimously agreed to give in-principle support to the preparation of a submission; all agreed to establish a company limited by guarantee; and finally, the cluster of bid supporters then spared no effort to find out what the public thought of the idea.

On Christmas Eve 1980, *Sydney Morning Herald* journalist Ray Gatt wrote an article with the headline, 'Canberra tipped to join Sydney League'. It began with a teaser: 'Canberra the hub of rugby league ... is it just a pipedream or might it eventuate?' Sydney was put on notice of an ambitious new kid on the block and Gatt went on to solidify the claim when he wrote that Kevin Humphreys was 'greatly impressed' by Bruce Stadium, referring to it as a 'magnificent sporting complex'. Gatt also alluded to more purposeful discussions that took place behind closed doors:

> The prime reason for the visit was to inspect the stadium but Mr. Humphreys is reported to have had talks with Canberra officials concerning a possible application to enter a Canberra-based team in the Sydney competition ... Mr. Humphreys' visit might result in Canberra applying.

It did, boosted by the league boss's encouragement and by some hastily gathered poll figures gleaned from 1,872 respondents in Canberra and

Queanbeyan. Nearly 80 per cent of them were favourable to the idea.

The hard work to produce a competitive submission began on an ultra-tight schedule of less than three months. The interim committee entrusted with the task comprised a balance of Queanbeyan and ACT League administrators, headed up by Les McIntyre and ACTRL President Don Elphick. Both were willing to set aside past disagreements and rivalry in favour of the common cause. To add clout to the committee, long-term federal politician the Labor Party's jovial Fred Daly was appointed as patron based on his enormous love of the game and lifetime barracking for the perennially struggling Newtown club. Daly was casting about for another team because his beloved 'Blue Bags', under pressure to survive in the competition at the beginning of the 1980s, disappeared forever at the end of the 1983 season. The interim committee also hired the Arthur Laing consulting firm to advise on promotions and marketing—in effect to add spit and polish to the final product. It all came together in a submission that *A Centenary of Rugby League* later described as 'compelling'.

There were several strong arguments in Canberra's favour: the region had two splendid local grounds, Seiffert Oval in Queanbeyan and Bruce Stadium in the Belconnen area of northern Canberra, capable of immediately hosting competition games and representing the code effectively in televised games; the region's junior ranks had gone from strength to strength, in 1982 boasting 136 teams in the district and several thousand players, statistics which prompted Les McIntyre to boast that Canberra–Queanbeyan had 'the strongest junior League in NSW Country and the third strongest after Parramatta and Penrith'; in advance of the final decision, league authorities knew that a Canberra–Queanbeyan team would have the services of one of the game's most experienced and respected coaches, Queanbeyan's own Don Furner, a man with an unmatched knowledge of the game in the Monaro region, Sydney and Queensland, both as player and coach; and lastly, a Canberra–Queanbeyan club in the premier competition would not have to contend with the sort of financial problems bedevilling the

Sydney clubs because it was bankrolled by the Queanbeyan Leagues Club, an organisation whose profits seemed to be cemented into an endless, upwards trajectory.

With the day for submission of presentations closing in, it became a race between two after the NSW Central Coast–Newcastle bid was withdrawn. That left only Canberra and Campbelltown. It was always going to be a close-run thing but in the countdown of the final fortnight in March a few things worked in Canberra's favour. For some years Newcastle had been regarded by almost everyone as the team most likely to be the first non-Sydney club in the competition. Its late withdrawal boosted Canberra's stocks, as the *Daily Mirror* headline of 17 March declared: 'Canberra's favourite for No. 14'. When a few of the CEOs of Sydney's struggling clubs expressed the fear that travelling their team to the nation's capital might prove a costly proposition, Les McIntyre responded instantly to the threat. Journalist Ian Hanson's *Daily Mirror* article in league's most widely read daily newspaper cited the Monaro boss' confident reaction: 'Our financial support down here is fantastic and our backers are prepared to do almost anything to get Canberra into the Sydney premiership.' Canberra, he confirmed, would be happy to reimburse all visiting teams for costs incurred. Surrounded by clubs crying poor, Kevin Humphreys and his committee welcomed this bold declaration from a potential club certain of its economic future.

With the benefit of hindsight, it was probably the public stance adopted by the league's executive director in the last few days before the vote that created the environment for what finally occurred. Humphreys' position on the renewal the game had to have was revisited by the most respected league journalist at the time, the *Sydney Morning Herald*'s Alan Clarkson, in an article of 27 March 1981 under the headline, 'Next season will set precedents'. In it, Humphreys' opinion on league's need to expand beyond Sydney or perish was extensively quoted:

> We are in Rugby League . . . we are not here just to run the Sydney premiership but to run the game in NSW and to assist its running throughout

> Australia . . . The only thing you need to make the Sydney competition better is less [Sydney] teams . . . teams outside Sydney need to be in the Sydney premiership.

The proximity of Campbelltown to Sydney weighed against it. This time, the tyranny of distance favoured more distant Canberra.

But wait. Would there be another twist or two before the final decision? Straight-shooting league Immortal Bob Fulton definitely thought so when, on the very day of the vote for the fourteenth team, in his regular *Daily Mirror* column he cautioned both contending clubs to beware the mischievous behaviour of Sydney league teams protecting their patch:

> Campbelltown and Canberra will know what the old doublecross is about when they make bids to enter the big-time tonight. They'll learn a promise is a promise—except in rugby league. Clubs who have given their word they would support one or two of the country areas are going to brush them both off. Instead, they will push for 13 teams . . . I know of at least four Sydney clubs who will sidestep the issue! Everyone on the street knows the big push is for Canberra and they may still make it. But more clubs than not will show a bigger sidestep than Steve Mortimer when the issue is raised.

There would indeed be a 'doublecross' to come, and a few tricky sidesteps as well. The delegation from the national capital had some more surprises in store for them.

The Canberra delegation was made up of eight individuals, most chosen for their capacity to respond to any technical questions that might arise concerning a Canberra team's unprecedented place in the competition and its ramifications. Les McIntyre and Don Elphick were there as the voices of decades of country football administrative experience, and the prime movers in Queanbeyan and Canberra league circles. They were ably supported by George Tooke and Graham Ayre, secretary and treasurer respectively of the Canberra District Rugby League (CDRL); Ron Edwards, the Queanbeyan Leagues Club secretary–manager; and Don Furner, the Raiders' coach-in-waiting. The other two members of the group gifted Canberra its genuine point of difference—ageless politician and sometime comic, Fred Daly, the 'King of Canberra' as the newspapers dubbed him at the time; and Ros Kelly, the recently elected member for the federal seat of Canberra. Importantly, Kelly was an attractive and intelligent woman whose background was Sydney working class. All three attributes had value on the day in a decidedly old-school male domain.

The two politicians were given the job of presenting the case, Daly to address the Canberra community's 'public and civic' support for a future team and Kelly to explore the team's potential place in the future development of the national capital. The two Labor Party colleagues were clever choices. Both worked the room expertly, with a charm offensive directed at the league's crusty bureaucrats and astute application of the politician's powers of persuasion.

Ros Kelly, who before entering politics had only a few years earlier taught English at Yass High School, and Dickson and Narrabundah Colleges in the ACT, fondly recalled the experience of presenting the submission 25 years later in a special Raiders supplement in the *Canberra Times*:

> Fred Daly and I were the joint-patrons and had the responsibility to put the case from the Canberra community perspective. I was told at rugby league headquarters as we walked into the room that no woman had officially set foot in that room before. I knew I had their attention for at least two minutes and told them it was their opportunity to grow rugby league in the region. Fred of course made them laugh. They couldn't resist us and the great argument put by the McIntyre clan.

The memory is about right. In the end the NSWRL administrators could not resist the argument, but they very nearly did. Kelly's memories fail to include the last-minute problems that surfaced in a meeting that went for nearly five hours. The Raiders' delegation encountered a particularly cunning nemesis in Campbelltown solicitor John Marsden. When he again raised the issue of team travel costs to Canberra, Les McIntyre reiterated the club's intention to cover the transport of opposition teams. This time, though, the wily McIntyre went one better, stating that Canberra would cover opposition *airfares* while paying its own fares for away games. The Canberra boss was not about to let cost considerations undermine the bid at this late stage.

Perhaps anticipating Canberra's reaction, Marsden then played his last chess move when he alerted the committee to the latest available air-travel statistics he happened to have handy: in 1980, the NSWRL committee was informed, Canberra's airport had been closed 39 times due to fog between the months of March and September, in effect the span of the footy season. While the Bureau of Meteorology would later record that not one game was affected by fog in the national capital in either 1982 or 1983, in March 1980 in the stifling atmosphere of the NSWRL's meeting room the heads of some of the room's decision-makers, about to cast their vote, nodded in apparent agreement with Marsden's eleventh hour news. The Canberra delegation gasped. A sure thing had suddenly become a 50–50 bet; Marsden had seen to that.

When the vote was finally taken, the tension was palpable. A first vote on a rogue motion *not* to include a fourteenth team—in other words, to proceed with only thirteen, Bob Fulton's anticipated double cross—was defeated 26–16. Comfortable, but by no means convincing. The vote to *accept* Canberra that followed was even tighter. Finally, by 24 votes to 18, a new chapter in the history of the 'Sydney' competition was written. The age-old brand, the Sydney brand, would have to be updated—twice. It was a Palm Beach to Sutherland competition no more. Canberra and Illawarra had stormed the barricades.

One of the game's most sensible voices, Frank Hyde, a former representative Newtown, North Sydney and Balmain Tigers player, the unofficial leader of league's radio commentators for decades, summed up the situation in one concise sentence in his *Sydney Morning Herald* column: 'Acceptance of Illawarra and Canberra into the Sydney Rugby League competition was inevitable if the game was to avoid extinction.' For those in Canberra and Queanbeyan, Les McIntyre put the local view with similar clarity when he said that 'Rugby League has a golden opportunity to take its place as the premier sport in the showplace capital of Australia'.

Time to roll up the sleeves

The Canberra club's preparations started at full throttle. By April 1981, thirteenth team Illawarra had benefited from over three months of bonus time to sound out players and officials in search of a competitive team and viable club. They were embedded in the player market with money to spend. This was a problem for Canberra from the outset and, just as serious, the first competition game was a mere eleven months away.

It was a recipe for failure and there were those in the Sydney media only too happy to predict such an outcome. The loudest of all was Channel Nine's chief sports commentator, Ron Casey, the 'mouth from the south', who described the addition of the two clubs from outside Sydney as 'an unmitigated disaster'. The feisty Casey, always on the lookout for a controversy that he could initiate or exploit, took it upon himself to be the prophet of doom: 'I feel like the man on the Titanic who has seen the iceberg . . . and no-one else has seen it'. In Canberra, rearrangement of the deck chairs was not an option. It was a time for everyone involved to roll up the sleeves.

Testing months lay ahead, although there was some good news for the locals in mid-May when the City–Country game at Bruce Stadium attracted a whopping 17,912 spectators. It was a statement for the future, many thousands more than even the most optimistic local league supporters had anticipated. The timing was perfect. Kevin Humphreys called the game a 'very worthwhile experiment', pleased that the Canberra community had shown in the best possible way that it was an audience keen to be won over.

A competition was announced to find a name, colours and logo for the team, with the winner to receive a trip for two to the Gold Coast, a week's accommodation and $200 spending money. Unofficially, a few media outlets had already begun using the 'Raiders' name, despite the *Canberra Times* insisting that no official decision on any naming–design matters had been made. Entrants were advised that the club's colours and logos could not replicate those of the Australian, state or other Sydney sides, and that the winning entry had to be endorsed by the NSWRL. The timeframe for the final decision hardly inspired potential entrants, who were given the bare minimum of time to submit original ideas. They appear to have had all of a week to the closing date and were told that 'entries should be lodged in boxes at the leagues clubs' or sent to a PO Box in Queanbeyan. The process looked rushed, and it was.

Like at least two earlier ACT public naming–design competitions—in 1912–13 to give the national capital its name, and in 1928 to produce a Canberra coat of arms—this one too was oddly flawed: a week was not enough to attract a decent crop of entries; the 'Raiders' name appeared to be mysteriously locked in already; and questions were being asked about whether the winning entry would in fact determine colours, logo and name, as first advertised.

There was a minimum of transparency. The Raiders' publication, *25 Years in the Limelight 1982–2006*, informs us that it was inaugural coach Don Furner who came up with the 'Raiders' name. Furner, it states, had visited the Oakland Raiders 'to study their coaching methods' and favoured the name. However, he did not come up with the name or colours, as some have suggested. The truth of the matter is that the name was effectively settled according to the views and market research of the NSWRL. Their communications section wanted the two new teams to have names with instant recognition. The decisions were made at a time when America's NFL and NBA had already achieved significant penetration into Australia's sporting market. The Pittsburgh Steelers and

San Francisco's Oakland Raiders were well known to audiences Down Under, along with a host of American basketball players. Local names both serious and tongue-in-cheek put forward in the naming competition, such as the 'Fat Cats', 'Brumbies', 'Diplomats', 'Cockatoos', 'Senators', 'Warrigals', 'Griffins' and 'Rovers', never stood a chance.

Not that this deterred a few of Canberra's more imaginative sporting citizens from promoting the 'Yowies' as their proposed choice—a hairy half-man half-beast, similar to the Yeti in the Himalayas, with a long and fanciful history of 'sightings' across the Limestone Plains. While the name no doubt ticked the necessary boxes for the locals, a Canberra 'Yowies' side catapulted into the Sydney competition amidst conservatively named teams like the Tigers, Magpies, Bears and Rabbits would have been a step too far. The NSWRL was changing, reforming, but not to the extent of embracing a mythic Monaro beast. The league's marketers favoured the 'Raiders' name for the fourteenth team, and so it would be.

If the circumstances surrounding confirmation of the name are obscure, the same can be said of the club's colours. The public competition in May 1981 attracted over 120 entries and was won by a local resident, 'Patricia Taylor'. She proposed that the colours ought to be a combination of the ACT's blue and gold, together with the green and white of the Hall village rugby league team of yesteryear. The uniform design, approved by the NSWRL in August, consisted of a lime-green jersey with white hoops above the elbows and blue and gold bands, white shorts with blue and gold stripes, and lime-green socks with banded blue, gold and white tops. 'Patricia Taylor' was in fact Patricia Elphick, the wife of local ACT Rugby League identity Don Elphick. It was felt that his prominent place in the Raiders' submission and presentation team might make the competition look like an exercise in nepotism. So 'Patricia Taylor' won the competition—well, half a competition—and most were pleased with the result. In a letter she sent to NRL Chief Executive Todd Greenberg in February 2019, 82-year-old Mrs Elphick pointed out for the historical record that she had nothing to do with the

Canberra Raiders' suggested jersey design or its colours. The 'original designer', she wrote, was her late husband Don, and the 'Taylor' name used in the entry was her maiden name.

A circular badge of the Canberra District Rugby League was sited on the jersey's left breast with the words 'Canberra Raiders' in blue on a gold outer circle and a Viking Raider's head on a green centre. The badge, nostalgically recycled in some of the club's gear for sale in 2018 and 2019, was also designed by the NSWRL's marketing section. It too was a top-down decision. The initial response was mixed at best; the Viking figure's cartoonish appearance in the middle of the logo failed to pass the Queanbeyan and Canberra pub tests of the early 1980s.

Time can be a great healer though. These days the original 'Victor' is affectionately recalled by the club's large contingent of baby-boomer fans. For almost as long as the team has existed, the appearance of the ever-popular club mascot, Victor the Viking, has validated the original. Given such energetic life by Tony Wood in the Victor suit since 1984, the Raiders' mascot stands tall as a nostalgic link to a less slick, less market-driven past.

When the chosen club colours were first displayed, there were howls of dismay from those for whom the lime of the 'lime green' was too loud, even disrespectful. It *was* a statement, a colour straight out of John Travolta's *Saturday Night Fever*, and it upset traditionalists. Not anymore. While it is true that over the years the vibrant green has occasionally been modified, it has a habit of returning to the original green, much to the satisfaction of the Raiders' faithful. The last word on the subject belongs to 1982 'Pioneer' Lloyd Martin when he said: 'I remember first seeing the gear. God strike me. I'd come from Balmain which had a traditional jumper, and then this one. But after the initial shock it became a jumper to be proud of in the end.'

The *Sydney Morning Herald* interviewed Les McIntyre for an article published on 24 May 1981. Intended as a promotional puff piece, the article delved more deeply into the new venture's future and the obstacles that lay ahead. Top of the list was, according to McIntyre, 'the restrictive 13-import rule, which didn't exist when Cronulla and Penrith entered the competition'. The rule, he said, was 'a big handicap for a new club'. Put simply, it amounted to a restriction of trade and the cash-flush Raiders suffered initially because of it.

There were, however, several bright spots to encourage the fledgling club's ambitions. First among these was that while Don Furner had not yet been officially announced as the team's coach, he may as well have been. Through April and May 1981 he went about utilising his main coaching strength, canny assessment of talent, with a view to achieving smart, cheap recruitment of players. Labelled in the *Herald* article as 'one of Canberra's trump cards', the easy-going Furner took the opportunity to publicise one of a Canberra-based team's most valuable assets: access to a 'lifestyle that should attract young family men. It's a better place to raise children'. Together with cheaper housing availability than either Sydney or Brisbane, this constituted an attraction every bit as important for coach Ricky Stuart today as it was for Don Furner 40 years ago. Canberra's laid-back rural appeal was from the outset a stark contrast to the bright lights of the other cities.

How successful was recruitment in the months before the 1982 competition year began? Under the circumstances, perhaps a seven out of ten. Queenslander Jay Hoffman was the first import to be signed, and this was confirmed at a televised media event on 30 August 1981 which also made official Don Furner's appointment as coach. At the same gathering it was announced that two more 'local identities, Billy Sullivan and Bob Camden—reliable men who brought with them a long association with the district's football culture—would fill the reserve grade and third grade coaching positions'. Furner indicated that he had a 'shopping list' of 50 players and that he fully intended to fill the thirteen import spots. He was not willing to elaborate on the progress already made in case it affected a few of the trickier player negotiations taking place.

Jay Hoffman was an inspired signing. A representative hooker with the Brisbane Brothers club, coached by a young and progressive Wayne

Bennett, he was a surprise omission from the South Queensland team to play Papua New Guinea during the 1981 season and he was not too happy about it. Aged 23, having changed his day job from Brisbane city council clerk to construction labourer in order to get extra physical work, Hoffman judged the next few years as vital to the development of his footballing career. Canberra offered him the freshest of starts. He was brought in as a marquee player, a team leader, and that is exactly what he became in the club's first six formative years, 'bricks and mortar' years, to 1987.

There was something else, something symbolically significant that Hoffman brought to the club: a direct connection between Canberra and the rich recruiting pastures of Queensland. Jay was the first off a Sunshine State production line that, more than any other single factor, enabled the Raiders to be competitive well ahead of schedule. Two more Queenslanders put pen to paper shortly after Hoffman—Mackay's Wayne Smith and Rowan Brennan, a utility player who proved his worth in the Raiders' early years.

In the final hectic months of 1981 Don Furner used every contact he had, and went to as many games as he could in Sydney and the bush, to get the signatures of players he felt would fit into the team culture he wanted to create. He informed Les McIntyre that he regarded the job ahead as a five-year plan, asked for a guarantee that he would be coach for at least that period, and got it on a handshake. Unknown to both men at the time, this agreement established one of the Raiders' most dearly held principles—coaching security. With only one exception over nearly 40 years, it has been the case that if you signed to coach the Raiders, you left the job on your own terms.

In the weeks following the Hoffman signing, the new coach received a number of knockbacks and he had several players pull out of deals at the eleventh hour. Furner was able to confirm the signatures of Ian Hamilton and Gary Ellis from Leeton, John McLeod from Wests in Sydney and a Novocastrian with the right attitude for the club he had begun to build, Craig Bellamy. For a young man, Bellamy was a deep thinker about the game, and he could play just about anywhere in the backline.

Furner eventually invited 100 local players to try out, the final list of signings including Terry Wickey from North Canberra; the Queanbeyan Roos' Sam Vucago, Chris O'Grady and Peter Elliott; Peter McGrath, Lui Bon and Gerry De La Cruz from the Queanbeyan Blues; livewire halfback Chris O'Sullivan from the Canberra Gallopers, a youngster with untapped talent; Ashley Gilbert from Crookwell; and Tony Pobjie and Gary Britt from just over the border in Yass.

Furner narrowly missed the signatures of Manly's Bruce Walker and the fiery personality player Geoff Robinson from Canterbury, though he could be well pleased with a succession of later signings that brought to the club: the Balmain Tigers' Lloyd Martin and David Grant—a monster of a man who gave the Raiders' pack the steel and belief in its first season that they could mix it with the Sydney sides; the Sharks' Scott Dudman; Mick Tilse, Dane's father, from Newcastle; and Steve O'Callaghan, as important as any of the first wave of signed players. O'Callaghan was yet another Blues player who, like his Queanbeyan teammates, brought a winning culture with him. The question to be answered was whether that culture could be successfully transplanted into the cauldron of Sydney football. For many years past it had been the case that any talented country footballer from the southern region who wanted to stay in the country headed to the Blues to get a game. Could the Queanbeyan brand successfully adapt to Sydney football? It was about to be put to the test.

The first training sessions at Queanbeyan's Taylor Park in the summer of 1981–82 were exhausting in the Christmas heat. It was lucky that coach Furner had already encountered the difficulties of training 'big fellows', as he called them, like Dick Thornett and the legendary Artie Beetson, a known connoisseur of the meat pie. This experience was invaluable for the attention he needed to give to the highly talented David Grant in particular. The former Tiger weighed in at about 112 kilograms on arrival in Canberra though he vowed to lose eight of those kegs by the first round. His coach must have gone a little weak at the knees when he lapped a totally gassed Grant in the marquee import's first training session in early November.

Geoff Peard, the brother of former Test player John Peard, was hired to train the squad, along with Brian Bourke—who came to the Raiders from West Belconnen, and before that the Blues. Those players Bourke had whipped into shape at either of his local clubs well knew the kind of commando regimen he would put together to meet the demands of Sydney football. Bourke and Peard expected the players to give their all at training. The Raiders were going to be a long way from the best side in the competition to begin with, so they better be one of the fittest.

Bourke and Raiders' secretary John McIntyre gave the club an additional connection that helped recruitment. They had both attended St Edmunds College. As old boys, they kept a close watch on the talent coming through at one of the best rugby (and Rugby League) schools in all of New South Wales and the ACT. The renowned Brother Wallace, in charge of St Eddie's football and a relentless taskmaster, continued to produce a succession of outstanding players who, after leaving school, made their mark in both codes. Champions of the future Ricky Stuart and Dave Furner both attended St Edmunds.

It was clear that, in preparation for their inaugural year in Sydney football, the Raiders left no stone unturned in their bid to be respectably competitive.

3

THE CANBERRA PHENOMENON

1982–85

Two powerhouse clubs, Parramatta and Canterbury, dominated the NSWRL competition in the first half of the 1980s. Mick Cronin, Kenny, Sterling, Price, Grothe and their Eels teammates shared the spotlight with Steve 'Turvey' Mortimer, Terry Lamb and an intimidating pack of Bulldog forwards. Champions were on show.

It was a glittering era full of star players, yet the game continued to have its problems.

Sink or swim

In 1982, a year which celebrated the seventy-fifth anniversary of Rugby League in Australia and two new clubs in the competition, an unassuming Sydney solicitor named Jim Comans took on a difficult public role deemed necessary for the code's longer-term survival. A former player and amateur boxer, Comans was asked by League Chairman Kevin Humphreys and his board to rid the game of those players who were restricting its growth and popularity because of their thuggish behaviour. Comans was the right man for the job, fearlessly handing out severe penalties to the likes of Western Suburbs' Bob Cooper and Les Boyd. The message was clear. Rugby League was determined to clean itself up. Careers built on violence and intimidation came to an end.

This stand by the NSWRL benefited the Raiders' prospects in the club's first decade for a couple of reasons: firstly, the attractive, attacking football at the heart of Don Furner's coaching philosophy gained implicit support; and secondly, the aim of Comans and Humphreys to give skilful ball-players more protection created the environment in which the supremely talented Raider teams of the later 1980s could, unhindered, ply their trade with innovation and adventure.

But that was also in the future, a fanciful dream as far as the Raiders' players and officials were concerned in their first season. They prepared cautiously for a tough initiation—hopeful, determined to win a few games if possible, and even more determined to gain respect as a viable addition to the most demanding Rugby League competition in the world.

First things first. A decision about the Raiders' home ground had to be made as soon as possible, given that the team admitted into the competition was, after all, the *Canberra* Raiders. A larger question loomed: how would the sometimes brittle relationship between Queanbeyan (NSW) and Canberra (ACT) Rugby League authorities evolve in the short term? Would the rivalries of the past recur in the present and future?

Les McIntyre wanted Seiffert Oval to be the Raiders' home ground. His stance on the issue, together with an unflattering assessment by real-estate firm Raine and Horne regarding Bruce Stadium's capacity to host regular competition games in its present condition, meant that into the immediate future the city of Canberra's first generation of league fans had better get used to heading out to Queanbeyan to watch the region's team.

The first important public occasion for the club in its year of entry took place on 19 February 1982 at a 'Meet the Raiders' luncheon at the Queanbeyan Leagues Club, the official launch of the fourteenth team. The long list of 'no-shows' foreshadowed the rocky road ahead. There would be no favours for the new club, not an iota of collegiate spirit among contending clubs. The total club representation at the launch for the Raiders' first-ever promotional day was two out of thirteen. To their credit, Cronulla and Balmain took the trouble to send a representative.

Manly stalwart Peter 'Zorba' Peters, who had carved out a successful career in the media after football, headlined a *Rugby League Week* article he wrote about the event, 'Snubbed! Cold shoulder for Canberra'. Peters noted that 'what should have been a historic occasion for Sydney's fourteenth club lost a lot because of the absence of the majority of the glamour clubs . . . the four and a half hour drive from Sydney or the $129 return air ticket seems beyond the Sydney clubs'.

In his news column the same month as the launch, Frank Hyde expressed his sympathy for the Raiders' forthcoming bus excursion every second week up the Hume Highway to play. There was no money for flash travel back then. Bus there, bus back, stop at Mittagong Motel for meals and put your head on a pillow on a motel in Ashfield on Parramatta Road. But Hyde also flagged an environmental advantage the team would always enjoy during every future season's months of June, July and August when Canberra's 'chilly winter winds' were set to make life difficult for those opposition players accustomed to, and spoiled by, balmy Sydney weather. Canberra's cold has undone many a visiting team over the years. Some opposition coaches, acutely aware of the psychological impact of the Limestone Plains' frost and bitter westerly winds, have been known to deliver an edict to their players on game day. Don't mention the cold! Hyde was spot-on.

Forty-eight hours before the Raiders' first competition match, against Souths at Redfern Oval, the coach finally announced 52 graded players, leaving three spots open to him. This group, the 1982 'Pioneers', were about to embark on a journey which would earn them an honoured place in the first chapters of the club's illustrious history. All deserve to be named:

> John Algate, Jim Antonakos, Bruce Bacchetto, Craig Bellamy, Lui Bon, Mal Bradley, Rowan Brennan, Col Brinkley, Gary Britt, Dennis Cherry, Richard

Cooke, Gerry De La Cruz, Scott Dudman, Peter Elliott, Garry Ellis, Greg Fitzgerald, Carl Frommel, Ashley Gilbert, Gary Givens, David Grant, Ian Hamilton, Jon Hardy, Neil Henry, Jay Hoffman, Chris Kinna, Barry Kirkup, Peter McGrath, Tony McGurgan, John McLeod, Angel Marina, Lloyd Martin, Tom Nickels, Steve O'Callaghan, Chris O'Grady, Chris O'Sullivan, Tony Pobjie, Mick Press, Herb Rauter, David Reid, Frank Robby, Derek Schaeffer, Peter Scott, Jeff Simons, Alan Smith, Trevor Smith, Wayne Stonham, Michael Tilse, Sam Vucago, Robert Warner, Graham Waugh, Paul West, Terry Wickey.

If the players required a reality check on their personal expectations with the competition about to start, they got it in spades from the betting market for the season ahead. Parramatta was 5–2 favourite; Canberra the rank outsider at 500–1. The first year was only about credible survival.

The Pioneers, 1982

The first few competition games of the Raiders' inaugural season amounted to a tough initiation, different entirely to the experimentation and mix and match on show in the pre-season trials. Two precious competition points were on offer as Souths made clear in the season's first game. As expected, the Raiders lost all three grades under Redfern's dim floodlights, the thirds going down 25–2, reserves 18–13 and the firsts being handed a hefty 37–7 loss. Welcome to Sydney football.

Raider trivia buffs are well aware of the team's first and only try-scorer against the Rabbits, indigenous halfback Gerry De La Cruz. Gerry had originally been recommended to Don Furner not by a talent scout but a truck driver he'd met in Brisbane who said he knew about a good local kid going great guns in Darwin. Don had said himself that he would go anywhere to have a look at players. Experience had taught him over the years that you could never be sure where talent might be unearthed.

The truck driver was sure that Gerry was one out of the box and, given the impression he made on both coach and club officials in the first months of Raider training, it was a bitter disappointment when severe injury curtailed Gerry's promising career after only four games in lime green. His fleeting appearances were enough to get him into the record books, however. Against Souths, in front of a fiercely partisan crowd, the Top End product momentarily lit the place up with a try described as 'bewildering' by one Sydney daily. Oh, what might have been had he been able to stick around for a few years at least.

For Raiders' historians, the trickier quiz question to answer is who scored the team's first points, and it was not the flashy indigenous lad from up north, number three in the club's all-time list of players. Answer? The first points were scored by five-eighth Peter McGrath, numbered eighth of all time, who kicked two penalties before his teammate crossed the stripe.

Canberra born and bred, a product of Daramalan College's rugby program, Peter these days is a respected lawyer in town, a partner in a firm called Griffin Legal. His off-field sporting CV since the Raiders is an imposing one. He was chairman of the Brumbies and, after that, chairman of the Australian Rugby Union. On-field in his twenties, Rugby League was his game of choice. Peter still remembers the pit in his stomach when running out onto Redfern Oval to the jeers of the Rabbitohs' plague of fans who had not a skerrick of sympathy for the star-struck visitors, upstarts from the bush who would have to learn the hard way. He also vividly recalls a tackle he attempted on Souths' lock Robert Simpkins, who exploded through his flailing arms as if shot out of a cannon. In that moment, frozen in time, Peter's four premierships with the Queanbeyan Blues were a distant memory.

After Souths, the next few games only got tougher. Game number two against the Western Suburbs Magpies, at Seiffert under the club's quality lighting, saw a respectable 10–4 deficit at half-time blow out to a 33–4 loss at the final whistle. Norths, Canterbury, Saints and Manly inflicted much the same punishment in the weeks that followed, leading into the fixture on 11 April at Belmore Oval against the formidable Parramatta Eels. It was an encounter that threatened to raise the competitive bar. Reporting the game, the *Sydney Morning Herald* suggested that while the Raiders did not play all that badly, the Eels were 'just too good'. Mick Cronin scored 27 points in a 54–3 thrashing; 'Guru' Eric Grothe terrorised the fragile defence line when scoring four tries; and the wizard, Peter Sterling, scampered in for three of his own.

It was a tough day at the office for the men in lime green. As they trudged off the ground, a lone try by John McLeod the only time the Eels were troubled by their presence, the 500–1 offer for a Raiders' premiership seemed about right. Ron Casey's squawk that the team would not win a game all year must have been ringing loudly in the playing group's ears.

Not a single Canberra player overwhelmed by the irresistible Eels could have anticipated the result a week later at Seiffert Oval against the Newtown Jets. Only a few games into the season, Don Furner was forced to defend the squad and his own strategic decision-making to the media. He asked for more time, pointing out that it had been no different for any of the new sides injected into the Sydney competition in decades past. Under pressure, Furner reassessed his best-case scenario of four wins in the season. He opted for two, conscious that a second win needed a first. And where would it come from?

Cometh the day, cometh the Jets on a sunny Seiffert afternoon, 18 April 1982, in front of nearly 10,000 fans who craved a maiden victory. Their team—or rather, the team they were heading along to cheer for against the latest band of Sydney marauders—was probably staring at yet another heavy defeat. At half-time, the Raiders were down 8–2 and battling with no less than four of their best fourteen players out injured. The second 40 minutes, however, was nothing short of a revelation. Captain David Grant, John McLeod and Jay Hoffman led from the front, gaining the ascendancy over a back-peddling Newtown pack. A McLeod try was reinforced, late in the match, by a wonderful touchdown scored by local boy, former Canberra Galloper, Chris O'Sullivan. He had built a convincing case for early promotion to the top side, many in the club feeling that he was a star in the making. Certainly his try received a mighty roar from the crowd, none cheering more loudly than Janet and Bob O'Sullivan, Chris's mum and dad, his two most devoted fans.

Newtown now led 11–10.

So it was Steve O'Callaghan, quickly gaining the experience that would enable him to be Player of the Year in 1983, who lined up the crucial conversion in his first pair of sponsored boots—a cheap pair of ASICS that gave him awful blisters in the Canberra cold for months. As he bent over the ball with his hands trembling, skipper Dave Grant casually walked past his nervous teammate and, no pressure, offered an assessment of the moment: 'This is the most important kick you'll ever have.' Steve converted and the Raiders had their first-ever win, 12–11. It was a memorable day for players and supporters alike. Centre Paul West, recruited from Souths, years later recalled the chant that went up. It was a 'Glorious First' according to one local paper, sweet music for everyone, and especially sweet for club President Les McIntyre. Known to have a liking for a punt, at the start of the season he happily took 20–1 on the Raiders winning at least one game. It was a big payday.

When Frank Hyde, covering another match on radio, crossed to Paul Quinn at Seiffert to get an update, all he and his 2UE listeners heard was an overjoyed Quinn shouting 'We won! We won!' The day after the famous victory, Ron Casey sent a telegram to Raiders HQ which simply read: 'Sincere congratulations—JC is infallible, RC is not'.

Despite a really gutsy win, media scepticism continued unabated. Only four days before the Newtown game, *Sydney Morning Herald* journalist Brian Curran devoted his regular column to an appraisal of the Raiders under the title 'Capital punishment for Rugby League'. What followed was a classic of its kind. It had taken only a few weeks for the team to be the latest subject for the popular sport of 'Canberra-bashing'. This was a sport with a long history. Brian Curran was itching to join the fray:

> The national capital is depressing at any time of year, more so during the winter months when even the politicians have the good sense to leave the

> place as often as possible. Depression sets in from the moment of arrival at what is called Canberra Airport whose terminal holds the distinction of being the most claustrophobic structure foisted on mankind since the invention of the backyard dunny. Visiting motorists have long found Canberra's chief landmark, its road system, to be almost as unintelligible as the workings of Federal Parliament.
>
> Indeed, our forefathers obviously knew what they were doing when they selected the site of Canberra for Parliament House—the two deserve each other. But do Sydney Rugby League followers deserve to have Canberra inflicted upon them? ... The competition is weaker for their presence. Canberra may win a game at home, so to speak, when Queanbeyan is gripped by mid-winter cold. But then a team of Eskimos could probably do the same as long as the match was played at the North Pole.

Curran's column proved too much for Raiders' convert and federal politician, Ros Kelly, who took him to task in her workplace. On the floor of the House of Representatives, Kelly had the hapless Curran firmly in her sights:

> Obviously Mr. Curran has never ever bothered to watch the Canberra team ... This man displays total ignorance of the game ... The competition has in fact been greatly enhanced by the presence of the Canberra Raiders ... If Curran had watched Canberra play and visited Canberra he would not have written this nonsense.

Nonsense it was, but the undignified pattern of the past had found crude expression in the present. The Raiders were in for their share of 'Canberra-bashing'.

If Ros Kelly was thrilled with her team's first taste of success, she and many other like-minded fans were ecstatic when three more wins were added during the season. Yes, the wins were interspersed between the odd belting at the hands of Illawarra 45–0, Cronulla 44–5, Balmain 35–0 and Penrith 42–8. But each win was another solid brick in the club's construction. And each one helped to make good on coach Furner's original prediction of four wins.

The Raiders got their prized second win when they beat co-competition leader Souths, 23–18, in front of nearly 13,000 spectators at Seiffert in early June. It was immensely satisfying, demonstrating that the Newtown game was no fluke and reversing the lopsided result of game one at Redfern. In the best team effort of the season, the *Canberra Times* coverage refused to nominate a man of the match: 'They were all men of the match'. The win was even better than it looked on paper, considering it was achieved without a number of regular first-graders. When recalling the first few seasons, most of the '82 Pioneers maintain that when skipper David Grant produced his best stuff, the Raiders won. After the Souths game, one Sydney paper's headline summed up: 'Raiders on Rampage. Grant lights the fire'.

The Raiders chalked up their third success against St George at Seiffert Oval to enthuse a massive crowd of 13,758. The ground record was broken again in a dramatic 25–22 victory. If the new brigade of supporters was 'delirious' when the team beat Souths, the Saints game was close to mayhem. The local boys in eye-watering green had begun attracting fans both from its heartland in the Queanbeyan area and across the border, from the city that the cynics said had no soul, no character.

As in the Souths game, big boppers David Grant and John McLeod again led from the front while Chris O'Sullivan delivered another cheeky performance. Local boy Angel Marina, gifted with heaven-sent fleet of foot, scored the winner just before full-time to break a 22–22 deadlock. 'Nana' Grant was again man of the match (according to Saints' coach Roy Masters, completely outplaying his own team's Australian representative prop Craig Young), Marina was elusive all day and O'Sullivan 'gave the St George defence headaches'. Another Sydney paper summed up: 'All honours to Raiders as they slay St George'. The spectators filing out of Seiffert after the Raiders' win had made up their minds. They were coming back.

The last win of the season was perhaps the most enjoyable of all. On Anzac Day, 25 April, fellow newcomers the Illawarra Steelers had hammered the Raiders in Wollongong to the tune of 45–0. Just over three months later, it was the Steelers' turn to travel to Seiffert and the tables were turned. The Raiders scored six tries in a gritty 26–19 win after being down 12–10 at half-time. Yet again Dave Grant was outstanding, ably supported by Chris O'Sullivan, who scored twice in another super display. Craig Bellamy provided further evidence of his value as a utility player, getting well on top of his more illustrious opponent, Steelers' captain John Dorahy. Jay Hoffman, Jon Hardy, Scott Dudman and 'Iron Man' Carl Fromel tackled everything that moved, something they had done for most of the season. Peter McGrath, the club's first-ever point-scorer, had his best game of the season. One headline said it all: 'Canberra reap revenge'. In fact, if the reserves had managed to resist a late surge from their opponents, the club would have won in all three grades.

In their first season the Raiders had over-achieved, and the assets that accumulated during the year went well beyond squad solidarity and four precious wins. There was much to get excited about for the first generation of Raiders supporters. First and foremost, the enthusiasm and resilience shown by the fans themselves. In only one year, a solid supporter base had been built well beyond expectations. Over 140,000 people came through the Seiffert turnstiles, the fourth best home figures of all teams. The average attendance was close to 11,000 people and the ground record was broken no less than four times. Club officials had to respond in the early season to big crowd numbers by cramming as many cars and trucks into the outer ground as they could. The backs of pick-ups were especially popular. Tightly bunched suburban groups of friends made themselves heard from their four-wheeled baby-grandstands.

The hardy few who began the Raiders Supporters Club at the beginning of 1982 had by round twelve found themselves forced to temporarily close the books (with 1,000 signed up) in order to organise the necessary administration to cope with the numbers. Perhaps the happiest cluster of new fans was a small group who had the optimism and belief to take 25–1 on the Raiders winning a single game in their first season. It didn't take long for a collect. They pooled $800 and pocketed a tidy $20,000. Les McIntyre was not the only Raider punter to exploit Sydney's anti-Canberra bias.

The performance of the Pioneer Raiders reinvigorated Rugby League in the area. So much so that the VFL's historical 'free kick', some 60-odd years of Victorian public servants and their families re-locating from Melbourne to Canberra to take up Commonwealth Government jobs, disappeared.

Late in the year the Raiders went public with the fruits of their recruiting of recent months and it was a plentiful crop. In early October, Terry Fahey, Mark Brennan and Nigel Wilson all signed up. Fahey was a coup. A big and rangy winger, at 29 years of age he still had good years ahead of him, to go with considerable international experience (Tests against England, France and New Zealand) and 150 first-grade games for Souths and Easts. This was experience and talent that, fortunately, money could buy. The later October recruitment announcements were, collectively, just as good: a young second-rower, Paul Elliott, enticed away from the Illawarra Steelers after strong performances earlier in the year against the Raiders; veteran Ron Giteau, a 100-game first-grader with Western Suburbs who brought heaps of experience and guile with him, as well as being one of the competition's leading goal-kickers; Percy Knight, formerly with Woden Valley and the Queanbeyan Kangaroos, returning to the Monaro after five successful years with the Balmain Tigers; and Ray Blacklock, ex-Penrith and Newtown, an energetic winger known for his ability to drift off his wing and get involved in the middle to give his forwards a breather. The talent pool was deepening.

Whether intentional or not, Furner's recruitment strategy placed great faith in the ability of a core of indigenous players to lift the Raiders into a more competitive category. Perusing the new Raider talent in

1983, one Sydney TV commentator described the Raiders' backline as the 'blackline'. It didn't want for speed, agility or scoring punch.

The signings of the last week before Christmas capped off a good year. Allan McMahon brought added international experience with his World Cup, Kangaroo tour in 1978 and 150 first-grade games. He was joined by Gary Spears from the Balmain club, who also came with a bit of rep football on his CV. One other off-season buy, money in the bank, cannot be overlooked: Ingham (Queensland) junior Sam Backo. 'Slammin' Sam's resume didn't look all that flash on paper with stints in Cairns, Group 8 for the Valley Statesmen and Yeppoon, but when the Raiders secured his services from the Yeppoon Seagulls, it turned out to be one of the club's most astute early signings. A few games in the Raiders' lower grades ultimately led Backo into the top grade and stardom. Sam became a personality player adored by the fans.

The Raiders' inaugural end-of-season awards night added fuel to the growing optimism. The best and fairest resulted in a tie between hitman Jon Hardy—one of the few forwards in the comp who had opposition players changing their running line to escape contact—and will-o'-the wisp Chris O'Sullivan. Hardy, who played all 26 games, got the nod on a countback. Sully had every right to question the disparity in the awards dispensed. The countback winner got a car; the all-tied runner-up, also voted the season's 'most improved' first-grade player, received a vacuum cleaner.

The 'most improved' player in any grade went to Ashley Gilbert. This was a sign of things to come, signalling a career that would establish the unheralded Crookwell junior as an essential contributor to the Raiders' future era of dominance. The Sydney media always undervalued him; Raider fans never did.

In the last weeks of the year the club received the best kind of recognition for overall performance. An early Christmas present came on 9 December 1982 when the Woodger Corporation's managing director, 31-year-old Jim Woodger—a local boy made good—announced a $100,000 sponsorship of the club. An established real-estate firm with a recognised regional brand that included fuel, food and insurance interests, Woodgers added to the support package with the promise of providing employment opportunities for players and assistance with promotional activities. The firm announced its new slogan, 'Woodgers grow with the Raiders', and the Raiders placed the Woodgers' logo on its game jersey for the next season. The sponsorship announcement put an exclamation mark on the first year's hard work.

'Upset of the decade' and other achievements, 1983

At the beginning of the second season, Don Furner kept firmly to the course he had marked out in the club's maiden season. He had two aims for the team in 1983: gradual improvement and six wins. The most committed core of fans headed to Seiffert in the second season in the belief that the team could exceed the coach's 'steady' improvement.

Good things started to happen early with convincing home wins against Norths and Wests bookending a desperately unlucky one-point loss to Souths at Redfern. The team secured its first away win with a visit to the Cronulla Sharks at Endeavour Field on 2 April, a workman-like 24–8 victory. Even the Sydney papers took notice, with headlines such as the *Sun*'s 'Canberra Now a Force to be Reckoned With' and the *Mirror*'s 'Respect Now for the Raiders'.

The latter headline and the effort maintained in the first few games must have pleased the coach enormously, particularly since his off-season buys had slotted in so well, so quickly. Allan McMahon, Fahey, Blacklock and Spears got among the tries (Fahey with a treble in the Magpies game), Ronny Giteau found the target with his kicking, Sam Backo in a few cameo appearances showed enough to indicate that a new enforcer had arrived in town, and a number of the '82 Pioneers took their game to the next level. Chief among these were Chris O'Sullivan, Jon Hardy, Steve O'Callaghan and David Grant. As reliable as a metronome, Jay Hoffman produced 80-minute performances every match and newcomer Percy Knight, once he found his feet a few games in, produced some scintillating displays.

By the end of May, the Raiders had already stretched beyond the '82 win total, with five wins on the board. Yet it was probably a loss in the first couple of competition months and a sixth win in mid-June that got fans, officials and, most of all, the players fired up about what lay ahead. The loss was against Manly at Seiffert on 23 April, a 34–14 scoreline that in no way reflected the closeness of the game. It was all tied 6–6 at half-time. The Raiders had a number of players out injured and still managed to extend to the limit the star-studded Sea Eagles, premiership runners-up to Parramatta in 1982 and 1983.

The best was yet to come.

When the team played Parramatta away in the second game of the season, they had been flogged 46–16 after the Eels went on a typical scoring rampage in the last 30 minutes of the game. The Raiders did manage to cross the line for three backline tries of their own, two to Percy Knight and one to Ray Blacklock, but the defeat was comprehensive. In fact, in the Raiders' three games against the Eels since their inception, the team had been outscored by a combined 137 points to 24.

Now fast forward just over three months to 12 June 1983. Seiffert Oval. The return clash in front of a massive crowd. The result? An epic 8–0 win for 'our boys'. The Eels, the try-hungry Eels, held scoreless! They hadn't been blanked since the second round of the 1979 season.

Those lucky enough to be there in the packed Raiders' dressing room after the game, or at the Queanbeyan Leagues later on, celebrated like they'd won some silverware. Massive pride was mixed with (if truth be told) an element of disbelief. It was a victory for the ages, a stepping stone to the future. The players who got the job done have never forgotten it, the so-called 'Bobby Sands' win, named after the courageous Irish republican who starved himself to death in a 1981 political protest. 'That's what it was—we shut them out,' recalled Jay Hoffman, the scholar of the side. Club Secretary John McIntyre hailed it as the 'greatest upset in the history of Rugby League', while well-known Sydney journo Tim Prentice went searching for an appropriate analogy: 'If one could draw a sporting parallel, it was Australia vs Zimbabwe at cricket all over again as the 1,000–1 longshots shrugged off their lowly rating to slay the giants.'

Dave Grant went forward all day, joined in a starring role by Steve O'Callaghan, Terry Fahey, Percy Knight, Craig Bellamy, Chris O'Sullivan and big John McLeod who, according to one report, 'tackled himself almost to exhaustion'. Between them, McLeod, Jay Hoffman, Ash Gilbert and Gary Spears racked up 120-odd tackles. All tackled themselves into exhaustion.

Ron Giteau scored the only try of the match and struck the only two goals in what was far and away the Raiders' sweetest victory since entering the competition, a win that prompted a range of David and Goliath headlines capturing the moment: 'Raiders League Shock—Eels Humbled in Boilover'; 'Warned About Fierce Raiders'; 'Eels Stunned'; 'Raiders Lower Boom on Parramatta'; and 'Rampant Raiders Continue Plunder'. It was only fitting that Parramatta's best player on the day was poached Canberra player, Stan Jurd. What a day for Rugby League in the region.

An inevitable let-down followed the Everest high of the Parramatta game, though the team still managed to add three more wins to their season output, the best of them the defeat of a fancied Eastern Suburbs at Seiffert, 36–8. The Raiders put six tries on their opponents, all to the backs except a Dave Grant special. Beginning to play a style of football that had everyone taking notice, the team scored 495 points during its second season, seventh best in the league, to go with seven wins. It was a sound return for splendid effort, enough to place the team in tenth position on the final premiership table ahead of Penrith, Newtown, Illawarra and Wests. The Raiders climbed over the top of Wests and Newtown in the club championship, and finished level with Illawarra. They managed six victories and the thirds a very creditable ten wins and two draws.

But this was a season where achievement was to be found in a number of other areas as well. A substantial list of 'firsts' kept the Raiders' statisticians busy. To go with a first away win and the first defeat of seemingly impregnable Parramatta, the S.G. Ball team was the first Raider side to qualify for a semifinal; in the round against Newtown on 22 May, the Raiders won all three grades for the first time; Jon Hardy, whose tackling was described as 'lethal' by Jack Gibson, was the first Raider chosen for representative honours when selected for city seconds; and Ron Giteau seemed to break Raider point-scoring records each time he stepped onto the paddock in the season's second round.

And there was one other important 'first'. On 8 June when the Raiders played Easts in a K.B. Cup game at Leichhardt Oval, the team took the field cheered on by the club's first (and only true) mascot, Victor the Viking, aka Tony Wood. In season 2019, Tony is still cheering the boys on in the distinctive suit that has gone through a series of alterations. He continues to be an integral part of the club, a popular citizen of his hometown of Queanbeyan, and one of the national capital's most well-loved personalities.

The unexpected results the Raiders' first-grade squad had during the year enabled the team to lock in the signatures during September of Dean Lance (then a 'young Newtown centre') and Ivan Henjak, both players destined to play key roles in the team's premiership ambitions a few years down the track. Don Furner continued to put an increasingly robust squad in place, chess piece by chess piece, in search of the week-by-week consistency that the Sydney competition demanded if you were to make a run for the semis.

Against this, the Raiders had to see off attempts to lure their own players elsewhere. Gary Wurth, a Canberra youngster, was lost to Sydney in 1983 as the Sydney club scouts began circling ominously. In-form Raider players seeking upgraded contracts were in their sights: namely, Chris O'Sullivan, Jon Hardy and Steve O'Callaghan. Don Furner, gaining a reputation among the players as a hard negotiator where contracts were concerned, refused to mince words when asked about the individuals involved: 'The players obviously value themselves more highly than we do and they are shopping around for better terms.' A Queensland club went close to getting O'Sullivan's services at this time and the wily Jack Gibson went after Jon Hardy, a defender after his own heart. Furner refused to countenance him changing clubs. In the end all three re-signed, despite the coach's undiplomatic public remarks. Perhaps it was all part of his strategy.

The O'Sullivan re-signing was significant. He was a player on the up in a club on the up. At such a key point in the Raiders' development they simply could not afford to bleed their best and brightest. Rex 'the Moose' Mossop was on record as saying that Chris O'Sullivan was 'the best half back prospect I've seen for many years'.

At the Raiders' second presentation night, workaholic hooker Jay Hoffman was named as Clubman of the Year. For this he received a handwritten, congratulatory note from Raiders' patron Fred Daly, a lifelong fighter in the federal parliament for the rights of workers and a lifelong defender of hard workers. Daly wrote that Hoffman was 'a great credit to the Raiders', wished him well in the years ahead and expressed his belief that Jay would go on to higher honours in the 'Greatest Game of All'. Working as a brickie's labourer to ensure match fitness, Jay was Clubman of the Year again in 1984 and gave the Raiders yeoman service in whatever role asked of him until his retirement in 1987. When interviewed in 1985 and asked to name the 'person you most admire in the world', he answered: 'Bob Hawke—I'm a bit of a Labor man.'

The unfolding relationship of the Raiders with their environment and the politicians in it was always going to find some expression in the club's evolution. Fred Daly and Ros Kelly had already played important roles in the team being admitted to the competition. Then, in March 1983, right on cue, the Labor Party ended nearly eight years in opposition when down-to-earth, sport-loving leader Bob Hawke comfortably won the federal election against the odds. As the Labor Party got down to business, so too did the local Rugby League team.

Despite growing up in Western Australia as a keen player and follower of Australian Rules, Hawke found himself in charge of a party newly in government with links already to a footy team in the league code's premier competition. The media enjoyed the symbolic connection. When the Raiders grabbed their first away win against Cronulla, a matter of weeks after the election, Sydney's *Sunday Telegraph* newspaper headed its game story: 'Canberra Landslide Swamps the Sharks, and Raiders Do a Hawke and Make History'.

Mungo MacCallum, with his barely disguised left-of-centre political views, could not resist connecting the Raiders to recent political events in his 'Mungo and Sport' column. He criticised the Sydney establishment for its 'parochialism'. According to Mungo, 'the Raiders ... since last year have made a recovery rivalling that of the Federal Labor Party' but, like Illawarra, they continued to be marginalised as second-class citizens. He speculated on the prospect of Hawke becoming the Raiders' number-one ticket holder to add a bit of clout to the 'brand' and, when club officials decided later in the year to approach the new PM to suggest just that, he accepted. The announcement was made on 11 September. Unlike all its rival clubs, the Raiders were now connected to the federal political arena. It gave them a marketable point of difference. Later in the decade the connection would become a valuable one.

Two steps forward, one step back, 1984 and 1985

When Jay Hoffman was interviewed in 1985 for *The Raider* magazine as a distinguished 'Pioneer', he said that the club 'reached maturity' in the 1984 season. There is plenty of evidence to support the comment.

At the start of the team's third season a growing number of the Raiders' hard-working officials and celebrity associates sensed that coach Don Furner's five-year plan might be successfully implemented ahead of schedule. Prime Minister Hawke understood the propaganda role expected of him when he penned his introduction to the Raiders' first-ever publication, *Canberra Raiders: The First Three Years*, which came out in March 1984. Given a few mutterings in Sydney the previous year about cutting the two newcomers, Canberra and Illawarra, out of the comp and consigning the experiment to the dustbin of league history, the Raiders' new number-one ticket-holder was having none of it. Unlike the Sydney sceptics, the prime minister pointed to evidence:

> The record shows that the Raiders have fully justified . . . the decision to admit them to the stronghold of Rugby League . . . Since their first match on 27 February 1982, the Raiders rose in 1983 from the bottom of the ladder to 10th position and were the highest scoring team outside the top six . . . The Club slogan—'Growing with the Raiders'—exemplifies the increasing confidence, determination and skilled effort which seems certain to drive the 'Raiders' further up the ladder with each new season until they reach the top.

Wins over Cronulla and Wests in the first two competition rounds were integral to the players believing that they might go even further in 1984 than first thought. After the Wests game, Magpies President John Brooks admitted that he was 'full of envy for the way the Seiffert Oval crowd lifts the Canberra teams'. Journalist and well-known rugby league historian Gary Lester added his observation that for 'Sydney-based teams, a trip to Canberra in the middle of winter is about as inviting as a tour of the Antarctic'.

Away games were a different story, though a little 'TLC' for the long bus rides to Sydney every fortnight helped. Take the game against the Bears for instance: it was reported that 'for the trip to North Sydney Oval . . . the players and their families and friends were treated to a tureen of soup, courtesy of John McLeod's wife'. Julie Giteau, Ron's wife, was also happy to bring along (in addition to the kids) homemade cakes for all. The routine was for the wives and girlfriends to go up in the supporters' bus and come back in the players' bus. It worked well. No mobiles, no headphones back then, but an abundance of good cheer among the players, family bonding too, and the occasional in-bus movie.

A few of the more distinctive journeys are still remembered fondly. Like the one heading home in the first season when only the players—fortunately—were on board. Refreshments flowed freely. After a few courtesy stops on the roadside, in-house bus driver and popular team strapper 'Griffo' declared that there would be no more stops, it was getting ridiculous. He was determined to head straight home. The edict worked for a short while, until it proved too much for a few of the squad with average bladders. The protest resulted in a liquid stream pouring down the bus's front steps. Griffo was horrified. He grudgingly accepted that when nature called he was powerless to resist. The bus had to be pulled up.

On another trip home when the women and children *were* on board resulted in an unscheduled stop that the whole bus demanded. Julie Giteau had changed the nappy of her infant son Matt (yes, the Canberra footballer who would go on to become one of Australian rugby's most creative backs). The smell was suffocating, so bad that the offending item had to be dispensed of immediately.

It is hard to imagine anything like that happening today. Wasn't it a character in British novelist L.P. Hartley's book, *The Go-Between*, who said that 'The past is a foreign country; they do things differently there'. Times have changed. Footy road trips today, with their apparently compulsory headphones and assorted technological paraphernalia, have changed completely.

In the Raiders' third season, grit and determination were there for all to see. And this from an outfit described by noted *Herald* journalist Alan Clarkson as 'Canberra's bits and pieces' team. A narrow, decisive win against Saints enabled the spare-parts squad to stay at the top of the table after six competition rounds and then, in round eight, as confidence grew further and in front of Channel Ten's TV audience, the Raiders beat Easts 44–8. The Sydney TV guide's write-up for the listed fixture has to be quoted: 'After visiting such renowned tourist spots as the War Memorial, the Institute of Anatomy, Parliament House, Mugga Way, Red Hill and Bob Hawke's cottage, the Eastern Suburbs Roosters will be too pooped to face up to the "local" lads from Sydney, Brisbane, Cairns, Thursday Island and Woop Woop who make up the Canberra Raiders.' There must have been way too much sight-seeing. The visitors were pooped and got walloped.

Philip Derriman in Sydney's *Sun-Herald* was intrigued by the team's premature emergence as a competition force. He wrote a long article under the headline, 'From Furner's Faders to Canberra Phenomenon in Two Years', and his apt opening sentence, 'It has come to be called the Canberra phenomenon', might well have served as the opening line of this book. Derriman also helped to advertise a new and lasting description of the team as the 'Green Machine' and he posed a simple question for his readers: 'How did Canberra come by their strength so suddenly?' He gave majority credit to Don Furner—the coach's determination to hunt 'far and wide' for potential.

Most of Sydney's league writers commented on the Raiders' impressive start to the year. Leading journalist Peter Frilingos took up Derriman's hypothetical in even more expansive terms: 'Don Furner's Canberra Raiders are the League's biggest success story since Cronulla's charge into the 1973 grand final'. For his explanation of the 'phenomenon', Frilingos suggested a number of reasons, or more specifically a number of players, the sung and unsung, old and young, including Ron Sigsworth, wingers Terry Fahey and Billy Walker, skipper Ron Giteau with his ultra-reliable goal-kicking, utility discovery Craig Bellamy, the nearly unstoppable halves combination of O'Sullivan and Henjak, ex-Newtown centre turned hard-hitting lock Dean Lance, second-rower Paul Elliott in the form of his career, big Sam Backo learning the tough-man trade and lethal Jon Hardy.

The two interchangeable halves, O'Sullivan and Henjak, were at their best in the Easts game, and the *Daily Telegraph*'s Ian Hanson got quite carried away with their dominance:

> Canberra's 'heckle and jeckle' halfback combination ... certainly gave the rampaging Raiders plenty to crow about at Seiffert Oval yesterday. Just like the two mischievous cartoon birds, the dynamic duo ripped the Roosters apart in the seven tries to two massacre.

The 'dynamic duo' led by example, so capably that in the round 23 game against Penrith, the second-last round of the season, the Raiders found themselves in a position to make their first semifinal series.

Outstanding wins against top sides Canterbury (18–14), Parramatta (14–10) and Manly (16–12), plus a rock-solid home record, had put the Raiders in contention for the play-offs. They easily defeated Penrith at Seiffert, with the 'Heckle and Jeckle' halves again leading the assault. The coach summed up: 'It was a gutsy performance . . . Things came together for us in the second half and O'Sullivan and Henjak started to exploit the gaps.' It was a big day for the Green Machine as they got up in the minor grades as well to make it a clean sweep. The firsts' victory moved them to 30 points on the competition table, one ahead of Penrith.

A win against competition leaders, Canterbury, at Belmore Oval in the last round would see the Raiders safely into the semis—in only their third year. The team had the fleeting luxury of being in charge of its own destiny but the occasion proved too big. The Dogs, flexing their muscles for another premiership, crushed the pretenders 36–0.

Could the classy Parramatta side do the right thing and beat Penrith, thus allowing the Raiders to play off for a spot in the semis? Yes, they could, gifting Canberra a post-season game against Souths for fifth place. Again, the occasion was overpowering, a case of too much too soon. The foreigners from the south, all pluck and hustle, were no match for a hardened Rabbitohs team and went down mid-week under the lights at the Sydney Cricket Ground by 23–4. An awful injury toll meant that the Raiders went into the game without strong-men Sam Backo, Terry Fahey, John McLeod and Jon Hardy. These absences proved impossible to overcome. Equally significant, Souths' clever halves, Craig Coleman and Neil Baker, kept their opposition halves relatively quiet.

The overall performance in 1984 gave everyone involved in the club legitimate cause for confidence in the immediate future. In addition, the third-grade side sweetened the season when it made the semis, the first Raiders grade team to do so (only to be beaten by Wests 23–16 in the elimination semifinal). To the Green Machine supporters, it seemed as if the club had embarked on an unstoppable march, one that would take their club into the top five in 1985.

Could it be done? The swelling crowds at Seiffert in 1984 thought so, the Queanbeyan and Canberra faithful voting with their feet throughout the season. A ground record 17,407 spectators headed to Seiffert for the July victory against Parramatta, 'the Raiders' finest hour'; 14,754 watched the Easts game in April; while 15,679 took in the Canterbury clash. This magnificent fan support lifted all grades to such an extent that the Raiders finished a creditable seventh in the club championship, ahead of six other teams.

O'Sullivan and skipper Ron Giteau played in all 25 first-grade games, Giteau's unerring boot producing a personal tally of 159 points, good for third best in the competition. Craig Bellamy produced his usual reliable stuff throughout the season, readily plugging gaps across the backline when injury occurred and in the process crossing for enough tries to place him equal fifth in the final try-scorer statistics (in the elevated company of the likes of Terry Lamb, Steve Morris, Phil Blake and Eric 'the Guru' Grothe). For good measure, Bellamy had claims to the Raiders' 'tackle of the year'. In a game against Easts in Sydney, Roosters tearaway Scott Gale raced away for a try late in the match that would have equalled the scores, only to be cut down by a bootlace Bellamy tackle. It was a 'Ron Coote' special according to Tony Adams in the *Telegraph*. 'A match winner if ever there was one,' said a happy and relieved Raider coach. The Raiders held on that day for a gallant 10–4 victory.

The most intriguing story of the 1984 year was told in the aftermath of the Raiders' narrow win over the Bulldogs at Seiffert. Tony Adams related the details in his account of the match under the headline 'Voodoo!' Why 'Voodoo'? Had the Raiders added a touch of black magic to their expanding repertoire? Had Don Furner secretly visited New Orleans or Haiti when he led the 'USA Sport Seminar Tour' to America in December 1981? The answer is clouded in mystery, but Canterbury's inscrutable coach, Warren Ryan, could easily have been convinced that foul play was involved as he mused post-game: 'I had the dubious distinction of being the first coach to lose to Canberra when they entered the League in 1982 and beat Newtown. Just look at what I've started!' It was the mid-1980s and, as we now know, Ryan didn't know the half of what he had uncovered. 1989. Tigers. Raiders. Grand Final. Extra Time. Unlikely field goal. Steve Jackson. The gods of fate would stay unhappy with coach Ryan and again use the men in green as their messengers of doom in the near future. But their plan needed several more years to reach a culmination.

The Raiders took momentum and belief into 1985. However, it would prove to be a bitterly disappointing year for them and for the game itself. When Sydney's *Daily Telegraph Mirror* ran a series of four-page supplements in the mid-1990s under the title *The Winfield Cup Story 1982–1995,* the 1985 feature included a short summary by Tim Prentice. 'It is doubtful,' he wrote, 'that rugby league has ever had a more sickening opening to a season than 1985. League record books carry an ugly black smudge in the chapter which records the felling of Cronulla's Steve Rogers in the very first Winfield Cup game.' Canterbury's Mark Bugden was the culprit and, as things turned out, the match was to be Rogers' last in Sydney football. It seemed grimly appropriate that the final game of the season, which pitted the hard men of Warren Ryan's Bulldogs against the Roy Masters–coached St George, should end in a bare 7–6 scoreline after 80 minutes of brute defence by both sides.

For Raider supporters, a season that had promised so much failed to deliver. Assessing the thirteen players signed in the 1984–85 off-season, on face value it appeared that the coach had recruited with a view to strengthening the depth of the lower grades. Brett Atkins, Phil Carey and Terry Regan would go on to give the club's senior side some good years of blue-collar service, Atkins and Carey through seven seasons of busy utility play, and the eccentric Regan for three combustible years. There were no highly touted recruits at all.

Don Furner and the training staff misread 1985. If the coach was of the opinion that he could sit pat with the hand he had, based on the unexpected output of the previous year, then he was mistaken. 1984 had produced a pleasing club result, reflecting stable administration and intelligent, sometimes imaginative coaching that got the best out of the players. The training schedule imposed by Brian Bourke, with its 'mad hour' that had the players 'running like idiots', undoubtedly led to tight Raider wins based on the players' superior fitness. All the players knew that they could go hard for the full 80 minutes. But in the elite Sydney competition, with so much money circulating and experienced scouts never sleeping, it was crucial to keep up with the hounds or better yet get yourself one step in front. Fitness alone would not take the club to the next level.

The team started well enough with a few early victories, including one against Norths at Seiffert (28–20) in round three, followed by a better performance against Souths (26–12) at Redfern. Even more impressive, the Raiders stretched the high-flying Manly Silvertails to the limit at Seiffert in early May, finally settling for a 20–20 draw. Terry Regan was on fire in those early games, 'scattering' the defence lines of opposition teams according to one report, and either winning man of the match awards or being ordered off to take a premature shower.

The declining mid-season results for the Raiders were a mixed bag. There was plenty to like in the ultra-physical display of the Raider forwards in the hard-fought 20–10 win over St George at Newcastle, one reporter maintaining that 'some of the collisions between Hardy, Regan, Robert Stone and Craig Young must have shaken coaldust from the hills around the Sports Centre'. There was also legitimate quality in the Raiders' 42–12 massacre of North Sydney in late June. However, when Chris O'Sullivan was hurt late in the season the Raiders struggled, sputtering to a tenth place finish.

The season did produce one stand-out achievement: Allan McMahon's gutsy second-graders became the first Canberra team to make a grand final, only to go down to St George 22–16 in a result mired in controversy. Who can forget the last desperate 30 minutes? The Raiders tried valiantly to defend a 16–14 lead only to see Saints' fullback Brian Johnson throw an obvious forward pass to Alan Neil, enabling the halfback to touch down for the winning try with a bare eight seconds left. It was heart-breaking stuff. The Raiders had been the better team for most of the match, a superiority built around the solid performance of the forwards. Les Morrissey, Peter Davis and Paul Thompson scored for the Raiders and Angel Marina kicked a couple of goals. It should have been enough.

Easily the best for the Raiders on the day was big Sam Backo. Jim Buckley in the *Queanbeyan Age* summed up the ex-Yeppoon Seagull's standout performance: 'His crashing runs, his determination and dedication brought continual applause from the stands at the SCG. Backo played beyond himself to get a Raider victory. That victory was denied, but Sam could still hold his head high.' President Les McIntyre rightly acknowledged the game as 'an historic event for the club' and, fittingly, the club's number-one supporter, the prime minister, dropped into the dressing room to add his congratulations and commiserations. The team was later honoured with a Parliament House reception. Co-patrons Fred Daly and Ros Kelly, stitched-on supporters of the battling club, were no doubt responsible for the function, a first at the nation's meeting house. It would not be the last.

The *Queanbeyan Leagues Club Journal* for the month of October 1985 is a true collector's item. The cover features a terrific photograph of the prime minister and Allan McMahon sharing a joke at the boisterous reception. There were several pages of advertisements, slices of the past, for popular entertainers such as Chad Morgan (the 'Sheik of Scrubby Creek'), Slim Dusty, Col Elliott, Les Girls and the ever-present Julie Anthony. And there's also a photograph of feisty MP Ros Kelly in knee-high boots and jeans, kicking off the footy to start the A-League Grand Final between the Queanbeyan Kangaroos and West Belconnen.

In the aftermath of an ordinary 1985 season for the top-grade side, Raiders officials and players were anxious to steer any talk towards the future. Les McIntyre did his best in his president's message at the wind-up of the season when he wrote that with 'the signing of Australia's

Test players and other leading footballers, I share coach Don Furner's confidence that the first-grade side could be in the final five for the 1986 premiership'. These bullish remarks require some context.

Sometime late in the '85 season, the Raiders' brains trust decided that after a few years of consolidation a major player overhaul was needed. Serious house cleaning resulted in the release of some twenty players, including Angel Marina and Percy Knight. This was extreme surgery and it took many Raider fans by surprise. However, while the ground was shifting disconcertingly at the time, no-one then or since has ever questioned the vision and courage of the decision to explore the potential availability of a number of classy footballers north of the NSW border, to spend the money required to get them and, ultimately, to inject a mother lode of extraordinary new talent into the club. The list so confidently promoted by the club president in anticipation of a bumper 1986 season—Queenslanders, locals and an ex-Newtown winger regarded by some league commentators as over the hill—surely comprises the most talented group of recruits ever assembled by one club in a single off-season. Who are we talking about? Mal Meninga, Gary Belcher, Gary Coyne, Steve Walters, Chicka Ferguson, Paul Martin, Steve Jackson and Mitch Brennan. Judge for yourself, reader.

As every Raider fan learns as a part of their football education, Malcolm Norman Meninga was the essential piece of the puzzle. His signature did not come easily. It was a close-run thing. The nerves kicked in for Don Furner, Secretary John McIntyre and the support staff when, at the end of August 1985 and as reported in *The Raider* newspaper's headline, 'Meninga delays decision 48 hours'. Permanently cashed-up Eastern Suburbs and the permanently cashed-up Manly Sea Eagles were formidable competitors in the market for the burly Queenslander. On behalf of the new club on the block, the minnow among sharks, Furner was only being realistic when he told Raider fans that 'the longer these decisions are delayed, the less chance we have'. What he meant to say was that more money would be put on the table by his competitors, both of them used to getting their way, getting their man.

When Chris O'Sullivan, Dean Lance, Jay Hoffman and Craig Bellamy all re-signed at this time it was welcome news, yet rugby league realists within the club knew that top-tier performance for the Raiders in the coming seasons hinged on the outcome of the Queensland player negotiations. Get Meninga and the others would follow. In later years, all the blue-chip players who *did* follow the great Meninga to Canberra have confirmed this interpretation of events. All were happy to come to Canberra to get the chance to play with Mal.

In the last few months of the '85 year, one of the main topics of conversation across the entire league was which club Meninga would join. Here the story gets more interesting. It might surprise Raider fans, young and old, that the club owes a debt of gratitude to Manly CEO Doug Daley. When Easts dropped out of the race to sign Meninga, the impatient Daley rang him one night and insisted on a decision being made by the next morning. Unhappy with the crude pressure being applied, Mal did make a decision by the following morning. He rang Daley to inform him that he was going to Canberra. John McIntyre still relates this story with a twinkle in his eye.

Mal signed. They all signed.

In a recent note to the author, Meninga wrote that he had always wanted to prove himself 'in the best Rugby League competition in the world . . . I came to the Raiders for many reasons. Don Furner, regional not Sydney living, a club on the up and an off-season with St Helens in the UK seeing that one-town teams could be successful.' He added that the sheer quality of the new recruits was vital to future success. The whole group, to cite Mal again, was 'impressed by the way John McIntyre and his team treated us'. As luck would have it, the August day that Mal and Gary Belcher arrived in Canberra to look the place over was sunny and warm. The football gods had blessed the Raiders' enterprise and its precocious endeavour, just as they had in 1921 when Bob Craig arrived in Queanbeyan to start the league code in the south.

So when Don Furner addressed the inaugural Raider silver plate dinner shortly after the 1985 finals series, and with Allan McMahon's feat with the reserves fresh in everyone's minds, he too shrugged off the caution of the past and boldly predicted that 'next year it will be the first grade's turn . . . In 1986 I can assure the other Sydney League clubs that we will be making our presence felt . . . and will be aiming high.'

4

A MOVIE SCRIPT COME TO LIFE

1986–89

To understand what happened in 1986 you have to rewind to the last game of the Raiders' previous season against St George at Seiffert. After twenty minutes, Saints had a narrow 8–2 lead, with the Raider pack holding its own against a very good St George six. By half-time the visitors had added eighteen unanswered points and by full-time the score had blown out to 50–6, the Raiders only try, a consolation, coming after a Saints player spilled a Chris O'Sullivan bomb.

Steve O'Callaghan, injury-free and playing fullback in Allan McMahon's high-flying reserves, remembers the game well. He maintains that some of the players in green stopped tackling. It was an awful capitulation in front of the home fans. Whether through lack of effort or lack of talent, or both, the Saints game highlighted a separate and larger problem. During the 1985 season something in the club had started to go wrong, a disconnect between some of the first-grade players and the coaching staff. The Saints game exposed the issue for all to see.

One long nightmare, 1986

Potential causes were not addressed in the off-season. The problem festered, and the early games of the new season reflected this. After six losses in the first seven games of 1986, Don Furner labelled the horror start as 'one long nightmare', a 'holocaust'. His audacious prediction of imminent success only a few months earlier had evaporated. 'I can't get out there and do the tackling and passing for them', lamented a frustrated coach.

What was going on? After an infusion of such rich talent into the club, talent destined soon to play its part in the creation of a Green Machine dynasty, what explains a performance so poor in the first year of the new era that at one point it threatened to derail the turbo engine even before it was in motion?

Answers can be found once we acknowledge that, in the mid-1980s, Rugby League itself was at a crossroads. Steve Rogers' terrible injury only accentuated the problem. Old-school thinking about the game was being challenged by a host of new ideas and innovations introduced by a younger generation of coaches. Like a number of other clubs, the Raiders were caught up in this generational shift.

At the conclusion of round seventeen of the 1986 season, the Raiders had won just four games. In the entire year the side would manage only eight wins. Statistically, this was an even poorer return than in 1985. A few points can be made which help to explain the number of losses: it was a refurbished team that needed more time to find its rhythm; there were some serious injuries to the likes of David Grant, Terry Regan, Jon Hardy, Mitch Brennan, Mick Aldous and Craig Ellis; Mal Meninga needed more time than some of his less talented teammates to produce his best every week; and, at season's end, ten games had been lost by eight points or less. But all these reasons stitched together fail to account for a desperately disappointing eleventh-place finish.

No, the main problem was a deeper one. Buried on page ten in the same April 1986 issue of *The Raider* newspaper that published Don Furner's exasperated comments, a columnist writing under the pseudonym 'Juan Tooh', probed for answers to the nightmare start. He looked behind the scenes at the prevailing methods of coaching and fitness training. A 'stalwart, long-time friend and teammate' of Don Furner's is anonymously quoted as saying that his good friend was 'still coaching in the sixties' and an unidentified present-day player, reviewing the miserable 1985 year, said that 'the training didn't change one bit during the year, it was the same in September as it was in January'. The frankness of these assessments leaves little doubt that the writer was privy to inside information. Players were confiding in him, venting their frustrations:

> Is the club keeping up with modern, scientifically proven methods? For instance, years ago sprains and strains required heat treatment—now it's ice. Do the players need their bodies wrenched to pieces with a mad hour instead of putting their hands on that precious piece of *cuero,* commonly called a football?

A reckoning was not far away. Between May and September a player 'revolt' occurred, as one newspaper termed it, a 'rebellion' according to one of the Raider players who went through it. Piecing together exactly what happened during these months is a difficult task. It depends on who you talk to, and any understanding is not made any easier by the fact that, for service to the game of Rugby League and his coaching acumen, Don Furner was rewarded in mid-1986 with appointment as coach of the Australian team. He would go on to carry out his national duties with professionalism and considerable success—duties quite different to the demands of the Sydney competition with its grinding, week-to-week pressures. The representative squad appreciated Don's relaxed style. His affability. The job description in part involved mending the fractured relationship between feuding New South Welshmen and the Queenslanders in the team. There were plenty of big egos and the Raiders' coach managed the national job with calm diplomacy and skill. At year's end, he was announced as Queanbeyan's 'Citizen of the Year'.

Ironically, though, Furner's representative duties led directly to an increase in the pressures at home. With the Raiders having managed only a few wins deep into the season and Furner off for three weeks to coach Australia, reserves coach Allan McMahon took over the top-grade side for rounds eighteen to twenty. The result? Three wins by a combined 90 points to 18. This was compelling evidence indeed for McMahon's coaching credentials at the top level, reinforcing the case his reserves' record had already presented. Mr 'Tooh' stirred the pot when he wrote that 'Allan is a coach of the new breed who believes in statistics'. McMahon had played at Newtown under Warren Ryan, a confirmed believer in the value of researched game plans which analysed opposition strengths and weaknesses. Ryan studied game film endlessly and applied the results. McMahon would do something similar as he acquired the skills of his new trade.

Reviewing the variety of reactions to the Raider upheaval in 1986, it is clear that no one individual can be singled out as the villain or even the primary cause of the conflict. Mal Meninga has on many occasions publicly acknowledged his debt, as he put it in a recent note to the author, 'to the McIntyre and Furner families'. From the earliest days, all newly recruited players had received the same warm introduction to their new surroundings. The McIntyre and Furner families had played a prominent part in nurturing a family atmosphere. This too added to the discomfort of several tense months during the 1986 football season.

In May, the first rumour of discord began to circulate in Canberra and across the league. All was not well in Raider country. The players met to discuss their grievances and shortly after captain Dean Lance and Meninga had a chat with their coach to convey, as Meninga put it several years later, 'a few home truths'. In the same interview (with his biographer John Macdonald for *Big Mal: The Inspiring Story of Mal Meninga,* published in 1990), Meninga focused on two fundamental grievances: the 'mad hours running like crazy under trainer Brian Bourke' and the coach's endless teamwork drills:

> We'd just run up and down the field passing the ball. Don had this crazy idea we couldn't train in tracksuits or beanies because it would give us the edge over opposing teams when they came down to the freezing conditions. All we were allowed to do was pull our socks up. I told him we needed skills

> work under pressure. His answer was to make us run up and down the field passing the ball.

Meninga had played under Wayne Bennett in Queensland, a coach whose ability was already well known both north and south of the border. He was a prototype example of the 'new breed' and Meninga was familiar with the fundamentals of his technique, based on carefully compiled statistical analysis and high-level skills work. Meninga contrasted Bennett's approach with the 'very archaic' methods on offer in Canberra.

On 26 June one newspaper reported that a petition had been signed by twelve Raider players, all of whom refused to play another season under Furner. The club secretary was furious with the unwanted publicity:

> Furner can't do anything more than he is doing now, we are very pleased with him. To sack a coach when he has been appointed Australian coach is insanity. He can't get out there and catch the dropped balls or do the tackling for them.

John McIntyre was battening down the hatches, determined to ride out the sudden squall. He produced a defence not unlike his coach's own: you can't do it for them. This did not wash with a large number of committed Raider fans, 4,500 of whom signed their own petition insisting on Furner's resignation. It was reported in the media that, at this point, a speculative offer was made to Canterbury coach Warren Ryan, five years at a lucrative $70,000 a season. While the report was wrong, he was contacted.

McIntyre then re-signed his coach for another twelve months in what he called 'a tremendous boost for the club'. If this was a tactic designed 'to nip the trouble in the bud', as he put it in a *Canberra Times* article by Graham Neeson, then it failed, as events in the coming weeks showed. McIntyre was incensed by the behaviour of his reserve-grade coach, Neeson writing that he 'implied yesterday that McMahon had prior knowledge of the recently reported unrest in the club'. It is probable that McMahon did, though some players who went through the distressing period strongly deny that McMahon was the trouble-maker, the 'mole' as McIntyre would label the individual concerned. For a short time the situation worsened, not helped by a provocative *Rugby League Week* feature article suggesting that internal discussions in the Raiders' camp had the power to 'blow the Canberra club apart'.

This was never going to happen. Too much work from too many people had gone into moulding a resilient community club that prized its tightness as a group. After the passing of a few particularly traumatic weeks, common sense once again prevailed. Sound decision-making reasserted itself. Some have suggested that at the secret players' meeting their petition was eventually ripped up by a senior player, one of the respected Pioneers, who felt that direct confrontation was not the best way forward. It was likely to exacerbate tensions rather than lead to a long-term solution. He was right.

A path of innovative and necessary compromise followed. Mal Meninga's assessment of the matter in his biography would probably have received support from all the participants when the dust settled:

> I think Don felt threatened by Allan's success while he was away with the Australian team. I can sympathise with McMahon. I'd like to be a coach one day. A coach can stay too long. The players get too familiar, the coach gets too familiar and both suffer without realising what's gone wrong.

McIntyre knew something had to be done to break the impasse and, with a transition stage suddenly the number-one priority, the Queensland connection did a little more to pay its way. The close relationship that Mal Meninga and Gary Belcher had with Wayne Bennett contained within it the makings of a solution.

There must have been a heap of phone calls and intense lobbying during the month of August because, on 1 September, South Brisbane Magpies coach Wayne Bennett, full of ambition and self-belief, on a handshake deal entered into a three-year contract with the Green Machine. Virtually overnight the Raiders' torment was replaced by widespread curiosity beyond the club and renewed optimism within it. It was announced that Bennett would share the coaching duties with Furner in the 1987 season before taking over the head coaching job in 1988. He was anxious to retain his Queensland State of Origin job, which he could do as the coach of a non-Queensland club. For their part, the Raiders were hopeful that the excellent appointment, secured under intense pressure, might also result in the club obtaining the services of highly talented South Brisbane centre Peter Jackson, tipped for an Australian jersey in the near future.

The Bennett coup was achieved with Furner's agreement and involvement. The Raiders coach knew that the contracts Meninga and Belcher had signed with the club contained a special 'get-out' clause. They could leave at any time if they were not satisfied 'in any way' with the club's situation. Hiring Wayne Bennett was the perfect compromise: the Queenslanders were happy to stay and look to a more successful future; the local players, a number of whom had been coached by Furner for most of their senior footballing lives, were excited that they would be challenged by a young, innovative coach set to introduce new ideas into training and game plans; the awkward situation with Don Furner would be eased immediately; and the aura of a Bennett–Meninga partnership, bolstered by a number of Queensland's best players, had the potential to bring more big names to the club.

After the ruptures of the previous few months, this was a result almost too good to be true. The only losers were Allan McMahon and his coordinator Brian Slatterly, the man who had the distinction of bringing Dean Lance and Chicka Ferguson to the club. McMahon resigned in later 1986 when his contract negotiations to coach the reserves again in 1987 stalled. He had wanted to be an agent for change and with some justification had felt that the coaching position for the senior Raiders team might be his in the near future. It was a misjudgement, both of those in positions of power in the club and the strong family roots that stretched back decades. Ultimately, McMahon was kept on for a year in a diminished capacity as marketing manager. The blood on the floor was his.

Mal Meninga, who had rejected the coach's approach to captain the Raiders in the 1986 season because he first wanted to settle in down south, began to assume more responsibility at this time. To prepare the ground ahead of the Bennett announcement, he gave a statement to the *Canberra Times* in mid-August that tactfully suggested the way a compromise arrangement might work:

> Having two first-grade coaches could be a problem I suppose, but Don is a very reasonable man and I am sure that he would not interfere if Wayne came down here. Don would obviously advise Wayne in some way, but I think Don would step back and give Wayne room to move. Their coaching methods are very different and they have a lot of different ideas. On field their proposals are probably very similar.

After the formal announcement, Bennett visited Canberra as special guest at the Raiders' silver plate luncheon. He praised all the hard work that had gone into establishing the club and stated his determination to build on solid foundations. He cautioned Raider fans not to expect 'instant success' though he definitely did not anticipate finishing 'twelfth next year'. He took on the new job with expectations tempered by reality.

What sort of team had he inherited? Over the Christmas period, when Bennett compiled the ledger of strengths and weaknesses of his newly acquired squad, he must have been thrilled with the enormous potential of what he found. For example, in the Raiders' round nineteen win against Penrith, Panthers' coach Tim Sheens—soon to submit his own extraordinary chapters to the Raiders' story—took responsibility for the failure of his game plan. 'I made a mistake with the tactics,' he said. 'I told our guys to play them in the forwards, down the middle, but it didn't work out the way I thought it would.' There would be a number of coaches after Sheens who would make exactly the same mistake in the next decade or so. For 1987, Wayne Bennett and Don Furner had some impressive if largely untapped grunt up front. Backo, Gilbert, Coyne, Lance, Hoffman, Rowan Brennan, a young Steve Walters and an even younger Glenn Lazarus. There was a lot to like.

So, too, with the glittering backline talent waiting to be primed effectively and unleashed: among them Gary Belcher, coming off a superb season in a losing team; exciting winger Paul Martin; the halves combination of Chris O'Sullivan and Ivan Henjak; ever-green Chicka Ferguson, the Seiffert crowd's favourite; and, of course, the looming figure of Mal Meninga, whose full book of skills was yet to be opened by a coach able to appreciate what he was dealing with. Local boy Chris O'Sullivan, selected in the City Seconds' side in 1986 with Gilbert and Ferguson, continued to find ways to improve his game. *Daily Telegraph* journalist (and future sport biographer) Grantlee Kieza captured the halfback's evolving talent with a dash of Canberra-centric creativity:

> At the National Gallery in Canberra, every art lover worth his beret and easel is lining up for hours to see the finest drawings from the Modern Masters . . . It's the most popular show in the national capital, winning rave reviews and capturing the imagination of a city more used to the equally abstract, but frequently less intelligent, offerings from Parliament House.
>
> But this year, as it has done every year since 1982, Canberra is also playing host to another modern master, a local prodigy with the inventiveness, flair and daring displayed in the great works hanging in the country's foremost art gallery. Rather than hushed murmurs, his skills draw rousing cheers.
>
> Chris O'Sullivan is a Rugby League halfback. A brilliant one . . . Sadly Sydney League fans only ever see O'Sullivan painting his masterpieces of mayhem when the Canberra Raiders venture from their home base at Seiffert Oval.

All that was about to change—for O'Sullivan, his duo of coaches and his array of gifted teammates. The Raiders' team, the 'Green Machine', was set to make a first indelible impression on all league fans. Sydney was about to be introduced to the way the game should be played.

So close and yet, 1987

It was inevitable in the first few months of 1987 that the Sydney media's passing interest in the lowly Raiders concentrated almost entirely on the team's novel coaching arrangements. Could it work? Would it work? Or would the unlikely partnership implode? Could an ageing coach, clearly a product of old-school Rugby League culture, bond with a representative of the new wave? Success was bound to hinge on the attitude of the older partner, the one being phased out. Don Furner was adamant that continuity had to be maintained: 'I determined long ago,' he said, 'that when I went, I wanted the coach who was taking over to work with me. To make the change smooth and easy.' To his great credit, this is exactly how it played out.

Two nonchalant rugby league men with a lifelong love of the game, as players and as coaches, struck up a relationship one journalist called the 'perfect partnership'. Two of league's most respected writers were intrigued by the experiment, Norman Tasker writing in January that 'the Furner and Bennett show could be the season's most exciting act' and Alan Clarkson discovering in April that, as he put it, 'at the Canberra Raiders, who have twin Rugby League coaches, too many cooks don't spoil the broth'.

Pre-game and half-time talks, never a strong suit of Furner's, he willingly handed over to Bennett as one of the game's proven motivators. When team meetings occurred, Bennett ran them; when the media rang, Furner took the calls. With a microphone under his chin, Bennett could be testy; old fox Furner was perfectly relaxed being interviewed. He enjoyed it, usually giving the journalist a good quote or two to nibble on.

Furner was so pleased with the initial impact of the change that he ventured another prediction: he promised Raider fans that humiliation was 'a thing of the past' and that the team had the talent base to 'lift themselves into the big time'. Don was excited by the latest crop of recruits, particularly Peter Jackson, the 22-year-old centre who had dazzled at South Brisbane in recent years (playing with Belcher and Meninga), and another 22-year-old, the sixteen-stone New Zealand international prop Brent Todd, an important buy. Todd would help tighten the middle, enabling the backs, the try-scorers, to shine. Steve Walters' younger brother Kevin, able to slot in virtually anywhere in the backline, completed another round of premier acquisitions. Add to this the fact that Sam Backo turned up at training for the new coaching combination in the best shape of his life, and a rejuvenated Terry Regan so impressed Bennett with his pre-season work ethic that, after being told his services were no longer required, he was offered a new contract. Later in the year, his presence would come in very handy.

Behind the scenes there were a couple of other significant alterations. Mitch Brennan, Rowan's older brother and a seasoned first-grader at the end of an impressive career, had signed on with the Raiders in 1986 only to have injury restrict him to a handful of games. Brennan was named as the Raiders reserves coach and John Osborne was appointed to look after the under-23s. Then there was the school teacher from northern New South Wales, Shaun 'Bomber' McRae. Mal Meninga, among others, had heard that McRae's new training methods were as good as any being used in football. Mal and Dean Lance paid him a visit and the result was the hiring of an individual whose approach to fitness neatly complemented the Bennett coaching vision and, after him and more importantly, the position taken by Tim Sheens. The Raiders were lucky to retain McRae for six years before he moved on to senior coaching positions. He was a bonus.

After the first few modest games of what would develop into an extraordinary season, it became apparent that there was plenty of work still to be done. Flashy trial form failed to reappear when the season proper began. The turning point for the team came in a satisfying if unpredictable way in round seven, a game against Penrith at

Penrith Park. Chris O'Sullivan was sent off in the first ten minutes of the match for an alleged high tackle on young Penrith star Greg Alexander. The setback inspired the Raiders, who managed to hang on for an 11–4 win. The usually reserved Wayne Bennett could not contain himself: 'I've been involved in football for a long time, but that was the gutsiest performance I've ever seen from a football team.' Ivan Henjak was the key. In the pages of *The Raider* newspaper Ron Norton described the diminutive half's super-human effort where he covered 'himself in glory in what will go down as one of the greatest games produced by any Canberra player in the side's six years of premiership football'. Henjak produced his most outstanding year in top-grade Sydney football to that point.

Excited as the Raiders were by the Penrith game, the roadblock presented by the leading Sydney sides remained. Three successive losses to heavyweight teams—Parramatta, Manly and Canterbury—came as another reality check. Don Furner had to revisit his latest prediction. While the Bulldogs kept the Raiders tryless in their comfortable victory, it was the game before against Manly at Seiffert that rocked the aspirations of the entire Raiders club. The second of May was a bitterly cold and wet day in Queanbeyan, a Shakespearean kind of day, portending ill. The fates delivered. When Mal Meninga went racing across the field to tackle the Sea Eagles' Cliff Lyons he crashed into the goalposts after sliding wildly out of control. There was a sickening thud. Lyons and his teammate Darrell Williams knew immediately that it was serious and signalled for help. The arm was badly broken. When Meninga left the field, his arm in a makeshift sling, his distraught look said it all. The shocked crowd went silent.

Worse was to follow. Over the next eighteen months Meninga's arm was fractured no less than three more times.

This first dreadful accident, in mid-1987, only stiffened the resolve of all the players. If anything was to be salvaged from a season so suddenly threatened, they would have to adjust to the absence of a teammate who by his imposing presence gave all his teammates confidence and assurance. Sydney's naysayers declared that whatever flimsy chance the Raiders had of making the semis had been erased. The Raiders, they chortled, would fade once again.

Not this time. The team rallied in adversity, revelling in a rich vein of form that saw them win seven of their next nine games. Management did its bit off the field too, and it was only fitting that the injured Meninga was the catalyst. Less than a month after the Manly game, he signed a new five-year $500,000 contract. The reasons he gave for re-committing to the Raiders make for fascinating reading.

In the days leading up to the signing, John McIntyre informed the media that his board had directed him to retain Meninga whatever it took. They need not have worried. The Queensland import felt much as he did in the first months of 1986: Canberra–Queanbeyan was effectively a 'one-team town' which made his family welcome. They felt at home. Lucrative approaches to entice Meninga away from the national capital were made by the cashed-up Barry Maranta consortium (bankrolling Brisbane's successful bid to be admitted to the Sydney premiership in 1988), by the St Helens Club in England and by Allan McMahon, who had landed the head coaching job at Newcastle for the team's first premiership season in 1988 and was on the look-out for a marquee player. Despite the offers, Meninga chose to stay. For the benefit of the media present at the signing, McIntyre offered another reason for the Meninga decision. In the *Canberra Times*, Mick Kassay took up the story:

> McIntyre said the presence of Bennett was a major factor in Meninga's decision to stay with the Raiders and he discussed reports that Bennett, in the first year of a three-year contract with the club, could leave to coach the Brisbane team next year . . . Any such suggestion by the Maranta consortium . . . was kiteflying. McIntyre said: 'Under no circumstances would the club be prepared to release Wayne for any other than compassionate grounds, and certainly not allow him to coach a rival club'.

Meninga re-signed on 28 May. Within days it was announced that Bennett *was* in fact off to Brisbane in 1988. The Raiders had allowed him to renege on his contract for compassionate reasons.

About two weeks after that, Bennett was interviewed for *The Raider* paper. It was not his finest hour in the public arena. He stated that:

> Although I had not conferred with Club Administration about returning to Brisbane at the end of the 1987 season, the move was very much on the cards. I was starting to look for other options in Brisbane outside coaching and if I found something I was going to seriously consider taking it . . . The best way to describe what has happened is to say that the [Broncos] job fell into my lap.

There is no doubt whatsoever that Bennett had genuine, compassionate reasons for leaving, reasons 'of a very personal nature and my family and I aren't about to let the world know'. Those close to the Bennetts were aware that two of their young children had serious disabilities. It became clear that Bennett's wife, Trish, was too far away from the family support that she needed in difficult circumstances. Bennett refused to see himself 'as the bad guy', stating that 'players and coaches being released from contracts wasn't new in rugby league and [he] couldn't see why people were making such a fuss'.

The home situation in Canberra was obviously challenging for the whole family. Yet there was an off-handedness to Bennett's words in interviews at the time that rankled Raider supporters. His assertion that he had never entertained the thought of coaching the new Broncos outfit is, quite simply, implausible; his open admission that he had failed to inform Raider officials about a move back to Brisbane, a move that was in his words 'very much on the cards', was an oversight with consequences; and his statement that in returning to Brisbane he was 'putting his family before his career, the Raiders and himself' did little to satisfy the Raider base. At a bare minimum, he should have been able to see what all the fuss was about.

Wayne Bennett was saved by the maturing young man he had mentored for years. At a crucial point in the tricky discussions, Mal Meninga informed the McIntyres, Les and John, and Don Furner, that despite his closeness to Bennett, he would recommit if the Raiders allowed Bennett to go back to Brisbane. While it was a selfless gesture, Meninga did feel let down by his coach's decision to leave so soon, especially in the context of the Maranta consortium's aggressive pursuit of him. McIntyre and Furner labelled these tactics 'unethical', tactics that culminated in a contract Mal Meninga described as an 'under the table' deal. It was rumoured that Wally Lewis said he wouldn't sign with the Broncos without Bennett. Maranta stopped at nothing to obtain the King and his nominated coach—and they got both.

For John McIntyre, Bennett's decision was 'the cross he will have to bear'. Years afterwards, the man who gifted him a dignified departure, Mal Meninga, called it 'a black spot on Wayne's character'. When Bennett left at the end of 1987, Peter Jackson and Sam Backo followed him twelve months later. They too left for personal reasons. Many in the rugby league fraternity saw it differently. These were two wonderfully talented players, future internationals, who were poached by a coach recruiting a new squad by stealth.

As his record over the next 30 years has shown, Wayne Bennett can coach—and when he was younger, he was hungrier. Fortunately for the Raiders, his untimely decision had no effect on the performance of a playing group that was starting to blossom. The pressure off, Bennett worked hard at training while his co-coach masterminded strategically in the background. The whole club began to buzz. John McIntyre played his important part when he refused to let the coaching confusion interrupt growing momentum. Rather than allow the issue of who would coach in 1988 to affect the players, he went out coach-hunting immediately.

Alan Fitzgibbon, who grew up in Goulburn and in 1987 was assistant coach to the charismatic Jack Gibson at Cronulla, was given careful consideration. In the end, however, the club offered a three-year contract to another impressive young coach: Tim Sheens. Sheens was Rugby League's Coach of the Year in 1984 when he almost got his Panthers team into the semis for the first time, something he did achieve in 1985. In the next two years, in his own words, his team 'put up a fair fight . . . but by then, for me the time had come to move on'. The extent of his Penrith legacy came into clearer focus a few years later when the elite squad of youngsters he had gathered at the foot of the mountains developed into champions in a premiership-winning team. Sheens was a coach who could identify talent and mould the best of them into greatness.

On 26 June, only weeks after Bennett's shock decision, the Raiders offered Sheens a three-year contract. With the stocks of the Raiders' junior development programs overflowing, he was invited to be Canberra's 'coaching director', in charge of the first-grade side, yes, and also working closely with the junior development squad. This visionary idea appealed to Sheens who, when wined and dined in Queanbeyan as he considered the offer, said that he found 'enticing' the prospect of being in charge of a playing group with unlimited scope at a well-run club. 'It's not just money that rules the roost,' he added. Shortly afterwards, he signed.

The second mid-season crisis in two years was over, a potential season-wrecker handled with such professionalism that performance on the field remained untouched. This was a remarkable accomplishment for a young club. It ensured that the wins continued mid-season and after, and the good news kept coming.

If Meninga's broken arm was a setback to be overcome, the Raiders' more football-savvy supporters were amply compensated for his temporary absence when a 17-year-old Junee youngster named Laurie Daley debuted in the green jersey in July. Registered as a Queanbeyan Blues player at the beginning of the year, Daley played Jersey Flegg during the first half of 1987 and made a big impression. He certainly caught the eye of the 'perfect' coaching partnership and, after warming the bench in an earlier game to get the feel of the action, he was called up to play in the top side against Wests at Campbelltown as five-eighth (with Kevin Walters at half) after Chris O'Sullivan pulled out injured.

Daley's mum and dad, along with a few of his seven sisters, headed to Campbelltown to watch the game and, like the entire contingent of Raider faithful in attendance on the day, they were exhilarated by what they saw—and very, very proud. The Raiders won the game 30–12, Daley scoring two tries in a performance that ABC Sport's Gerry Collins wrote 'made the rugby league world sit up and take notice' of the next-generation Raider's 'undoubted ability'. The always tight-lipped Bennett was not about to let the game go to his young charge's head, advising him not to read the morning papers. Keep your feet on the ground. If Daley did happen to ignore the coach's instruction, he would have enjoyed perusing headlines such as 'Daley stars' and 'Raiders whiz blitzes Magpies'. Darren Hadland in *Rugby League Week* went into raptures about the 'red hot prospect' he had just watched tear the Magpies' defence to pieces:

> Canberra has unearthed a seventeen-year-old capable of taking the league world by storm. Laurie Daley, who follows in the footsteps of Phil Blake and Andrew Ettingshausen as seventeen-year-olds to shine in first grade, caught the eye of Canberra and Australian coach Don Furner when he was fourteen.

The Wests game featured one other unpublicised yet equally significant Raider debutante. Coming off the bench in Campbelltown was a hard-headed, steely-eyed youngster every bit as ambitious as his Junee teammate: Queanbeyan's own Glenn Lazarus, whose Monaro district pedigree stretched back a hundred years and more. The Lazarus name was about to be projected back into the public sporting arena.

Late in the 1987 season, the Raiders again lost to competition front-runners Parramatta and Manly to remove any semblance of complacency as the semis got closer. The game that restored the team's confidence was the round 25 fixture on 23 August against South Sydney, the last-ever game to be played at Redfern Oval, a ground dripping with tradition. If ever there was incentive for a high-flying Rabbitoh team and its ferocious pack (boasting the likes of Ian Roberts, Mario Fenech and Les Davidson), then it was this game in front of 19,000 rabid red-and-green fans spilling out onto the streets of inner Sydney. Only one point separated the two teams on the competition table going into the game. It shaped as a true test of mettle.

The result? A totally unexpected, crushing 26–2 win to the Raiders. Souths' coach George Piggins didn't mince words: 'Canberra were just far too good for us on the day. They killed us.'

In one majestic brushstroke the Raiders erased the demons of the 1984 semis play-off loss to the Bunnies, chalking up another milestone win in the club's brief history. John McIntyre wore a grin from ear to ear when he said that Penrith's coach, Tim Sheens, wherever he was watching the game, must have been as thrilled as anyone in the Raiders' post-game dressing room: 'I think he will be delighted with the team he is taking over. If today's win wasn't the best in the club's history, it was certainly the most significant.' Of that there was no doubt. Assessments of the Green Machine as enthusiastic pretenders, try-hards, also-rans who only made up the competition's numbers, were past history. The club had arrived. Five glorious tries to none at hostile Redfern Oval said it all. It was a first advanced lesson in Raider football.

Such a powerful statement of intent, however, did not come in the opening stanza of the game from some Chris O'Sullivan sleight-of-hand, or a dart from Ivan Henjak, or even an elegant, curving bust from Gary Belcher or Peter Jackson. It came from a tackle, a single Raider tackle, David versus Goliath, when massive Souths' prop Ian Roberts received the ball heading wide of the ruck only to be met by Dean Lance, no-name captain of the Greens, who hit him in a collision that shook the old Redfern stand. It was a nine-on-the-Richter-scale tackle, a Biblical encounter that probably still haunts Ian Roberts' dreams. He went backwards and down like a giant toppled. What a moment for the Raider faithful to savour. For the rest of the afternoon, Sam Backo had unaccustomed space in the middle of the ruck that he and the rest of the Raiders pack ate up.

After a 22–18 win against Easts in the season's last round, the third-placed Raiders played the Roosters again the following week at the SCG in the Major Preliminary Semifinal, only to go down 25–16 in a robust encounter. Easts' coach Arthur Beetson could not contain his enthusiasm. 'That was just to get the dust out of the nostrils. We were a bit rusty.' Artie was sure the grand final would have his team pitted against a hot Manly outfit.

With a second bite of the cherry the following week, it did not get any easier for the Raiders when their opponent was Souths—surely intent on revenge and fired up by a coach who as a player never took a backward step. Could George Piggins' much-touted pack recover from the shell-shock at Redfern?

They didn't even come close. This time round, a Raider team riding high on belief, despite the previous week's loss, handed Souths another if possible more comprehensive footballing lesson. Stumps were drawn at the SCG that day with the scoreline reading 46–12. Only weeks earlier, many knowledgeable league pundits had predicted a Manly–Souths grand final. The Raiders ruthlessly extinguished that presumptuous notion. The balance of rugby league power was shifting before their eyes.

The preliminary final had the Raiders once again up against an Eastern Suburbs team high on belief after a narrow 10–6 loss to competition favourites, Manly. The Sydney media predicted a comfortable Roosters victory. Manly only just got by the Chooks and hadn't popular pie-eating Artie proclaimed that he had removed the dust from the team's nostrils? In the pubs of Sydney most drinkers felt that the Raiders had already over-achieved. It was time for them to retreat to the national capital and enjoy 'Mad Monday' celebrations.

The week leading up to the preliminary final had its share of breaking news, the dominant item being that after an emotional request from his teammates, Mal Meninga would take the field, his arm heavily strapped.

The announcement alone had psychological weight, but it was no ruse by the Raider coaches. Meninga was willing and Don Furner saw no problems at all with the calculated gamble: 'He is a champion and he'll slot into our side as comfortably as pulling on a favourite football boot.' The players thought so too, though everyone felt for Brisbane teenager Kevin Walters, who had played so well as a utility back in Meninga's absence. His time would come.

The preliminary final was sudden death. An opportunity like this for a Cinderella team, the competition's newest member, might not come again any time soon. The Big Fella had to suit up! Wayne Bennett was typically matter-of-fact about the selection: 'Twenty minutes of Meninga can be absolute magic.'

The Raiders got many more minutes than that out of the inspirational Meninga, the most memorable moment coming in the twenty-eighth minute after a typically powerful burst from Sam Backo got his team within ten metres of Easts' try line. Meninga and Belcher combined smartly before Meninga, handling a second time, produced a three-metre burst, an unstoppable tidal surge, to score. He ran over poor David Trewhella, who looked as though he'd been hit by a semi-trailer. He stayed down for some minutes then left the field and did not return. The Trewhella moment flagged the sheer will and determination that Mal would need when his arm broke three more times in the months ahead. Those playing beside him knew it was a statement, Dean Lance years later recalling that 'as long as I live, I don't think I'll ever forget the time he just ploughed over David Trewhella. We knew then he was back.'

The final was in the balance for a long time before the Raiders clawed their way in front. When unsung Raider winger Matthew Corkery scored another vital try in a season where he had done it with regularity, a try converted by Meninga, the Raider lead got out to 26–18. Having done his job superbly, Meninga left the field and was replaced by Kevvy Walters. Fittingly, a deft Walters pass to Henjak led to a Peter Jackson try, fattening the advantage to 32–18. The game was as good as over, Easts getting a late consolation to produce a final scoreline of 32–24. It flattered Easts.

Artie Beetson was disgusted. 'We were hopeless,' he spat out. 'If we were gallant in defeat, I'd say so.' Easts' opponents, on the other hand, were gallant all day, none more so than tearaway Terry Regan, who came on for an injured Brent Todd in only the ninth minute of the match. Regan was dynamic, taking on the Easts pack all day. 'Rego gave his heart for us out there today,' said an exhausted Ashley Gilbert. 'He took a lot of pressure off the rest of us.' He sure did. Bennett's offer of a one-year contract to Regan at the start of the year, based solely on 100 per cent effort at training, paid off in spades.

And so the Raiders, in only their sixth year in rugby league's premier competition, were into a grand final. All season the team had strived to play a brand of attacking football that challenged their opposition to match it. Well ahead of his fellow journalists, the *Daily Telegraph*'s Grantlee Kieza alerted to something special happening, an approach by the Raiders that had the potential to change the face of the game. After the first semi against Easts, Kieza began his column with a quote from a man who had stood next to him at the game: 'See what happens when Canterbury and Parramatta aren't in the semis? You see tries. And plenty of 'em. Not that boring defence all the time.' It *was* the start of a new era.

On the Tuesday before the big day, Kieza tipped an upset, declaring that the 'Raiders' spirit can triumph over Manly's reputation'. Tens of thousands of mad keen fans of Canberra and Queanbeyan shared exactly the same opinion in defiance of the fact that the Sea Eagles were the shortest-priced grand-final favourites for at least a decade. The rapidly growing Raider fan base was on top of the world, hundreds turning up at Canberra airport after the Easts' semi to welcome home their conquering heroes. According to Brent Todd, they all felt like rock stars, not footballers. The overflowing enthusiasm presented the coaching staff with a problem they'd never before had to encounter. Everyone wanted a piece of the players, radio, TV, newspapers magazines, politicians, men and women and kids in the street—everyone.

Don Furner and Wayne Bennett did their best to keep a lid on things, even vetoing the prime minister's invitation to a team breakfast that he was keen to host. Their best efforts were futile. The unfolding story in the south—surely a fantasy?—transcended Rugby League. The day after the victory over Easts, workers at the new Parliament House site hoisted a super-sized Raiders' flag to complement the enormous Australian flag flying atop the splendid structure they were erecting. Milton Cockburn wrote in the *Sydney Morning Herald* that the Raiders 'might play, train and live across the border, and be largely funded by Queanbeyan money, but they have now captured the hearts and minds of Canberra'. It was true. Canberra was hooked.

Grand final week meant so much to so many, none more motivated than three Raiders players, 1982 Pioneers Chris O'Sullivan, Hooter Gilbert and Chris Kinna. Why did these three in particular hold a special place in the heart of their veteran coach, Don Furner? He explained:

> Only those three and I know all the pain and torment the Raiders have had to endure to make it into Sydney's big game. They were the ones who had to wait behind the tryline after the opposition scored, who had to look up at the scoreboard when we copped 50-point hidings, who had to put up with all the jokes and the insults. For those three, this game is probably more special than anyone else.

Don was right to include himself in the mix. Amidst all those hidings, he kept encouraging his team to play the kind of football that fans paid their hard-earned dollars to see. He continued conscientiously to build a team that would contend for the title, so that when he got to watch his three Pioneer originals, their hearts pumping with pride as they ran on to the SCG for the last grand final ever to be played at the beautifully sculpted, historic ground, he could have been excused for having the odd tear in his eye.

In the end, the grand final went the way the bookies and most league experts had expected. Manly were the better side, muscling their way to an 18–8 win. The Sea Eagles forwards, led by Paul 'Fatty' Vautin, Ron Gibbs, Noel 'Crusher' Cleal and Phil Daley, led the way for backs like Dale Shearer, Michael O'Connor and Cliffy Lyons to weave their magic. Manly were too good. 'The Day of the Raiders', as I called the first piece I ever wrote on the Raiders for the *Canberra Times* (the day before the grand final), would have to wait. But the day was fast approaching.

In all the media coverage, one article stood out head and shoulders above the rest for its refreshing insight. Summing up the grand final on the Monday after, Tim Prentice maintained that:

> Rugby league owes the Canberra Raiders a hearty vote of thanks ... the jolly green giant-killers injected a refreshing air of daring and enterprise to finals football ... Thanks Canberra for pumping a new strain of adrenalin into the Sydney league arteries. And thanks, Raiders, for making try-scoring in September an art form again.

Raider football was now an established expression of football at its best, with admirers spread right across the country.

The effect that the team's meteoric rise exerted on the local region can be effectively measured by the several thousand people who flocked to Canberra's normally lonely Civic Square to express their thanks. The spontaneity and joy of the civic reception shattered all the clichés about a dull Canberra full of robotic public servants. Even Ian Warden, the *Canberra Times*' columnist with the acerbic wit, was swept up in the emotion of it all when witnessing his city suddenly transformed:

> Mal Meninga, my hero, signed his magic name on the peak of the Raiders' cap I had worn with such pride at the SCG last Sunday. Someone asked me foolishly if I had got the autograph for my son!
>
> Meninga, displaying infinite patience and good humour, was still churning out signatures and the frightful fluorescent green jelly of the fountain had still not yet set as I left the square, the amplified strains of

the Raiders' sophisticated theme song—'We'll hit ya! Hit ya! Hit ya!'—biffing against the walls of Civic Square.

Raiders captain Dean Lance, on behalf of his team and the whole organisation, accepted the keys to the city in scenes never to be forgotten.

So when Tim Sheens took stock of the year that had been for his new club and sat down to dissect it with departing coaches Don Furner and Wayne Bennett, he probably pinched himself. For the 1988 season he had inherited a strong and mobile set of forwards already competitive with Sydney's best, a pack definitely on the way up, and a backline with the talent to be the best in the business. Any doubts about bench strength were now nonsense. All that was needed was a quick scan of the nine players named as reserves for the grand final: Phil Carey, Paul Martin, Terry Regan, Les Morrissey, Jay Hoffman, Laurie Daley, Kevin Walters, Rowan Brennan and Glenn Lazarus. It reads well.

No wonder one of league's shrewdest coaches, Roy Masters, predicted that the Raiders were on the verge of 'a golden era'. Perennial Raider critic, Channel Nine's Ron Casey, with form on this subject stretching back to 1982, was forced to eat yet another helping of 'humble pie'. The Raiders, he finally, grudgingly conceded, were the real deal.

Opportunity missed, 1988

Season 1987 was a watershed year for the young Canberra Raiders club. The platform provided by the '82 and '83 Pioneers, who had endured humiliation, grafted some hard-earned wins and spilt blood in the green jersey had served its purpose. The fantasy chapters of the fairy-tale had begun.

Symbolically, the page turned forever when the club held a special, silver-plate testimonial dinner for Jay Hoffman, the first import signed by Don Furner in 1982. Hoffman never gave less than 100 per cent and, as if to forecast the future, he was a Queenslander. Two Clubman of the Year awards gave some indication of his contribution both on and off the field. With the emergence of Steve Walters in the hooking position, a young lion knocking on the door of a representative career, Hoffman found himself in 1987 mostly playing in the reserves. As a back-up he again gave his all and no-one expected any different.

Mal Meninga spent two seasons observing at close hand what Jay meant to the club. So when he did not get on the field in the grand final (and felt too uncomfortable going up on stage and accepting a medal), Mal shook his hand and gave him his. For Jay, 'the fact that Mal gave me his medal meant more to me than if I'd gone up on stage and received it from the Prime Minister. He didn't do it to be in the limelight, it wasn't for show.' Mal later explained his reason: 'It's about not forgetting the people who helped get you there . . . You never forget those players, you make sure they're involved in the celebrations because they deserve it.'

Politician and Raider fanatic Fred Daly did not forget his mate, sending Jay another hand-written letter of thanks for his 'ability, dedication, loyalty and great club spirit. You are indeed an inspiration to all who play the Greatest Game of All.' Following his usual practice, Fred included a few bob in the letter, wanting Jay to take his wife Jenny out to dinner. The gesture perfectly encapsulated the down-to-earth kindnesses of a bygone era.

The Raiders' new breed of players was poised to put its stamp on the years ahead. Roy Masters' 'golden era' beckoned as the club welcomed several top-shelf recruits from the wider region, bush kids with backgrounds completely different to their city opponents.

Laurie Daley, the son of a Junee railway man, had spent some time working in an abattoir. He soon worked out that footy was a far more appealing career path. Glenn Lazarus was the proud son of a Queanbeyan shearer whose family, as we have already learned, could be traced back to the town's foundation years. Brad Clyde's father was also a shearer. Born in Culcairn, in south-western New South Wales, Clyde spent his early years in Holbrook and went to school in the Belconnen area of Canberra. He would make his debut in a Raider jersey in May 1988.

With youngsters like these pressing for selection in the top grade, it is not hard to understand why Sydney's *Daily Mirror* newspaper commented at the start of the year that the Raiders 'weren't exactly frenzied performers in the off-season player market'. One reason was the attention that had to be paid to solving the awkward coaching predicament; another was the team's form explosion late in the 1987 season. The main reason, however, was the club's glowing assessment of the ability of those working their way through the junior ranks.

Add to this group a brilliant young Rugby Union halfback, Ricky Stuart, another Queanbeyan youngster. He was pursued by a few Sydney clubs but had promised John McIntyre that the Raiders would have the last call on his services if he switched codes. He was as good as his word.

Raider signings of players from other clubs were thus kept to a minimum, with the likes of Chris Houghton (from Penrith), Phil Hurst (Cronulla), Brian Battese (Easts) and Dean Lonergan (New Zealand), and one or two others, added for insurance. Sadly, Brett Atkins, Steve O'Callaghan and Paul Elliott were all released, while Jay Hoffman had hung up his boots. From the four departing players, the Raiders had received some 20 years of dedicated service. The pages of the past had been turned.

The NSWRL's official guide to the 1988 season featured some interesting comments from the Raiders' new coach. Recognising that many in his squad had gone from the cellar to the penthouse in so short a time, Tim Sheens identified one of his challenges as the high self-esteem of the players. They 'expect to win when they go out onto the field'. Part of his job as he saw it was 'to instil into them that to lose a match is not the end of the world'. After a loss, the good teams always bounce back, regrouping for the next game. In the same pre-season interview, Sheens reiterated his belief that he was not 'on a hiding to nothing'. Only time would tell on that one. How would a playing group full of stars and stars-in-the-making respond to the change in coaching personality and demeanour?

Mal Meninga liked what he saw from the start. 'Tim,' he said, was 'young and had all the modern ideas. He was orientated towards skill but had a strong inclination to introduce weight training . . . He was like a young Wayne [Bennett] but didn't have Wayne's psycho speak and ability to say the right things at the right time. He had our respect, however.' As usual, Meninga was insightful in his assessment. Bennett and Sheens were very much of the new generation of coaches. The major difference was Bennett's unmatched ability to motivate. Sheens was steadier, a scholar of the game whose research, and methodical implementation of that research, proved second to none. At the beginning of 1988, his capabilities had yet to be demonstrated to a new audience.

Sheens relished the prospect of taking charge of a group oozing ability and he mapped out plans based on all hands being on deck. He did not, however, plan for injuries, certainly not before the start of the competition in early March. He should have. A horror few weeks unfolded in February, starting with the seemingly innocuous 'Super Sevens' tournament at Parramatta Stadium. Mal Meninga had only recently had a plate taken out of his left arm after the previous bad break. In the opening minutes of the game against the Broncos he broke his arm again, an injury set to sideline him for at least half of the season.

In the same tournament, Chris O'Sullivan went down with what seemed like nothing more than a badly twisted ankle. The injury turned out to be far more serious, a split of the ligaments near where the ankle and the shin bone join. He was ruled out indefinitely. Adding to the growing toll, Ivan Henjak twisted ligaments in his ankle and was forced to take a break.

The Raiders got $20,000 as runners-up in the tournament, but at what cost?

The terrible luck continued when Kevin Walters stepped in a pothole at training, twisting an ankle that put him out for a month and, in the Raiders' first trial against Parramatta at Seiffert, Kiwi enforcer Brent Todd copped a heavy hit from Geoff Bugden, resulting in his left arm being broken above the elbow. The local crowd let out a collective groan when he went down, expecting the worst. They got it. Tim Sheens and the whole Raider throng must have thought the footy gods had turned their backs on them.

Some exceptional talent occupied the sidelines for a while but there was a ton of ability fit and ready to perform. Six wins in the first seven games had the bookmakers shortening the odds on a Raiders premiership in a hurry. In the first three games, against Illawarra, Souths and Saints, the Green Machine sent out a warning to all rival clubs when it clicked into the same smooth gear as late 1987. The team put 96 points on their opposition, conceding only 24. Saints' coach Ted Glossop was full of admiration: 'Pretty devastating stuff. They sure know how to score a try'. Despite the injury toll, Tim Sheens' confidence soared as he watched his charges go through their paces in the early rounds. He particularly liked the side's ability to cash in on broken play errors by the opposition. No-one was more accomplished at instant counter-attack than Chicka Ferguson, the Seiffert crowd's favourite son. Chicka had skills every coach wishes he could teach: a spontaneity enhanced by extraordinary on-field awareness, lateral vision that could produce a four-pointer when nothing was on.

People still talk about a try in the seventh round against the Gold Coast at Seiffert in 1988 won in a canter 50–6 when the Raider backline, standing deeper than any backline of any era, got the ball through several lightning pairs of hands to Matthew Corkery, who had come across from the blind-side wing. Corkery received the second-last pass and put Chicka over in the open-side corner for one of his twenty tries during the season. It was breathtakingly simple, surgeon-clinical finishing. Gold Coast General Manager, Peter Muszkat, could only sit back and admire the potency of what he described as a 'point scoring machine' that was 'too brilliant'.

Chicka's re-emergence was just the boost the club needed. The 1988 Raider *Annual Report* referred to his return after a crippling knee injury the previous season, at the ripe old age of 34, as 'the greatest comeback of them all'. He'd been forgotten by league experts but not by Raider fans. What a joy to hear Seiffert once again reverberating with the

'Chicka . . . Chicka . . . Chicka' chant. The same pens which had written him off now wanted the 'Black Pearl', as he was often called, reinstated in the Australian side. Immortality for the gifted wing three-quarter, as we know, was still a season away.

Something special was percolating in the nation's capital in defiance of a mounting injury toll. In the round nine game against Wests, an 18-year-old school boy star, Brad Clyde, was picked in first grade to fill the injured Gary Coyne's second-row spot. The Hawker College product did more than that, producing a man of the match display on an Orana Park bog. The structure of Clyde's all-court game was there for all to see: non-stop defence for 80 minutes regularly punctuated by destructive, long-striding bursts in the heart of the ruck or out wide. He had size and pace. Clyde commented after the game that the mud heap had slowed everyone down to his speed. This was modesty in the extreme.

There was not very long to wait for the next new 'star' off the production line—only two rounds in fact, when a baby-faced Ricky Stuart was named on the reserves' bench for his introduction to top-grade football. And what a game for him to lock away and go to school on. The Raiders against Brisbane Broncos at Lang Park. The match-ups had all Raider fans and lovers of the game salivating at the prospect: in the forwards, Walters versus Greg Conescu, Backo versus Greg Dowling and Lazarus versus Bryan Niebling; and in the backs, even better, Belcher versus Colin Scott, Laurie Daley versus Chris Johns, Peter Jackson versus Gene Miles, Chicka Ferguson versus Joe Kilroy and Ivan Henjak versus Alfie Langer.

In Brisbane for an Australian Literature conference, I made sure I had no work commitments for the afternoon of 15 May. All roads that day led to Lang Park. It was the halfway point in the season and a win by either side would make it outright, or at least equal competition leader. Some days after the clash, won in breathtaking fashion by the Raiders 36–16, I wrote about the experience for the *Canberra Times* in a piece entitled 'Raiders '88—Footy for Art's Sake':

> Tim Sheens has built on the Furner–Bennett team with wisdom. This year's Raiders run even straighter and the defensive pattern, apart from the collapse against Parramatta, looks far better. Grand Finals, they say, are won in the forwards. We won't have any trouble there. But I've got a feeling that the 1988 Grand Final will be won by a creative set of artists who double as a rugby league backline. The Raiders just might do for rugby league what ice hockey phenomenon Wayne Gretsky did in North America a few years ago. Turn a thug's game into a sport of power, and even beauty.

By mid-year Sheens had learnt so much more about his gifted playing group. They were going wonderfully well, strengthened by the return of Mal Meninga. 'George' looked awesome from the opening seconds of his comeback match in round fifteen against Newcastle at Seiffert. The opposition unwisely decided to target him from the kick-off. There have been better tactics tried on a football field. Meninga caught the ball behind his try line and by the time the defence had put him on the ground, he was 45 metres down field. It was as if he had never been away.

Tim Sheens was maturing as a coach along with his players. By all accounts he put considerable work into Ricky Stuart to enable him to transition into the different code as smoothly as possible. Stuart's ability to throw ridiculously long torpedo passes to his outside backs and hit them on the chest did not need any adjustment, nor his ability to read a game, nor his brilliant kicking game, short, long and, when necessary, popping field goals. He would have to shoulder his share of defence though, since opposition sides were certain to target a player of his smaller stature, running their big forwards at him. He adjusted, starting in the round sixteen game against Illawarra and retaining his place for the rest of the year.

The coach was less hands-on with Glenn Lazarus, who was gaining a reputation as a front-rower of substance in attack and defence. He quickly acquired the subtleties known only to those who inhabit league's mysterious 'engine room', assisted by his coach, a Penrith front-rower in his playing days, and teammate Sam Backo, on-field instructor-in-residence. Lazarus readily credits his debt to the uncompromising former Yeppoon Seagull: 'Sam was one of the best front-rowers I've ever seen.' His advice to his young student was disarmingly simple: 'Stick with me, son, and I'll make you a star.' Lazarus did stick with him as the season developed, an education that prepared him to become one of the game's great front-rowers in the coming seasons.

At the end of round seventeen of 22, the Raiders found themselves leading the competition and were promptly installed as 2–1 favourites. Meninga's form was so good that he turned out in a president's team against the English in Canberra, followed by an appearance against the Papua New Guinea Kumuls in an unsurprising cricket score inflicted by the Australians, 70–8, Meninga scoring twice. He was selected for the Australians against a Rest of the World side in Sydney.

Disaster struck again. His biographer John McDonald summarised the moment in fatalistic terms: 'This was the end of Mal Meninga's career. Most everyone accepted what seemed to be inevitable when Meninga broke his arm again. Same arm, different place.'

The curse had struck yet again in a game that was hardly important. He returned to Canberra to consider his future, well aware that many in the league world felt that he should retire for his own wellbeing. Raider tragics found the ongoing ordeal especially painful. Reluctantly, some wanted their champion centre to retire and put an end to his suffering.

Fortunately his teammates felt otherwise, as did his coach. Meninga pressed on, bolstered by Tim Sheen's insistence that he involve himself as much as possible in the team's daily routines. Mal later acknowledged the show of faith:

> We kept the flow going. Tim had become a very good coach. He just grew and grew into maturity and got to know the guys better. He kept me involved. I'd take the backs for skills work and acted as water boy.

The Raiders knew how to overcome a crisis and after the hiccup of successive losses against Canterbury at home and Cronulla away, they re-grouped as good teams do to end the season with two necessary wins. This put them into the top three and the Major Preliminary Final against an arch-rival Canterbury team being guided by 30-year-old Phil Gould. 'Gus' was attempting to become the youngest non-playing coach ever to win the premiership.

The Raiders, despite racking up an astonishing 596 points at an average of 27 points a game, got into an alley fight with Gould's team, lured into a style of play that suited their opponents. A late field goal by Terry Lamb broke an 18–all deadlock, one which certainly did not go according to Sheen's plan. Ivan Henjak had a groin injury, Laurie Daley a hamstring strain and Peter Jackson knee and shoulder injuries. Decisions also went against the visiting non-Sydney team.

When the Balmain Tigers defeated the Raiders in the subsequent Minor Semifinal 14–6, the Raiders could not really complain. Two key games; two losses. They had been unceremoniously shunted out of the play-offs by hard-nosed Sydney teams with big packs of forwards. So despite having the Dally M Winger of the Year in Chicka Ferguson (who also scored the most tries) and the Front-rower of the Year in Sam Backo, and scoring easily the most points during the season of any club, they had been shown the door. Steve Walters put it concisely: 'At the money-end, we lost two semis.'

Gus Gould liked what he saw. With the arrogance of a relative newcomer to the coaching ranks, he repeated his opinion of the Raiders to anyone who would listen. The Raiders were soft in the forwards. Soft in the middle. Fatty Vautin's 'faders' tag, that he had used once or twice in the past, appeared again in a couple of Sydney papers. Tim Sheens was firmly of the belief that if Mal Meninga had not broken his arm again, had he stayed on the paddock, the Raiders would have won their first competition in 1988.

Unfairly, the Raiders' coach came under pressure from a few within the club who expressed disappointment with the way the season ended. Tim's wife, Rhonda, was angry at the naivety of such reactions. Her husband, on the other hand, eyes focused on the future, must have drawn considerable consolation from the club's end-of-season awards night. Ricky Stuart was announced as the Raiders' Player of the Year, Laurie Daley as Best Player, Glenn Lazarus as the Players' Player and Brad Clyde as the Rookie of the Year. All four were set to play crucial roles in guiding the Raiders' fortunes in the coming years.

'Inside each of you is a dream', 1989

For a season about to re-define the Canberra Raiders' status in Rugby League, 1989 had an unpromising start. Optimism about the imminent return—again—of Mal Meninga was extinguished when he went back into hospital in December 1988 only to have the surgeon discover that the rigid plate inserted earlier had caused another break in the arm. While the problem was fixed, it resulted in another enforced absence of four more months.

This setback, together with Wayne Bennett's signing of two Raider internationals over the summer (Peter Jackson and Sam Backo), was hardly the ideal scenario for those retaining the devout belief that the year of our Lord 1989 would finally be the year of the Raider, the first season to deliver on Roy Masters' prediction of a 'golden era'. Would Raider football finally get its day in the sun, or again succumb to those big Sydney packs and the spoiling tactics of their coaches?

In the off-season, Sheens had been busy. Ignoring the murmurings in the club that his job was on the line after failing to make the grand final, he went about securing a number of players drawn directly from the club juniors. A representative sample included Matthew Wood, Mark Lowry, Darren Fritz, Nigel Gaffey, David Barnhill and Roger Kenworthy. The depth in the club was the envy of a number of Sydney teams who had for far too many years paid scant attention to their junior ranks. Additional Sheens signings for the year included Craig Dimond and Steve Lidbury. Considered collectively, this was an imposing list.

In the first round of the competition in mid-March, the Raiders lost to Cronulla at Caltex Field, 32–14, giving up six tries and managing only two of their own. The Cronulla forwards got well on top of their opposition, allowing a slick backline, the likes of Jonathan Docking, Andrew Ettingshausen and Mark McGaw, to run riot. According to David Middleton in his season summary, the Raiders, forwards were 'shell-shocked and showed none of the form that took them into the top three in 1988'. The Raiders were without Meninga and Laurie Daley but that was hardly an acceptable excuse for a team aiming to be a contender again.

It did not get any better in round two, versus Souths at Seiffert, when Mario Fenech, David Boyle and Ian Roberts led a muscular Souths pack to a solid points win over the Raider six. Phil Gould's advice on how to play the Raiders was firming up as doctrine, the standard tactic to beat the Green Machine. Get on top of the forwards, and thus put the brakes on the slippery backs.

Against Souths at home, the Raiders failed to score a single try. Their season threatened to unravel before it had really begun.

Sheens introduced a positional reshuffle, on the face of it a selection gamble, shifting the elusive if small Ivan Henjak to the centres and leaving Ricky Stuart and a rejuvenated Chris O'Sullivan to develop a halves combination. Without doubt this was the most important adjustment of the entire year and it was helpful that it happened early. Henjak, O'Sullivan and Stuart, 'the mosquito squad' as they were labelled, were set to play havoc with opposition defences which insisted on sticking to the predictable 'up-and-in' style of Warren Ryan's Tigers and Phil Gould's Canterbury Bulldogs.

From round three, the Raiders put seven consecutive wins on the board, starting with a 9–8 squeaker against Easts and followed by several games that built durable team self-belief. Phil Gould's Bulldogs were thrashed 34–4 at Seiffert in round five, a rampant Canberra backline producing five tries to one as the 'mosquito squad' led the way. Covering the game, John Blanch entitled his article 'Mossies Put Bite on Dogs'. He singled out Canberra's 'little men', O'Sullivan, Stuart and Henjak, and threw in Laurie Daley, Kevin Walters and Phil Carey for good measure. *Big League* magazine flagged the new look with cover pictures of Ivan, Ricky and Sully under the headline: 'Tiny But Tots Run Hot'. Looking on, the injured Mal Meninga asserted that the Canterbury game was 'the turning point of the year for us'.

Next came Illawarra, put to the sword 44–8 in Meninga's comeback game. Once again, it was as if he'd never been away. The Steelers' game was followed by a narrow yet decisive win against Manly at Brookvale, made even sweeter because it was a record sixth win in a row for the team. What's more, the club tasted victory in all three grades.

The seventh win was equally satisfying, against Parramatta at Seiffert. The visitors no longer boasted a long list of super stars, as it had in the 1980s, but Sterling, Kenny, Peter Wynn and the burly Bugdens were in the side. Names of an earlier era meant nothing as the Eels were ruthlessly cast aside by the Raiders, 41–8, who piled on eight tries. If this 'next' Raider generation introduced itself to the club faithful about the time Jay Hoffman retired, then that same precocious group announced itself in lights to the entire league world in the Eels game in May. The Raiders were a force. They were here to stay.

An exhausted Peter Sterling gasped after the game that the Raiders 'are the best side in the premiership without a doubt. There's not a weakness there . . . they've got great speed, great size, they've got workers, they've got flair and they've got brilliance'. David Middleton was just as flattering as he noted that Canberra was 'fast developing into the hottest point-scoring machine in Rugby League'. Raider football was gaining a wider audience, a broader fan base, who wanted to see tries scored in numbers.

Inexplicably, yet somehow typically in a season the pundits found impossible to follow rationally, in the next eight matches to round seventeen the Raiders managed only two wins. To emphasise the zaniness of a miserable mid-season run, in round twelve the 'well-oiled' Green Machine ran right over the top of a star-studded Broncos outfit at Seiffert in front of a record crowd of 18,272. The final scoreline was 27–6, five tries to one, achieved on the back of a commanding display from Brad Clyde and all the Raider forwards. The very next week, perennial cellar-dweller Western Suburbs came to Canberra. In the 'upset of the season' Wests came back from an 18–6 deficit to win 25–22. Go figure. Tim Sheens was baffled, not for the first time, with his team of unpredictables. Consistency was proving difficult to achieve.

The most difficult loss came in round seventeen in late July when the Raiders headed to Sydney to play Souths for the second time in the season. The Rabbitohs had already chalked up one convincing victory through the forwards at Seiffert and, playing on their new home ground at Sydney Football Stadium, they repeated the dose. After the game Souths coach George Piggins expressed disappointment. His ladder-leading team had played 'cocky football', he said. The insult was implied though clearly there: Souths weren't playing at their best but able to win nonetheless. The opposition didn't really matter in the Bunnies' relentless march to the semis. Fatty Vautin ribbed his Queenslander mate Mal Meninga that the 'old Canberra faders' were at it again.

The Raiders were without seven first-graders, including four internationals, in the Souths game but it made not one scrap of difference to their predicament. Here they were, at the end of round seventeen, nine wins and eight losses for the year, teetering on the brink of elimination from the semis with five rounds to play. Every game ahead was suddenly sudden death. All five games had to be won. And . . . they were, though none of them in overly convincing fashion. After another victory over Canterbury, narrowly 18–14 at the WACA ground in Perth in front of 22,000 fans (the first premiership game ever played outside either New South Wales or Queensland—yet another Raider first!), Bulldogs coach Phil Gould declared that his team had once more shown how to beat the Raiders. Through the forwards. Never mind that his side had lost the match. Tim Sheens, typically circumspect, always analysing and re-analysing in search of the perfect game, said that the WACA match had taught him a little more about his pack. With bigger games looming, subtle adjustments were made.

At this point, club Secretary John McIntyre decided to advertise the claims of his team in public when he boldly tipped a Canberra–Balmain grand final, specifying exactly how his underrated side would get there. Don Furner's deficiencies as a clairvoyant in the past might have given McIntyre pause for thought. Not at all. He outlined the match-by-match results for the rest of the '89 season and, as the *Daily Telegraph* pointed out weeks later, he was 'spot-on'. For this, he was awarded the newspaper's 'Nostradamus award'. His predictions were about to be put to the test.

The Raiders edged into the semis as the fourth team on percentages. The previous year a courageous Balmain side went all the way to the grand final from fifth spot, in part at the Raiders' expense, only to lose to Canterbury. Under the prevailing semifinal structure, no team had ever won coming from outside the top three. And no league experts north of Goulburn imagined that the Raiders were about to rewrite history and do exactly that.

The Raiders' first game in the post-season resulted in a 31–10 win over Cronulla. It changed few opinions. All that Sydney fans could talk about were the prospects of the top-three qualifiers from within their own city: Souths, Penrith and Balmain. Canberra, Brisbane and the southern shire of Cronulla were peripheral to requirements, a distraction and nothing more. When captain Mal Meninga commented that 'we can play better than that', the league-mad citizenry of the mega-metropolis ignored him.

Royce Simmons and his young Penrith side were the Raiders' next roadblock.

The Panthers were a club on the up, with a solid pack and gifted young backline boasting the likes of Brad 'Freddy' Fittler, Greg Alexander and Brad Izzard—any one of whom could change the course of a game in an instant. The Panthers semifinal constituted the best measure so far of where the Raiders' topsy-turvy season was heading. Better qualified than anyone to comment on the ability of both teams, Tim Sheens anticipated a close tussle.

It was for most of the game. The Raiders led 11–2 midway through the first half, on the back of a controversial Matty Wood try awarded by referee Mick Stone. Most observers thought the four-pointer was suspect at best. Despite the call, Penrith steadily got themselves back into the game, so effectively that in the second half they hit the front 12–11. Then the Raiders changed gears. Stunning tries to Paul Martin, who had just come on, Chicka Ferguson and Kevin Walters produced seventeen Raider points in 22 minutes. The game was as good as over. Writing it up, Ray Chesterton in the *Telegraph* remained unimpressed by the visitors. They scored five tries, he noted, 'without ever looking like a team that might trouble . . . Balmain and Souths'.

Written off again. Could the Raiders continue to upset the Sydney media's cosy notion of an all-Sydney grand final, and one featuring 1908 'original' teams at that? The signs were not good. Tim Sheens was 'very disappointed' with the Penrith game and his team's inability to close it out with authority while Kiwi international Brent Todd was only being realistic when he said the side would 'have to play a lot better'. True, but the Raiders' audacious challenge was still alive.

Three sides remained. Two had played with commendable consistency all year and the other, the southern Raiders, had oscillated between the marvellous and mediocre. Which Raider team would turn up for the preliminary final to play a side that had already beaten them twice in the season? George Piggins' Rabbitohs, clear-cut minor premiers, felt that they had shown enough during the year to see off the Raiders' threat. But could they? Or would the Green Machine continue to have the wood on them in the big matches that counted?

Sadly for the tribal residents of Redfern and its surrounds, Raider dominance reasserted itself. David Middleton described the Green Machine display as a performance of 'dazzling brilliance'. Whenever the ball went wide to the Raiders' outside men they were 'almost unstoppable'. The problem was getting it there to men in space. Souths refused this time to fade meekly into the season's sunset. It was 12-all at halftime, despite the authority of the Raiders' first six minutes when they raced to a 10–0 lead. The second half developed into a titanic struggle.

It was fitting that Glenn Lazarus was man of the match. He and the rest of the Raider six, growing in stature with each pressure-packed, post–regular season game, matched the Bunnies' pack in every facet of the game for the full 80 minutes. With seventeen minutes remaining, the Raiders had a four-point buffer but they burst the shackles in the last eight minutes, running in two clever tries, one to Gary Belcher and the other, deservingly, to Lazarus. Chris O'Sullivan and Ricky Stuart, who continued to game-manage a hamstring injury, convincingly outplayed their tough opponents, Craig Coleman and Phil Blake. It was a vital match-up which went the Raiders' way.

While George Piggins afterwards blamed the refs for the result, the better team won. In the Raiders' dressing room, amid muted celebrations at qualifying for a second grand final, Tim Sheens insisted that his team had 'room for improvement'. Meninga, not one to skirt the issue as the Raiders chased their ninth consecutive win and first Winfield Cup, put it with characteristic brevity: 'I am pleased to be going into the Grand Final as captain, but more importantly as part of the team. It doesn't mean anything unless you win it.'

For the second time in three years, Canberra and Queanbeyan experienced the euphoria of having their team in the grand final. Shopfronts were decked out in the distinctive lime green, white, blue and gold colours; homes right across the region were decorated in a multitude of creative extravagances; the Commonwealth Parliament cafeteria had the previous week served up rabbit stew to get the pollies into the right frame of mind; Canberra Milk went green; and in offices everywhere conversations focused on the prospects of 'our' team. One wag at the ANU made an adjustment to the Daley Road sign on campus named in honour of a significant Australian public servant. For grand final week 'Laurie' was added. It stayed put for months.

Background stories in the national capital abounded, among them one by Phil Rothfield, who talked about the career of 'veteran'

Chris O'Sullivan and the fact that he had been watched and admired as a young Lakes United and Canberra Galloper by two ball boys—Ricky Stuart and Brad Clyde. 'I can still clearly remember them as seven- and eight-year-olds,' said Chris. 'They were cheeky little buggers then and still are.' Brad remembered Sully as 'a real pin-up player among all the locals in Canberra. You should have seen some of the tries he used to score.' Ricky agreed. Now all three were about to head to Sydney and battle for the Winfield Cup together.

What did not happen in the 1989 grand final week was a street parade like the one preceding the grand final against Manly. John McIntyre was as blunt as he was confident: 'We've planned a civic reception for Monday.' One of the cars, he felt sure, would have a shiny trophy on board.

Other than fulfilling their prescribed NSWRL commitments, the Raiders stayed at home quietly establishing the right mindset before venturing up the Hume Highway. Balmain, on the other hand, could not help but be a little distracted despite coach Warren Ryan's best efforts to keep the external chatter at bay. For a week, virtually all of Sydney became Tiger supporters. Balmain was both the sentimental favourite and the punters' favourite.

As the week progressed the money poured in, the Tigers firming even further as the bookmakers' rock-solid, odds-on choice. *Rugby League Week* put itself unapologetically into the Tigers' camp, running with an appropriately colour-coded cover and the quotation: '1939, 1969, 1989?' The Sydney argument ran that the Raiders could not create history by coming from fourth or fifth, Balmain's monster pack had enjoyed the week off to refresh the batteries, their coach knew how to win grand finals, and the crowd would be overwhelmingly barracking for the locals.

Prime Minister Bob Hawke tipped the Raiders, though everyone knew he had a vested interest. Besides, he grew up playing Australian Rules in the west. Tom Keneally also favoured the Green Machine after his Manly Sea Eagles had been eliminated, but everyone knew he was a spinner of yarns. No, the script was written. The boys from the south had put together another productive season. Three in a row. A pity, thought Sydney, they were about to fall short once more.

Phil Gould led the naysayers. He'd spruiked for months, years, that the Raiders were soft. 'They haven't got the forwards to go on with it. They have a class backline . . . but their forwards leave a lot to be desired. They haven't got the fire power . . . they can't beat Balmain.' Tim Sheens took issue with his conclusion. He cut out the offending Gould article and made it available to all his players in grand final week, probably directing his forwards to review it daily. Gary Belcher spoke for the group when he said that 'Gould's comments were just gold for Tim'.

The unsung second-row combination of Gary Coyne (who statistically almost never missed a tackle) and veteran Dean Lance took particular note of the dismissive comments. Brad Clyde made sure he paid tribute to 'Deano', who had struggled for form earlier in the season and as a result had lost the captaincy to Meninga and his position to Clyde. Deano remained an 'inspiration'. He had the happy knack of making ground-shaking hits on the biggest opposition forwards in important matches to lift his team's spirits. Could he do it one last time in his farewell first-grade appearance? Steve 'Blocker' Roach will testify that in the '89 grand final he kept his record intact. More of that shortly.

24 September 1989. The date with destiny had arrived, the stage set for a match about to produce the highest possible drama. It *would* be one for the ages.

At the toss of the coin, Balmain captain Wayne Pearce was nervous. He knew his dressing room had already had a moment of organisational meltdown. In an excellent feature article written shortly after the grand final in the *Brisbane Courier–Mail*, Billy Rule pointed out that when the edgy Tigers were handed their jumpers for the most important game most of them would ever play in, they were too big. The jumpers 'hung off their frames like kaftans'. This led to a hasty 'symphony of slashing scissors as fabric flew across the floor. Sleeves were cut off, jumpers were hacked from the bottom and electrical tape was used to lock loose material in place.'

The Raiders' dressing room was a sharp contrast. An atmosphere of calm and assurance prevailed. The players all sensed something special, a feeling which had its background story three years earlier when John McIntyre, an old boy of St Edmunds College, asked another, younger St Eddy's old boy, Reverend Monsignor John Woods, to come on board in the unofficial role of Raiders' chaplain. For McIntyre, the chaplaincy program 'was never a religious thing. We had a lot of young men come into town ... with no extended family.' He saw the role as one that provided the players with an additional source of pastoral care.

John Woods was 32 when he accepted the position, one that he has retained for over 30 years. He is as keen in his support of the players today as he has ever been. In the mid-1980s he was fit and loved his footy, so he often joined the team for training while always maintaining a low-key presence unless it was laps of the oval. If Father Woods was in front on the run, Ricky Stuart for one knew that he was 'in trouble'.

Father Woods knew that his task was to earn the players' 'respect and acceptance', and it didn't take long for that to occur. The role, he said, was a 'ministry of presence' and he became a trusted mate of many of the players. Mal Meninga for one. So on the Friday morning before the 1989 grand final, the Catholic priest was moved to send a typed note to the Raiders' captain, choosing his words carefully to motivate and fortify:

> Thursday 21st September 1989
>
> Dear Mal,
>
> Just a note to wish you and the other guys all the very best for Sunday.
>
> I consider it a privilege to have been associated with you as Chaplain over the years. These sentiments would be echoed by your families, friends and many thousands of Canberra fans.
>
> Simply stated, the Grand Final is a challenge for you to realise your God-given potential as footballers. Inside each of you is a dream. Dreams

do come true if you are willing to sacrifice what you are to become what your dream calls you to be. My prayer for you is that of St. Paul: 'May your hidden self grow strong.'

I believe that you are ready for this challenge because you have all been willing to pay your dues thus far. Sunday's game will be your most demanding payment. It is simply another game and yet this game sums up all the other games. In this game you will find out who you are. 'May your hidden self grow strong.'

May it be a great game played in the true spirit of the occasion. Good luck, God bless and see you Sunday.

John Woods

Father Woods drew in part on a song by Rod Stewart, 'Never Give Up on a Dream', a song inspired by the extraordinary 18-year-old Canadian Terry Fox who ran most of the way across Canada with a prosthetic leg (due to cancer) to raise money for cancer research. The nation was transfixed; the world watched on too, amazed by his levels of courage. The song the TV channels played regularly as he hobbled his way from the east to the west coast was the Hollies' 'He Ain't Heavy, He's My Brother'. When death interrupted his journey, the world wept.

Father Woods had Terry Fox in mind when he penned his words to Mal. The note also included a short passage from a letter by St Paul to the Ephesians, 'May your hidden self grow strong'. Was it this passage or was it the popular priest's simple statement that 'Inside each of you is a dream'? Whatever the trigger for captain Meninga, he read the letter to his team on Saturday night and asked the club's resident chaplain to address the boys the next day in the sheds, immediately before the biggest game of their lives.

And so he did, inviting his gathering of young men to play in 'the true spirit' of the game. Not a word was uttered by the audience but, the instant he finished, Chris O'Sullivan, the best Raider on the field in the 1987 grand final and someone who had set a high standard of effort right from the club's maiden years in the Sydney competition, cried out: 'Yeah, and if we get behind we'll come back, we'll come back. We'll keep fighting.' The atmosphere in the dressing room crackled with ambition. Inside each of them was a dream.

So at the toss, a calm Mal Meninga identified the strain on his opposing captain's face. While Wayne Pearce later questioned the validity of the observation, his head must have been swirling with so many thoughts. He knew he had for many years been something of a poster boy for the league code. Justifiably so. A polite, non-drinking and non-smoking role model, he played the game with intensity and always fairly. He had represented club, state and country hundreds of times, producing virtually identical 80-minute performances around which his coaches could organise the rest of their strategy based on the fixed compass position of what 'Junior' Pearce gave his team. Above all, like Bob Craig 70 years before, he was a one-club legend, a Balmain boy down to his black-and-gold socks and bootlaces.

For Pearce, there was only one thing missing in the trophy cabinet of an exceptional career, what he himself referred to as 'the missing piece of the puzzle': a Winfield Cup medal. In pursuit of this Holy Grail, he continued to put up with bad knees, a left eye he could hardly see out of due to a detached retina courtesy of a game nearly a decade before, and general body fatigue as a result of his unbelievable work ethic in the engine room of the forwards for some 200 first-grade games. Beaten in the grand final in 1988, Pearce knew that another opportunity might not come again. He wanted this one badly. He had a right to be nervous.

The skippers were both 29 years old. The difference was that after four potentially career-ending broken arms, every experience the game afforded the great Meninga was a bonus dividend. He also knew that he was in charge of a young team on the rise.

At 3.08pm the Raiders' captain kicked off the grand final and Garry Jack fielded the ball. The first half was absorbing for a few reasons the experts had not predicted. Firstly, the attack-oriented Raiders produced the best three tackles of the first 40 minutes. The first was a stand-and-deliver hit by Dean Lance on 'Blocker' Roach, contact so perfectly timed that it didn't matter in the slightest that Lance was giving away many kilograms in weight. He hit Roach with a shoulder aimed at the upper chest and sat him on his bum. Roach got up almost immediately, shocked and embarrassed rather than hurt, but the tackle set the tone.

The veteran Raider had left his teammates and all Raider supporters with the memory of one more signature assault in a long line of tackles inflicted by a little man on big men. The team, Ricky Stuart later said, had come to expect this from Lance. When Brad Clyde later spoke about the grand final he went for a different Deano highlight, an 'almighty hit' on giant Paul Sironen. For Clyde, the incumbent Australian lock, this was plainly inspirational 'kamikaze material' because Deano 'tackled him with no regard for his own safety'.

The other Raider tackle, unfortunately for Garry Jack, was inflicted by Meninga on the Tiger fullback a few minutes later. Ricky Stuart had again sent a long, pin-point kick into Balmain's defensive corner and Jack had the misfortune of carting it back. He too opted for a decision of courage—to run straight at the hefty Raider in another case of little man confronting big man. This time the result was different. Cruel. Billy Rule writes that Jack was 'pulverised'. Close to the action, Chris O'Sullivan was ecstatic at what he had just witnessed. 'Great hit, Mal! Great hit, Mal!' It surely was.

The Stuart kicking game was so efficient that Balmain often struggled in the opening stanza to escape from their own half. Given the fact that Stuart was nursing a hamstring injury, 'Rampaging Roy Slaven' and 'H.G. Nelson' (the uniquely talented John Doyle and Greg Pickhaver) could not resist the opportunity on radio to discuss the Queanbeyan youngster's calm performance under stress:

H.G.: 'He's been having injections every half an hour since he was born.'

Roy: 'He's had a needle in each buttock this arvo.'

H.G.: 'So he'll be numb from the wedding tackle down.'

Roy: 'Geez, maybe his wedding tackle will be numb, too.'

Not everything had to be as serious as the gladiatorial first-half action on the field. There, the Raiders were the better side. According to Jeff Wells in *The Australian*, they 'easily ... [had] the better of it'. The Tigers had only two genuine opportunities in the first 40 minutes to score tries and did so ... twice. The first, when James Grant intercepted an errant Brent Todd pass and scampered twenty metres to score, a try converted by Englishman Andy Currier (Tigers 6–0 after thirteen minutes); the other, by Paul Sironen minutes before half-time, would have been the best try of the match in perhaps 95 per cent of all previous grand finals of the modern era. Brilliant Tiger initiative, as the ball travelled through numerous sets of hands, had its exclamation point when a rampaging Siro completed a length-of-the-field effort to touch down moments before the break. It could have been the execution blow. The Raiders had a lone goal by Gary Belcher to show for its effort and superiority. It was 12–2 at half-time. No team in the modern era had come back from ten points down at the oranges break to win.

What was said in the Raiders' dressing room at half-time? Not a lot because Tim Sheens had always believed that, regardless of the score after 40 minutes, if his team was playing well, then keep it going. Luck usually evens out. The captain wasn't too impressed with the errors that had led to Tiger tries but Glenn Lazarus, having a whale of a game, spoke for the group in stating that 'we knew we were the better side'.

The game was still wide open, very winnable. When the second half got underway, winger Mattie Wood went close to scoring five minutes in, only to have Wayne Pearce bob up in classic cover defence to bundle him into touch a couple of metres out. Ten minutes later, Gary Belcher got the Raiders back into the game with a try after terrific lead-up work by O'Sullivan, Ferguson and Daley. The Meninga conversion made it 12–8. Now it *was* anyone's game.

End-to-end action characterised the next ten minutes of showcase Rugby League, both sides striving for a try that would assume disproportionate value as the full-time siren got closer. If it was the Tigers, they would get beyond the magical six-point buffer; if the Raiders, they would hit the front for the first time, justifiably believing they were finishing over the top.

Much has been written and spoken about the last seventeen or eighteen minutes of normal time in what was proving to be an epic encounter. During this period, the game achieved even greater heights. It started when the magnificent Meninga by his account was 'beaten cold' by Mick Neil on his right side. Somehow he reacted sufficiently to flick out a despairing hand that just clipped Neil's boot in what Billy Rule subsequently labelled 'the most famous ankle tap of all time'. Neil stumbled to the ground a few metres from the Raiders' line, giving Steve Walters just enough time to overwhelm him. Short. Neil quickly played the ball, which went through various hands to Ben Elias, who then threw a lofted pass to his captain. The ball approached from Pearce's left, his 'blind' side. He fumbled. Knock on! Tim Brasher and James Grant were outside him in a potential two-on-one on Laurie Daley. Grant later commented that the pass to the skipper was awkward, 'a floaty type ball, a real tough pass' and it went down. The threat was over. The mass of Raider supporters in Canberra and Sydney breathed again.

Meninga's biographer John McDonald has no doubt that, after consideration of all Mal's glittering career moments of attacking brilliance and crushing defence, the Neil ankle tap was '*the* moment of Meninga's career'.

Up to this turning point in the match, Balmain had enjoyed almost every bounce of the ball, every ounce of luck on offer. Their coach, Warren Ryan, had good reason to believe that the curse his teams had suffered for years in games against the Raiders, stretching back to 1982, was finally over. Extinguished. But wait! The Neil moment forced a hasty rethink. Covering the game for the *Sydney Morning Herald*, Tony Stephens began his lively account this way:

> God wore black and gold for 78 minutes of the Rugby League Grand Final yesterday, but He went home before full-time. That, at least, was the

> explanation from Balmain's winger Steve O'Brien. Or, perhaps 'the man upstairs', as O'Brien described him, switched to Canberra's green colours in the dying minutes.

In the spirit of the Balmain winger's spiritual post-mortem, I think it's more accurate to say that God swapped sides a little earlier. But swap He did.

What followed on from Meninga's desperate 'hand of God' was an unlikely sequence of historic Rugby League moments that put this grand final into the legendary pantheon of ultimate sporting contests.

With a bare twelve minutes to go, a Balmain penalty was potted by Andy Currier to get the Tigers out to a converted try lead, 14–8. Five minutes later, Benny Elias's field goal attempt hit the Sydney Football Stadium crossbar with full force, ricocheting back into the field of play (after an earlier shot had been charged down). John McIntyre mischievously noted that a later measurement of the relevant crossbar indicated it was a few millimetres too high—just enough to reject the Elias one-pointer that would have tightened the Tigers' grip on the coveted shield and probably won them the match.

With less than five minutes to go, the Raiders rucked the ball to the halfway and a scrum packed down. Billy Rule informs us that Steve O'Brien then caught sight of activity at the entrance to the tunnel as NSWRL officials led by John Quayle prepared to crown Sydney's beloved Tigers as the 1989 premiers. O'Brien evidently managed a hoarse yell to his centre partner, Tim Brasher, that their team was about to win the Winfield Cup. The truism of sport comes immediately to mind: 'It's never over 'til it's over'. Within seconds of O'Brien's premature celebration, Bill Harrigan made a huge call: penalty Raiders. Perhaps a 'get square' for the one minutes earlier in favour of the Tigers? Who knows? In the following six tackles, the Raiders searched from side to side for a gap which didn't appear. On the fifth tackle, ten out from the Tigers' line and with 90 seconds on the clock, Chris O'Sullivan zipped into dummy half and sent up a 'hail Mary'. The ball bounced into Laurie Daley's grateful hands and he threw it instantly to Chicka Ferguson as if pushing out a medicine ball. Not pretty but it found its mark.

How fitting that the Raiders' last gasp play started with '82 Pioneer O'Sullivan and found its way into the hands of the Seiffert crowd's perennial favourite, Chicka Ferguson. He could have opted to go for the corner, or as Peter Sterling pointed out later, he might have opted for any one of three less difficult routes to the line, but he went to his career-long strength, the left foot—not the injured right that had almost had him substituted when he waved to come off a few minutes earlier. No, the turbo-charged left. One glorious step wrong-footed the cover defence, a second step demolished the late Tiger arrivals, a third determined his ultimate route to the line, together with a wombat's determined burrow. Raiders' substitute, Mackay-born Steve Jackson, number twenty, got right in behind his Townsville-born teammate and made sure he got there.

The accolades that followed this special moment in the newspapers the next day did do justice to the feat. Tim Sheens, delighted to have Chicka confirmed for the 1990 season, stated that his remarkable 35-year-old 'showed he was a truly great winger out there today . . . You can't coach the guy because he's so naturally gifted.' Chris O'Sullivan put it simply with his observation at close quarters, 'The Tigers were all staggered and Chicka is lightning on his feet.' Journalist–historian Ian Heads gloried in the masterclass that was Chicka's astonishing try in a *Herald* article under the title: 'Youngsters cannot cramp style of grand old miracle man "Chicka"'. The youngest player on the field, Brad Clyde, won the Clive Churchill medal in the game. Yet for Heads (and a host of other judges) it should rightly have gone to the oldest, Chicka, 'the man who enabled Canberra to bring off the miracle . . . If there had been any doubt, rugby league's oldest first-grader confirmed himself as a marvel of the game yesterday.'

The conversion kick that Ferguson presented to his skipper was ten metres to the side of the goalposts. Much easier than from the corner but in the cauldron of this unbelievable match, the pressure at breaking point, no gimme either. Meninga, a career toe-poker, calmly potted the conversion. The Raiders' captain was never likely to be the League's most reliable kicker—unless it was a big kick on a big occasion. *Then* Raiders' fans knew it would fly over the black dot, ten metres up. It did.

Fourteen–all. Full-time buzzer. Extra time in a grand final for the first time since 1978. Ten minutes each way.

Minutes before the break, Warren Ryan replaced Paul Sironen with Michael Pobjie, just as a quarter of an hour earlier he had controversially put Kevin Hardwick on for Steve Roach. Roach was furious. Inconsolable. The Balmain coach was looking for quicker men to make tackles, to shore up a tiring defensive line. Yet at this point in the match it was surely all about belief. The Raiders' huddle had it and when extra time began, it was immediately evident.

Two minutes in, the Green Machine had calmly secured a scrum in Tigers' territory, twenty metres out and with the feed. In his senior role as caller of the plays, Chris O'Sullivan, the former Canberra Galloper, fearlessly took it upon himself to make the biggest call of the game to that point, arguably the biggest call of his footballing life. 'Angel'. Sully elected to kick a field goal on the first tackle, and he would be the kicker. It's impossible to overstate the significance of such a call at this precise moment. Miss and he would be remembered forever as one of grand final history's most selfish players. Gary Belcher said as much later on. Ah, but kick it and the impact would be a hammer-blow for an opposition team that had not been behind since they'd scored the first try 90 minutes earlier. John Hogan expressed it perfectly in his *Australian* newspaper report: 'Although it was worth only a point and the game still hung in the balance, it caused immeasurable psychological damage.' Sully knew it. He also had complete faith in his ability as another career toe-poker to be deadly accurate at short range. He liked the cushion of grass in front of him, called 'Angel', absorbed Ricky Stuart's stare and the captain Mal's shrug, not so much a shrug of concern as recognition that the five-eighth had made up his mind to take it upon himself.

He says he 'took the shot regardless. I have always been my own man and played enough football to know when to take a chance.' On footy's biggest stage he backed himself. The result? The sweetest of field goals over the black dot, 25 metres up. Raiders 15, Tigers 14.

With the Raiders dominating extra time, the teams got to the seven-minute mark of the second ten minutes—the point at which all lovers of Rugby League at the Sydney Football Stadium and everywhere else were witness to what Laurie Daley has forever described as 'the best try I've ever seen'. It was 'a moment', he declared, 'frozen in my mind's eye'. The *Sydney Morning Herald* called it 'the try of a lifetime'.

Surely the try in question must have been scored by one of the Green Machine's elite backline? A second miraculous try by Chicka? A steam-rolling four-pointer from Mal? A dash from dummy half by Ricky Stuart? Sully?

For the answer, we need to take a step back in time to 1986. Steve Jackson joined the Raiders as an unknown Queenslander from the town of Mackay, identified as someone who gave 100 per cent effort every time he took the field. The Raiders' hierarchy viewed him as forwards insurance they got cheap. Unfortunately, injury restricted Jackson to a mere seventeen games over three seasons, 1987–89, most of them in the lower grades. In a first-grade game earlier in the '89 season, it was Jackson's error that probably cost the Raiders the match. To make matters worse, he was injured yet again in the same fixture and out for a bunch more games.

Tim Sheens told Steve Jackson that despite the fact that he had not played in the finals series so far, he would be named as the Raiders' last reserve for the grand final. Jackson got to suit up, to his delight, though he never really felt that getting on the field was a possibility. He was quite content to have the souvenir of a grand-final jersey.

Back in real time, and close to full-time. Tim Sheens had said earlier to his assistant coach Phil Foster that he was contemplating pitching Jackson into the fray, given the right circumstances. Brent Todd was carrying an injury and Jackson was told to warm up. Jacko still didn't believe game time was a prospect and accordingly did what he called 'a couple of pretend calf stretches'. And then it happened, seventeen minutes from full-time. Foster to Jackson: 'Jacko, you're on for Todd.' Jackson: '... my heart almost jumped out of my mouth'. Sheensy had always felt that the unlucky Queenslander was a wholehearted attacking forward when able to play injury-free. This was the basis of his gut decision. A big man with surprising speed who gave you his all. When Chicka burrowed to score the game-tying try, it was Jackson who was on hand to make sure he got there. He bobbed up at exactly the right moment.

It was about to happen again.

Fast-forward fifteen minutes and Jackson was still on the paddock, intent on maintaining a work ethic to assist his far more illustrious teammates. There was less than five minutes to the end of extra time. The Raiders were rock solid sitting on their single point lead, so this time it was the Tigers who had to gamble. It fell to the English centre Andy Currier, not having one of his best games, to grubber kick on his own twenty-metre line. The ball skewed off, straight into Meninga's giant arms and, when Tim Brasher uneasily attached himself to the Raider's massive frame, like a limpet on a blue whale, Meninga popped the ball to his nearest support, the number twenty, who was buggered and by his own confession years later as he told the story for the umpteenth time, 'was having a bit of a bludge in the backline, where I shouldn't have been'. Mal popped the ball to Jacko. What followed is quite rightly mentioned in the Introduction to this history. Steve Jackson careered through the attempted tackles of Balmain's Edwards, Jack, Neil, Hardwick and, belatedly, Gary Freeman to muscle the ball over the stripe through sheer will. He looked up at referee Bill Harrigan and got the OK. It was the stuff dreams are made of and Jacko has dined out on it for 30 years. He deserves to. Raiders 19, Balmain 14. Ninety seconds later the game was all over.

The Balmain players slumped to the ground, some lost in tears. They were in shock. So too their army of supporters in the stands and across Sydney. Their best-known supporter, singlet-wearing, shadow-boxing

Laurie Nichols, tendered the psychologically wounded out on the ground. Many photos in the Monday newspapers gave some sense of the depths of the misery and despair. Ben Elias sat on the ground alone, deep in thought, perhaps regretting the fact that when he was asked by a journalist from *The Australian* why the Tigers were so cocky, days before the game, he replied: 'Because no side can beat us.' The defeat was shattering; so was the year-long aftermath. Billy Rule concludes his account of the match, a great tribute to a grand occasion, with a poignant epilogue:

> History would be cruel to the Tigers. Of the 13 players to start the match, only Steve O'Brien knew what it was like to win a Grand Final, having been on the wing for Canterbury in the 1984 team. None of the other Balmain players who took part in the 1989 decider—the greatest Grand Final in rugby league history—would ever win a premiership.

The visitors had an entirely different future sketched out, one largely defined by the heroics of 1989. If the Tigers were in mourning, the Raiders were euphoric. Mal Meninga's tears of joy and happiness, a spontaneous outpouring when the buzzer sounded and soon shared with teammates, have featured in some of the code's most iconic photographs. It was a day of extremes. Meninga called it 'the best day of my football life' and also 'the most emotional'. Tim Sheens, never one to show much emotion, was himself close to tears. He had made his way down to the sidelines to witness the extra-time minutes at close quarters. Raiders' ball boy, Queanbeyan youngster Mark Webber, couldn't wipe the smile off his face. The next time he wore a grin as wide he had just won his first Formula 1 race in the 2009 German Grand Prix.

The Raider players, along with family, friends and adoring fans, stayed out on the field for at least 30 minutes to soak it all up, hoping the feeling would never end. Unforgettable television images mesmerised the populations of Queanbeyan and Canberra.

When the speeches finally commenced, Wayne Pearce was as always as gracious in defeat as he was when victorious. He acknowledged the Raiders as the superior team and stated that, even if they'd lost, they were still the better side. The Clive Churchill Medal was disputed. Plenty of people went for Chicka Ferguson, Ray Kershler in the *Daily Telegraph* pointing out that the award was given shortly before the end of regular time by the distinguished panel of experts (Reg Gasnier, Bob Fulton and Johnny Raper). So Chicka's 'golden try', indirectly the match-winning try, was not considered.

Still, not one person begrudged the winner. What a year 19-year-old Hawker College student Brad Clyde had experienced. In July he had become the first Raider junior to be selected to represent Australia in a senior Test, for a game against New Zealand when he was also man of the match. He had already become a favourite of league's most celebrated lock forward of yesteryear, Johnny Raper, while the pride of Parramatta, Ray Price, felt the young Canberran was 'destined to become an all-time great'. In his acceptance speech, Clyde made sure he singled out Dean Lance, 'a battler all of his career'. Lance had certainly left a few signature marks on the game. What's more, when the dust of battle had settled, he was persuaded to turn out for one last year in 1990.

The evidence for Roy Masters' prediction of a 'golden era' for the Raiders club was mounting amid a number of confirmed 'firsts': a first premiership for the club in only its eighth year; the first premiership win for a team outside the top three; the first premiership win by a team from outside the Sydney metropolitan area; and a comeback from a half-time ten-point deficit that constituted the greatest comeback in grand final history. Better than all of these, the thrill and wonder of Raider football was paraded for all to see on the game's biggest stage. New fans signed up from all parts of Australia and beyond.

The club also basked in its most productive season across the grades with the Jersey Flegg team going through undefeated, the under 21s beaten in the grand final, the reserves beaten in the preliminary final and a number of Raider players chosen for representative honours.

The myth that the Raider forwards were soft was annihilated. They were magnificent.

When the prime minister made his way to the triumphant dressing room to meet the playing group, he received a far better reception than politicians normally get at sporting contests because he had played a stewardship role for the club in the tougher times.

A week of exuberant celebration began in earnest when the two DC3 aircraft carrying the Raiders home touched down at Canberra airport hours after the game, to be greeted by well over 2,000 screaming fans. The Raiders' 'Green Machine' song blasted out in scenes of unrestrained joy. As ABC's radio's Tim Gavel said, 'the city exploded'.

The Winfield Cup trophy had its own much-publicised adventure in the streets of the national capital when it ended up in Laurie Daley's car in the motorcade tribute that travelled all the way from Queanbeyan to Canberra. He should tell the story:

> I committed one of the game's worst handling errors. I was sitting in the back of a convertible and the trophy was next to me on the back shelf. The car stopped so I picked up the trophy to show it off to the crowd before placing it back on the shelf. When the car took off again, I went to grab it but I could feel it slipping. I thought that if I hang on to this thing, which must have weighed 15 kilos, I'd probably go with it. So I let go and it smashed onto the roadway.

The anecdotes, memories and controversies attached to the Raiders' 1989 premiership have multiplied over the years. One of them, however, has taken on a life of its own: the argument over whether the game was the greatest grand final ever. Reactions to this bold claim began even as the game was being played when television commentator (and former Canterbury Bulldogs star) Graeme Hughes, enthused by the vigour of the early clashes, declared that he was watching 'one of the greatest openings of all time'. As the Introduction to this history recalls, novelist Tom Keneally praised a remarkable game in the *Sydney*

Morning Herald, calling it 'a movie script that came to life'. Keneally opted for Biblical comparisons to try to represent the significance of what he had witnessed.

Was it the greatest? The question has attracted a number of expert opinions over the last 30 years. In the mid-1990s, Ray Chesterton authored the supplement for the 1989 year in the *Daily Telegraph Mirror*'s series entitled 'Blood, Sweat and 14 Years—The Winfield Cup Story 1982–1995'. He headlined his article 'Mal's Miracle'. Paying sympathetic attention to Balmain's 'enormous personal grief', he was in no doubt that the Tigers had dutifully played their tragic role in 'the greatest grand final'.

The Ian Heads–David Middleton *Centenary of Rugby League* (2008) is unequivocal in its assertion that 1989 was 'the Greatest Grand Final', while *Rugby League: A Modern History* (2015), full of praise, describes the game as 'epic'. Canberra historian Brian Kensey, motivated by the absorbing 2015 grand final between the Paul Green–coached North Queensland Cowboys and Wayne Bennett's Brisbane Broncos, wrote a paper in 2016 where he meticulously compared the special features of the 1989 and 2015 matches. The number of parallels between the Raiders and the victorious Jonathan Thurston–led Cowboys is astonishing. After many pages of argument, Kensey finally opted for 1989.

The votes of a number of experts have been cast, virtually all in favour of the Raiders, though none of them carries the weight of the Men of League Foundation poll announced in August 2018. The Canberra Raiders' inaugural premiership was 'declared the greatest grand final of all time'. It has stood the test of time.

5

THE TEAM OF THE '90S

1990–2001

When summing up the 1989 season in his annual report, Raiders' Chairman Jim Woodger proudly spoke of 'the most successful year for the club in its relatively short history'. The challenge facing the coach, players and staff into the immediate future was how to follow up a year of such unprecedented achievement. Brad Clyde put it well: 'All of a sudden we were the yardstick.' How would the Raiders respond to their newly elevated status?

Despite the fact that the Winfield Cup had vacated Sydney for at least a year, officials of the NSWRL were thrilled to welcome into the fold the code's new ambassadors of open, attractive football—football that tallied up tries scored rather than punches thrown. The league's determined push to outlaw brutality in the game had paid off in the best way possible. Crowds were on the up and profits increasing. It was decided to take a few promotional risks. One involved what *Rugby League Week* described as 'the most costly and flamboyant marketing strategy ever attempted by not just rugby league but any sport in Australia'. American rock-and-roller Tina Turner was signed up at virtually the peak of her solo career, mainly due to the fact that her manager was an Australian. As a favour, Turner accepted significantly less money than she could have asked for, enabling the NSWRL in March 1989 to freshly brand its game with Turner's 1987 hit 'What You Get is What You See'. The song was instantly successful and Turner's bubbly personality seemed a perfect fit with the league's aim to get more women and families through the turnstiles.

Oozing class, 1990

The campaign went up several notches the following season when, on 12 March 1990, Turner's 'Simply the Best' was used for the first time at a function in Sydney to launch the football year. The campaign ended up going for several years, and was in time acknowledged with justification as 'the most inspired piece of marketing ever introduced into Australian sport'. Turner's raunchy, athletic demeanour was vital; but so too was the fact that the campaign stretched right across the Raiders' glory years. No other club could have carried the weight of the promotion as effectively. The Raiders—young, adventurous and led with class—fitted it like a glove. It was as if the campaign had been shaped with the Green Machine solely in mind.

The manner in which the team gained its first premiership, together with the Tina Turner aura, took the Raiders into Australian lounge rooms they could never have dreamed of 'invading'. They had become a presence in the game, attracting new fans in and out of Canberra. President of the Senate, Labor's Kerry Sibraa, noticed the shift at his workplace: 'I'm president of the All Party Parliamentary Rugby League group. When Canberra first came into the competition, we would go down to the Transport [section of Parliament House] and see pictures of Parramatta, Manly. Now you see Raider posters everywhere'.

A shift of home ground when the Raiders became a premiership force was inevitable, from the country charm and bush boutique niceties of Queanbeyan's Seiffert Oval to the much larger spaces, better parking, better seating and more central location of Canberra's Bruce Stadium, a stone's throw away from the Australian Institute of Sport. Some fans were unhappy, high-profile politician and Raider fanatic Ros Kelly reporting that her support of the move to Bruce attracted one or two unpleasant, threatening messages. Tony Wood, a Queanbeyan boy through and through, refused to don his Victor the Viking suit for a full twelve months in protest. However, any escalation of this dissent was swamped by success. The Raiders were big news. The team needed a stadium befitting their newly acquired place in league's scheme of things.

There had been a bit of football between the grand final victory and the start of the 1990 season. The Raiders took their Australian title to England, less than a fortnight after securing the Winfield Cup, to play English club side Widnes at Old Trafford in what was billed as the 'World Club Challenge'. The Raider players were neither happy about it nor particularly interested. Straight after the grand final, Glenn Lazarus went on record with some straight talking that English league authorities would not have appreciated: 'We've played all friggin' year . . . we deserve a break, yet we've got to get on a plane . . . I really think it's a waste of time.' The Raiders were in England for two days, played the day after arrival and headed home the following day. After leading 12–0 at the eleven-minute mark, they lost 30–18. The anti-climax of the game was apparent to all.

The months of relaxation that followed were sorely needed. Tim Sheens and John McIntyre took a short break and then re-engaged with the player market. It was bitter-sweet. New signings included Brett Mullins (the son of champion Eastern Suburbs winger Bill Mullins), Steve Stone and Dave Woods. Against this, the club said farewell to Ivan Henjak and Steve Jackson, both of them going to the Western Suburbs club, while Wayne Bennett was at it again, this time obtaining terrific utility back Kevin Walters for the Broncos. All three were going to be missed for their valuable contributions on and off the field.

The premiership defence began against St George at the Raiders' new home at Bruce Stadium in mid-March. The fans were pumped, a bulging 22,527 turning out for the opener on a fine autumn day in Canberra. The Raiders played well within themselves for a 26–10 win and this was followed by an equally comfortable away victory against

Illawarra, 'a professional win' according to Tim Sheens. The side appeared to be slowly moving through the gears. Certainly Manly legend Max Krilich thought so in a piece he wrote for *Rugby League Week* at the beginning of April which found a receptive audience in the league world. Krilich made a comparison that was unimaginable only a couple of years before:

> Canberra will be to the early '90s what Parramatta were to the early '80s under Jack Gibson. Gibson gathered a marvellous mixture of talent alongside some experience and turned the premiership into a 'catch us if you can' event. It's early days yet in the 1990 premiership but the signs are flashing red that Canberra are going to be an awesome proposition for any side . . .

The round five game against Eastern Suburbs in Canberra will never be forgotten. Paul 'Fatty' Vautin, like Phil Gould a Raider sceptic in the face of overwhelming evidence to the contrary, had a first-hand look at the Raiders on the day. As the result of a falling out with his old club Manly, Fatty had become a Rooster. This was his inaugural visit to Bruce Stadium to play the team he was wont to call 'the faders' and he left utterly plucked. Canberra journalist Brad Turner termed it the 'Easter Massacre'.

> When stumps were drawn in the late afternoon the scoreline read Raiders 66, Easts 4.
>
> The Raiders racked up the most points they had ever scored in a single game while Easts experienced their worst-ever defeat since the club's formation in 1908.
>
> Mal Meninga scored 38 points, made up of five tries and nine goals, in a performance that Laurie Daley said 'monstered the Roosters and I swear there were players trying desperately just to keep out of his way'.
>
> Chicka Ferguson scored three tries in a backline that scored all twelve tries.

The three Raider teams on the day scored a total of 133 points, one every two minutes across the grades.

Poor old Fatty Vautin, behind the tryline to watch another Meninga conversion of his try, asked his teammates whether Mal was covered in spiders. Craig Salvatori chipped in that they might be funnel-webs. He also pointed out later that his coach, Russell Fairfax, 'banned grog on the bus and made us sit through the video of the game. It was like a horror show'.

The compliments being dished out to the Raiders, collectively and individually, were heading into the stratosphere. Was this cause for concern? Was it all too much too soon?

At the halfway point in the season, between rounds eleven and twelve, the Raiders led the competition by a point, and they kept their noses in front throughout the second half of the season in games which produced an interesting aside. After a one-sided loss to an emerging Penrith side in round fifteen, 23–2, at Bruce Stadium, the Raiders stayed unbeaten through the last seven rounds. In the last of these, an away game against Souths, the Raiders inflicted a bruising 48–0 defeat on a team that had, until recently, figured prominently as an unflinching and respected opponent in the Green Machine's rapid rise to the top. The bells of change were tolling loudly. As the precocious youngsters at Penrith demanded their shot at the Green Machine's title, the ageing Rabbitohs were on the slide, most of it self-inflicted. Sadly, in 1990 the foundation club got the wooden spoon.

As the Raiders prepared for their fourth consecutive semifinals campaign (without Brad Clyde, whose leg injury had ended his season), they were bolstered by the achievement of a couple more defining 'firsts'. When they beat a bewildered Easts (again!) in round twenty in all three grades, this resulted in the club leading the competition in all three grades for the first time. When each of the sides maintained form right to the end of round 22, the club had secured all three minor premierships, another magnificent first and a rare achievement in the long history of Rugby League in Australia.

The Raiders met the Penrith side in the major semifinal. Fresh from a victory over Brisbane in the minor preliminary final, the Panthers went into the Raiders game brimming with confidence. The Broncos had been widely tipped as a grand finalist, only to be soundly beaten, and the Panthers did not have to reach back too far when looking for the motivation to take on Canberra. In round fifteen at the Raiders' home ground, they kept the Winfield Cup holders tryless in an impressive win. In the major semifinal, they took results and momentum into the game and, for their coach Phil Gould, a near-flawless record. In three years of games played at the Sydney Football Stadium, Gould-trained teams (Canterbury and Penrith) had won seven games with one draw. He was unbeaten in four semis.

The 1990 major semi added to the unblemished record. A relentless, end-to-end struggle for 80 minutes had the scores locked 12–12 at full-time. The match-ups across the ground disappointed no-one and with only five minutes left, Greg Alexander, the Panthers' fresh-faced captain, kicked a pressure goal from 35 metres out to tie the scores. It was the boost he and his team needed. Alexander dominated extra time, ultimately scoring 22 points in his team's convincing 30–12 victory over the tiring Raiders. In the duel of the halfbacks, 'Brandy' Alexander finished over the top of rival Ricky Stuart.

Laurie Daley speculated that the week's rest did his team no favours at the back end of the contest. If so, the situation was about to be reversed, with the Panthers given a spell the following week as they marched straight into the grand final. On paper, the Raiders' preliminary final opponent, the Broncos, looked tough. They too had registered a last-start win over the Raiders which coach Wayne Bennett no doubt dwelt on as he put together his game plan.

Once again, the dominant pattern in the Raiders' extraordinary period of polished, winning football reasserted itself. A big game; another lopsided result. The Broncos were thrashed 32–4. Mal Meninga felt the game was one of his side's 'very best'. Teammate and dyed-in-the-wool New South Welshman, Laurie Daley, was not willing to be as polite. 'We blew Brisbane away . . .' The Broncos managed their only points two minutes from the end of the game with a try which saved them from being routed.

In the days that followed—grand final week—I wrote an article for the *Canberra Times* entitled 'On Faith, Hype and Green Machine Glory' in which I attempted to summarise the skill level of the Raider team poised to play the Panthers:

> They're good all right. Consider Sunday's decimation of the embattled Broncos. Brent Todd back to his bustling best and taking more yards at the advantage line than at any time this season. Glenn Lazarus confirming that he's not only the in-form prop of the competition but the speediest; Steve Walters shellacking his brother, the Test incumbent rake, with typical bursts through the soft belly of the Broncos ruck; Nigel Gaffey and Gary Coyne providing perfect foils, the one with strength and enthusiasm so reminiscent of Brad Clyde (is there any higher compliment?), the other with intelligence and rock-solid defence in tight; Dean Lance, a footballer in the old style, whose hits are legendary and still the most feared in Winfield Cup football; Ricky Stuart, extraordinarily gifted and with the sort of peripheral vision equalled only by Wayne Gretsky, the North American ice hockey superstar; Chris O'Sullivan, canny, a big-match performer and back to his best form since the blood-poisoning; Meninga and Daley surely as brilliant as any centre combination, ever; Chicka and Paul Martin, playing better than any two wingers in the competition have all season; and Gary Belcher, streets ahead of any of the present group of fullbacks here or overseas.

Panthers' coach Phil Gould must have been increasingly nervous when watching the professional manner of the Raiders' win over the Broncos, especially the smothering defence of the Raiders' forwards.

The heroics of 1989, with all its pressure and suspense, had not impacted at all on the Raiders' determination to go back to back. There was a second grand final to be won, the team's third appearance in league's showpiece in only four years. The Canberra–Queanbeyan community continued to enjoy all the emotional highs of finals footy, and this interested some of the media's more thoughtful commentators, who enquired into the Raiders' unfolding story. Milton Cockburn wrote a piece mid-year in the *Herald* where he discussed 'the de-bonding process' in Canberra that had happened so quickly: namely, the speed with which 'league-starved former Sydney residents' who had moved to Canberra broke bonds 'forged in childhood' with their suburban Sydney family team to become Raider fans. The attraction of the Raider football evolution had proved impossible to resist.

With game day approaching, Tim Sheens refused to buy into the Raiders' favouritism and glowing publicity. He was well aware of the untapped ability of the squad from the foot of the Blue Mountains, having coached ten of the thirteen players who were to start the grand final. What's more, the Panthers had played the Raiders twice in the year so far for two big wins. Sheens knew the Raiders had a difficult game in front of them.

All Raider true believers know, as if citing sacred text, that their team won the 1990 grand final 18–14 in a game that in truth was never as close as the final scoreline suggested. Mal Meninga summed it up well: the game 'lacked much of the electricity, emotion and theatre of the previous year's classic, but was still an exciting game that went all the way to the finish'. The Raiders had the best of the early action and tries to Chicka Ferguson and Laurie Daley saw them lead 12–0 at the 25-minute mark. The contest threatened to be one-sided but, to their credit and as Tim Sheens had anticipated, the Panthers roared back with such commitment that seven minutes into the second half it was 12–10, and game on.

An arm wrestle developed but, in the end, there was too much big-game experience, grand final experience, for this champion Raider team to call on. Looking for a bit of edge speed as all players tired, Sheens went to his bench and put on Matthew Wood. It was a typically astute substitution. Soon after, a Meninga bust, short pass to Laurie Daley, and another pass to Wood released the winger, who easily beat the cover defence in a 55-metre dash to score in the corner—and effectively wrap up the title. Greg Alexander scored a late consolation try for Penrith.

By all accounts the celebrations in the Raiders' dressing room and at their Canberra–Queanbeyan clubs in the evening were, in Meninga's words, not quite 'as raucous or as sustained as in 1989'. Laurie Daley said he felt more relief than excitement. And then there was the sight post-match of Brad Clyde on crutches, coaxed onto the ground by his Junee mate and happy for his team's second triumph—yet feeling 'empty' as he 'straggled behind'.

In the aftermath of a hard-fought grand final, commentators focused on two key elements: firstly, the strength of the Raider forwards led by Glenn Lazarus and Brent Todd, who overpowered their opponents. Peter Frilingos summed up their hard toil, effort often overlooked: 'As was the case throughout the year Lazarus and Todd got down in the pits and made the tough yards for the backs to operate.' Secondly, the almost flawless display by Clive Churchill Medal–winner Ricky Stuart. His kicking game was at times close to perfection. Peter Sterling bestowed high praise: 'Ricky had a super game, absolutely super. It was as good a kicking game as I've seen in a Grand Final.' Ray Kershler in the *Telegraph*, amazed by the skill on display, got a little more creative: 'Stuart, you will remember, has a rugby background, and managed to break the ball at right angles to the sideline. No-one has been able to do that since they invented the sphere.'

If the Churchill Medal in 1989 was mildly controversial, there was nothing contentious about the decision in 1990. Ricky Stuart produced a strategic kicking masterclass. He had been nervous about being selected for the forthcoming Kangaroo tour but his grand final was impossible to ignore. Stuart was named in the squad for England along with four other teammates, Mal Meninga (as captain), Laurie Daley, Glenn Lazarus and Gary Belcher.

What a year it had been for the Raiders. As the Heads–Middleton *A Centenary of Rugby League* puts it with admiration, the club had won 'almost everything in sight': the Channel Ten pre-season cup, the minor premiership, the club championship, the President's Cup Grand Final (with captain Steve Stone, Brett Mullins, Jason Death, Jason Gregory and David Boyle starring) and just missing in the Reserve Grade Grand Final after being in front 6–4 with three minutes left, only to lose in extra time.

1982 Pioneer and super-coach in the making Craig 'Bellyache' Bellamy described it as a 'once-in-a-lifetime year for the club', echoing the feelings of just about the entire league world. Bellamy was the captain of the desperately unlucky reserves but his disappointment turned to joy when he was called up to sit on the first-grade bench. 'I was 32 years old. I'd been through the club's tough times. I didn't play in the '87 Grand Final because of a shoulder injury and I missed '89. Out of all the years, all the time I was there, 1990 was the year I remember most.' Jason 'Toots' Croker has not forgotten the day either. Aged just seventeen, he played wonderfully well in the winning President's Cup team and sat on the bench for the reserves and firsts. When he headed back to Canberra with medals for all three grades, he felt a bit like Michael Phelps.

Little wonder that Club Secretary John McIntyre, having tipped the Raiders to go all the way weeks ago, jubilantly told the media that his young club was 'in terrific shape . . . in first-grade we have all our players tied to long-term contracts and there are dozens of richly talented kids rising through the grades, just waiting for their chance. We won the first premiership of the 1990s and talk of a dynasty is not ridiculous.'

Even the retirements of club stalwarts, Chicka Ferguson and Dean Lance, and the departure for England of Chris O'Sullivan, seemed well timed. They had all experienced the sticks and stones of the lean years and were all going out after two premierships in a row. What could possibly go wrong? What a difference twelve months can make.

Rise, fall and rise again, 1991–93

It was Mal Meninga who said that the 1991 season was 'one of the most turbulent of my career'. On the face of it, the comment appears absurd.

After all, the Raiders had banked consecutive premierships, Raider football had swept all before it and, in the 1990–91 off-season, the great Raider captain had combined with Ricky Stuart to add yet another magical moment to his illustrious footballing dossier. It happened when he captained the Kangaroos on the October–November 1990 tour of England.

Great Britain won a bruising First Test at Wembley, 19–12, in front of a record crowd of nearly 53,000. When the teams re-engaged at Old Trafford for the Second Test, the scores were tied 10–all with eleven minutes to go. The Poms had an opportunity to kick a penalty and hit the lead but it missed. With 60 seconds on the clock, Ricky Stuart broke clear close to his own line and went on a 70-metre jaunt downfield. Looking left and right for support, and the cover defence closing, he found his Raiders and Kangaroos captain on the inside for Meninga to score. The try will live long in the memory of all Australian lovers of Rugby League, a try *A Centenary of Rugby League* describes as 'among the greatest ever scored in Test-match football'.

The two Raider teammates had added more substance to glowing reputations. In Canberra, their club team had become a seminal part of the cultural fabric of the city and region. Cars now had Raiders' streamers all year round. Raider jerseys, socks and assorted gear were standard issue. The players routinely visited local schools, hospitals and aged-care facilities, and attended a wide variety of community functions as the invited VIPs. On local television, Raider players popped up everywhere: Mal amused by the outsized gear he was advertising; Brent Todd trying vainly to pronounce 'Frank Reynolds' Retravision' at speed; Chicka dapper in Working Gear shorts; Laurie Daley munching Jackos' pizzas; and Brad Clyde, Belconnen's own, promoting the latest car deal at Lennock Motors. A generation of youngsters was besotted. The Raiders were now centrally located in the city's conception of itself.

Why, then, was 1991 'turbulent'?

Tim Sheens was well aware that a successful premiership charge was built in part on the foundation of the team sustaining few injuries. Unfortunately, the 22 rounds of the 1991 competition became nothing short of a war of attrition. Results reflected the long injury list. In the first six rounds the team looked anything but the league's best, winning two at home and losing four other games. A big win against Parramatta at Bruce was counter-balanced by a disappointing loss against Wests. As expected, in spite of the average start, the Raiders slowly, conscientiously began to turn the season around. Indeed, the last eight rounds produced only one loss, against the Broncos at Bruce, enough to place the team fourth going into the semis.

The turbulence that Mal Meninga referred to had nothing at all to do with the courage being displayed each week on the field. On 6 May, the first reports appeared in the media about the Canberra club's financial situation. Newspapers stated that the combined debt of the Raiders Group (Queanbeyan Leagues Club, the Raiders' Mawson Club and the Rugby League football club) was somewhere between $5 million and $6 million. The Raiders had exceeded the 1990 salary cap by $85,853 (duly fined that amount by the NSWRL) and looked certain to overspend in 1991 by far more than that figure. The fine in anticipation was $100,000.

Heads had to roll. Both the Chief Executive John McIntyre and Chairman Jim Woodger were forced to resign from their positions. At one point in the unpredictable and troubled months of June and July 1991, the Raiders organisation was at risk of going into liquidation. Rumours spread that the team was up for sale.

The players were shocked by the suddenness of the NSWRL announcements and penalties, as both Sydney and English clubs circled the wounded beast. On 17 July, Mal Meninga admitted he was close to signing with an English club; on 25 July Laurie Daley threatened to sign with either Wigan, St George or Wests; and on 1 August the Gold Coast club dangled one of the richest deals in Rugby League history in front of Brad Clyde. The Broncos, always on the lookout for the best talent unearthed by other clubs, signalled their interest in Glenn Lazarus, as did Manly with Steve Walters. The Raiders' finest players were at risk of departing *en masse*.

What then happened in response to this predicament was simply remarkable. Labor Party minister and Raider tragic Ros Kelly talked Governor of the Reserve Bank Bernie Fraser into heading up a management committee to deal with the crisis. His stated reason for agreeing to do so—'I'm a sucker for a blonde'!—was only one small and amusing part of the story. In the 1960s, Fraser had turned out for both the Canberra Tigers and Canberra Workers Club in Group 8 as a utility of talent. He played lock, second-row and in the centres. A proud local, Fraser was exactly the right individual for the task ahead. He met with the ANZ Bank, to whom the Raiders owed some $5 million, and managed to get the bank to lend a further $700,000 to shore up the immediate liquidity threat—on the proviso that all players agreed to a significant pay cut. The players were rightly angry at being kept in the dark while the club hierarchy, led by new Chief Executive Kevin Grace, attempted to keep things afloat. All player contracts were declared null and void.

Emergency financial arrangements were essential. Even more important was the way in which the community responded to an alarming sequence of events. A club with less spine, a community with less belief would have recoiled. Collapsed. The Raiders' players, officials and their region of avid supporters dug deep. With July staggering into early August, small miracles began to happen.

I tried to sum up the phenomenon in the *Canberra Times* newspaper, which willingly played a leading role in the rescue operation:

> Tim Sheens signed on for 1992. 'Someone', he said, 'had to take a positive step.' Given the uncertainty, it was miracle No. 1. When Sheens agreed to terms, he admitted reluctantly that Mal Meninga probably would sign one of the big English contracts being waved in front of him. August 7: Meninga re-signs with the Raiders. It was the second miracle. Miracles three, four and five: Clyde, Daley and Walters sign. All took substantially

less than they could have obtained on the open market. Other signatures followed, despite the precarious Raiders economic position. In this era of aggressive professional sport, of unashamed club hopping, lawyer involvement and management consultants, why? When asked this question by hardened, incredulous Sydney reporters Sheens, Meninga and co. kept returning to unfashionable notions like loyalty. Friendship and enjoyment. Mateship.

On 30 August, Ricky Stuart, Steve Walters and Brett Mullins all re-signed. Walters did so, he said, because it's 'a tremendous club with so much talent and camaraderie'. Stuart gave as his primary reason that he wanted to remain in his home town and 'continue to eat the world's best cooking—my mum's'.

The character of the players inspired the community. How else to explain the likes of Prime Minister Bob Hawke, his Labor colleagues Ros Kelly and Fred Daly, Bernie Fraser, Ron Murray of Murray's Buses, David and Richard Farmer, and a host of Canberra's highest-profile citizens rallying to show their support.

Richard Farmer, a prominent wine merchant and political lobbyist with close ties to the Labor Party, kicked off a 'Save the Raiders' trust fund which sparked the 'Rescue-a-Raider' campaign. Money poured in from all quarters of the community. Canberrans big and small wanted to help.

The Royal Australian Mint's Geoff Izzard conceived the idea of having the mint produce a limited edition of 'Road to Victory' medallions to raise money. It was underwritten by Ron Murray and David Farmer, and got the go-ahead three weeks later. Only the Raiders could get government red tape cut so quickly.

On 23 July the *Canberra Times* editorial gave its reasons for the astonishing response: 'The Raiders live, train and play right here in Canberra. We can watch them play every second week at Bruce Stadium and hear and read reports of the away games. They belong to us . . . the Raiders have put Canberra on the map.'

Several days later in a *Canberra Times* piece called 'Glimpses of Heaven' I expressed my thoughts as a stitched-on Raider fan and father of Raider fans, singling out the elevated stature of the captain:

> Mal Meninga just might be a contemporary icon. Putting my four-year-old to bed at half-time in the Test mid-week, she asked me for the umpteenth time in the last fortnight 'Is Mal Meninga going away, Dad?' Clearly, the Meninga-to-England saga was beginning to assume 'death of Santa Claus' significance.

The horticulture columnist in the *Canberra Times*, 'Indigofera', in the same few weeks declared that Meninga, 'breathtakingly famous in his own lifetime', should have a plant named after him. He settled on the very sturdy *Eucalyptus melliodora*, the yellow box, which he suggested might be renamed *Eucalyptus meningaoides*.

Canberra closed ranks. But so did Sydney in spiteful reaction, its media at times merciless. The *Sun-Herald* entitled a lead article 'How the Raiders Cheated to Win' and John Harker on 2GB and Channel Seven criticised the Raiders for months. Journalist Peter Frilingos summed up the response when stating that 'Raider-bashing is challenging league itself as the most popular sport on the eastern seaboard of Australia'.

Months of criticism meant that the Raiders' forays into Sydney for the 1991 post–regular season action were met at times with abuse. Laurie Daley put it best. 'We felt it was us against the world', and some in the world were fuming, especially the supporters of Wests, Manly and Norths supporters when the Raiders, though wounded by injury, were able to beat each of the Sydney teams in turn. Gary Belcher was back from serious injury in the Magpies game and had a blinder in a solid 22–8 victory. Manly came next, and in a high-scoring match in which the final margin flattered the Sea Eagles, the Raiders served Sydney up with yet another display of Raider football with a difference. In a game of end-to-end action, the Raiders' ever-reliable second-rower Gary Coyne helped himself to four tries in a 34–26 win. 'I've scored four in a game of juniors,' Coyne said, 'but never before in senior football.' How fitting that his four-try haul, the last of them a bit of sleight-of-hand with his captain that Manly fell for, should make him the Raider forward with the most tries in a single game, all time.

The North Sydney Bears, who had experienced one of their best seasons in decades under coach Steve Martin, were the Raiders' next opponents in the preliminary final. The Bears got off to a flyer, 12–0 after fourteen minutes, but they could not withstand the quality of football which steadily, typically, pegged them back over the remaining 65 minutes of calculated Raider attack. At the end of the day it was Canberra 30, Norths 14, before 39,665 people—a huge number of those spectators travelling up to the SFS from the national capital. John McDonald, having written the first edition of Mal Meninga's biography the year before, produced a new and imaginative reaction to Raider football for the *Sydney Morning Herald*:

> Canberra may have redefined the nature of football as they progressed to the grand final . . . It's now almost like a horse race, with the weight-for-age performers having to carry the grandstand via points start in a handicap. Football teams aren't supposed to win that way week after week. It's just like Super Impose carrying 63 kg and coming from last on the turn in a big Randwick mile . . . There was just too much power and poetry from Canberra's incomparable artists for Norths' honest artisans.

In a very real way, the Canberra club's grand final had been run and won just getting through the long process of the previous three months. In the season finale, against a committed Penrith team, the minds of the Raiders were still willing but some of the bodies were weak. They laboured all afternoon but the sheer number of players struggling with injury took its toll as Penrith reversed the previous season's grand final to get up 19–12. Champion lock Brad Clyde got his second Clive Churchill Medal as the game's best player, a decision many Panthers fans contested, but it was Penrith's day.

After the grand final, the *Canberra Times* headlined its front page: 'When Grown Men Cried'. It was that sort of emotional season. Drama, despair, loyalty and immense courage, despite all odds. In 1991, the mythology surrounding the club grew even more.

Six days before the grand final the 'Raiders Players Trust Fund' held a 'Rescue a Raider Dinner' at Canberra's Lakeside International Hotel. Prime Minister Bob Hawke spoke with admiration and drew the raffle. There wasn't a person in the room who did not admire the fight back by the club. In 1991, with Ricky Stuart and Laurie Daley virtually playing on one leg, they failed at the final hurdle. Only just. The season's highlight lay elsewhere, something summed up well by radio commentator Alan Jones at the trust fund dinner: 'The Raiders have young men who, when push came to shove, weren't prepared to swap the guernsey.' In doing so, they ensured the long-term future of the club.

1992

If 1991 was the Raiders' most 'turbulent' year then 1992 was, according to another of Mal Meninga's in-house assessments, the 'toughest'. The team's sharply reduced salary cap, self-inflicted by management it should be emphasised, made the year a difficult one to negotiate, much less perform well in. League's best journalist, Alan Clarkson, wrote an article in the *Herald* in the last weeks of the '92 season entitled 'When the Raiders luck ran out'. The implications of dramatically altered circumstances were bound to have consequences. Clarkson objectively stated the case: 'The Canberra Raiders' chances of making the 1992 Winfield Cup semifinals went out the door before the first round of the premiership had been completed.'

For five years the Raiders had thrived due to the close attention the club paid to junior development and astute perusal of the player market, but that all changed after the imposition of the NSWRL's punitive measures. A colossal 60 per cent of the Raiders' playing group was turned over during the 1991–92 off-season. Virtually overnight it was a completely different club. Quality players and promising lower graders were forced to leave in numbers, among them David Barnhill (to Saints), Mark Bell (Wests), Brett Boyd (Penrith), Glenn Lazarus (Broncos), Nigel Gaffey (Easts), Jason Gregory, Brent Todd and Paul Martin (all to the Gold Coast). Paul Beath and Phil Carey headed to Newcastle to join the Toronto Workers Club while Craig Breen, Gavin Price-Jones, Glenn Ryan and Michael Twigg, unable to be retained under the restricted cap, drifted into local Canberra clubs. Alex Corvo departed for the Riverina and '82 Pioneer Ashley 'Hooter' Gilbert took over the coaching duties of his old hometown club, Crookwell.

On the plus side of the ledger, the Raiders obtained the services of Phil Blake, Paul Osborne, Craig Bellamy (back after going with Chris O'Sullivan to Swinton in 1991), Rugby Union convert Albert Fulivai, and a few other young players. Sully too had returned from his stint as captain–coach of Swinton. But the 'buys' were relatively few; the players who had to be traded away were many. As one writer said, so aptly, 'the Raiders became the Raided'.

Tim Sheens knew the scale of the task confronting him in 1992:

> My main concern at the moment is to get a football side put back together after starting what was basically a new club . . . This is a brand new club . . . We've had to put everyone on [a new] contract and you really start from scratch . . . It's going to take six games, eight games, ten games, or a season to get some of these kids out of A-Grade mode and into playing grade.

In late February 1992, the Raiders appointed a new chief executive, Kevin Neil, when interim CEO Kevin Grace opted to focus on the job of Raiders Group general manager. Neil immediately sought to defuse expectations when stating his main task was to 'help make sure the Canberra Raiders have a 1993'. A 36-year-old former St George lower-grade player (and for three years coach of the Raiders' S.G. Ball side), Neil had resigned from a good job as the ACT manager of the prominent Linfox trucking company. When some of the dust had settled in his new position, he listed his top priorities: 'Priority one is to retain the coach, priority two is to retain players and three is to make the off-field management as professional as the on-field management.'

None would be easily obtained. The club's debt, though stabilised at last, was an open bleed. Several Winfield Cup clubs were hovering, salivating at the prospect of signing the likes of Ricky Stuart, Steve Walters, Brad Clyde and Brett Mullins. How would the club balance contract discussions with survival necessities?

In May, Neil re-signed Laurie Daley and signed New Zealand winger Sean Hoppe, first spotted by Tim Sheens at a Raiders trial in Auckland. Meninga was locked away but the rest were potentially on the market and the Manly Sea Eagles were identified as the club most likely to swoop. A few weeks along, Stuart and Belcher re-signed, leaving Brad Clyde and Steve Walters the only internationals not yet secured. The Canterbury Bulldogs, admirers of 'Boxhead' Walters' full-throttle approach to his football, signalled a strong interest in him, so strong that television and radio personality Ray 'Rabbits' Warren confidently declared that they had him in the bag already. They didn't. When Clyde and Walters re-signed, all the internationals (with the exception of Glenn Lazarus, heading north to the Broncos) had renewed their Raider contracts for less money than they were worth. Again.

Under the circumstances, the Raiders did pretty well to finish with a 10–12 win–loss 1992 season record that placed them twelfth overall. One game, a 33-10 win against the Gold Coast at Bruce, deserves a special mention because there was some emotional history attached to it. With injuries decimating the club, Tim Sheens asked Chris O'Sullivan if he'd consider playing one last time as the team's five-eighth stocks were bare due to injury. Sully, having chalked up his two-hundredth game for the club in round four against Illawarra after returning from his second stint in England, suffered serious medial ligament damage in June, the injury casting a shadow over his testimonial year. He was out for months. And what was his response to the coach's request to pull on the green jersey one last time: 'Yes', naturally.

It was a grand 80 minutes against the Coast, King Wally Lewis' last game south of the border and a worthy last contest: O'Sullivan versus Lewis. Again, the Raiders shone all around the paddock, scoring a number of tries. There might have been one more in the last couple of minutes when Sully received the ball in centre field about twenty metres out. With the cries of teammates ringing in his ears Sully paused, eyed the black dot, and calmly slotted the single point. It was a moment full of nostalgia, one which must have triggered so many cherished memories for the local-boy-made-very-good.

There were some positives to take out of 1992, and they did not take very long to have an impact. The torrent of traded players and a disastrous injury list created opportunity in the top grade for a number of talented individuals coming through. After surgery, David Boyle and Brett Hetherington quickly confirmed their superior credentials; New Zealand-born winger Sean Hoppe, the club's Rookie of the Year, was an instant hit with Raider fans for a robust running style that recalled the exploits of Terry Fahey; Ken Nagas, the Indigenous lad who had grown up in the New South Wales town of Kyogle, was a superstar, one out of the box; another rugged Queensland forward, Darren Fritz, impressed the coaching staff with his aggressive work ethic; the St Edmunds College nursery of footballers kept ticking over, producing Dave Furner, Don's son, and Michael Maguire; and two regional recruits drawn from the development program, Jason Croker and Brett Mullins, impressed enormously as potential stars of the future. The Raiders also managed to pick up prop Paul Osborne on the rebound from St George. Never lost for a word, 'Ossie' would write his own chapter in the Raider's history. But not yet.

The long-term importance of one last piece of good news that appeared in the later part of Mal Meninga's 'toughest' year cannot be overstated. It was reported in September 1992 that the club was 'emerging from the red at last'. The Raiders Group that financed the football team—the Queanbeyan Leagues Club, the Mawson Club and the Canberra District Rugby League—had compressed the $6.5 million debt (at its peak in July 1991) into $4.5 million. Bank debt had been reduced by nearly $3 million and the debt incurred by the Mawson Club, at a peak of $1.3 million in the previous year, had been pegged back to about $450,000 in 1992. As Kevin Hepworth summarised it in his *Canberra Times* article aptly entitled 'Rebuilding the Green Machine', 'the club's recovery from a suffocating debt level has been little less than Lazarus-like'.

The Raiders were staying put. The club's worst crisis since 1986 had been seen off with skill, enthusiasm and large doses of loyalty. The players, coach and fans looked forward to 1993 with a sense of renewed optimism. The Raiders were set to rise again.

1993

At the end of the 1992 season the club farewelled another of its favourite sons, Gary Coyne. Every high-achieving club must have its visible stars, yet equally important are the workers harder to spot on the field. Coyne, who played 158 games for the Green Machine over seven seasons including four of the five grand finals, was just such a player. He always made a contribution that counted, whether at club, state or international level. All his teammates said that they liked to have Coyney standing next to them in the defensive line. He never ducked an assignment. He was going to be missed.

Perhaps it was the prospect of life without Coyne (and Todd and Lazarus after the forced player migration) that motivated Tim Sheens to venture down less-travelled footballing roads. New Zealand's All Blacks had been successfully raiding the islands of the Pacific for talent for many decades. Tim decided to do the same. He and reserves' coach Dean Lance—and their wives—visited New Zealand to run their eyes over the local competitions. CEO Kevin Neil was not too happy about the expenses involved but the rewards followed when the club enticed three players to try their luck in Rugby League's best competition in the world. John Lomax, Quentin Pongia and Ruben Wiki re-settled in Canberra in a coup that Tony Adams, in his *Masters of the Game: Coaches who shaped Rugby League* (1996), described as a 'scouting master-stroke'.

Excited by the signings, the Raider coaches attended the Coca-Cola World Sevens tournament at the Sydney Football Stadium in early February. A big, strong, fast Fijian winger named Noa Nadruku had everyone talking with four brilliant tries in the Plate final. The Raiders wasted no time in signing him up. Noa's sensational first season, followed by four more years of the same, had the competition's other coaches attempting to emulate the Raiders' audacious recruiting foray.

With the start of the '93 season getting closer, and the Raiders regarded by the Sydney media as yesterday's news, the dimensions of the club's fresh recruiting went relatively unnoticed. Under the radar. Furner, Croker, Boyle, Mullins and Nagas were fit and ready to exhibit the range of their talents; Noa was ready to score tries and plenty of them (a club record 22 by first season's end); Lomax, Pongia and the young Ruben Wiki, once they became accustomed to the speed of the Australian game, developed into the enforcers the Raiders needed across the paddock; two 17-year-olds had been added to the roster through the efforts of Laurie Daley and Kevin Neil, the PNG-born Cairns High School student, David Westley, one more big body, and Simon Woolford, halfback (and hooker), like Brett Mullins a Cherry Picker from the NSW country town of Young. Two Belconnen locals, Mark Corvo and Luke Davico, were also identified, along with Jason Burnham, Bruce Mamando, Jamie Kennedy and Steve Trindall.

Evidence of a revitalised Raiders team in 1993, well ahead of schedule, was flagged when the side won the pre-season Toohey's Challenge Cup against a useful Western Suburbs in Dubbo. It was the first silverware for the cupboard since the 1990 grand final. Looking back, the game had its good news and, as it turned out, its grimly prophetic forecast as well. The good was easy to identify. Any cup win at this re-grouping stage was a boost to the confidence. Newcomer Quentin Pongia lugged the ball up all day against a willing Wests' pack. On the other hand, the Magpies came back from an 18–2 deficit to make a real game of it, losing 21–18. As *Big League* magazine reported, Wests 'pulled back ground when Canberra lost playmaker Ricky Stuart with a groin injury and the halfback's problems take on tremendous proportions to the club'.

It was a casual observation which ultimately summarised not only the Raiders' season to come but the outcome of Rugby League's year. Ricky Stuart owned the 1993 season, his personal fortunes directly affecting the premiership itself. Exaggerated claims? Let's see.

The Raiders began the year finding their feet as a new unit with fresh faces, three games won and three lost. Two of the losses came against Saints (at home) and Parramatta (away), though it was the round four game against the previous year's premiers played in Brisbane that caught the eye of most league commentators. The Broncos won 12–10 at QE II Stadium. There was not much in it and the game put a spotlight on the untapped ability of the 'new look' Raiders. A handful of debutantes had appeared in the lime-green jersey in the early rounds of the competition. They were beginning to gel. When the *Raider* newspaper considered the prospects of all teams in the pre-season, it provided an accurate assessment of the home team:

> You wouldn't know it from last year's statistics, but this is probably the only side with a serious claim to what the Broncos already consider to be theirs—the Winfield Cup and J.J. Giltinan Shield. Stacked with individual talent and—in contrast to much of last year—with the lower-grade players to fill the gaps whenever they are called on . . . Will be there at finals time.

The fifteen games from round seven to round 21 delivered on the paper's prediction, the Raiders notching up thirteen wins, one loss and one draw.

In this sequence, the round nineteen game against the Broncos, their second meeting of the season, needs special mention. What a game it was, a mouth-watering fixture full of classic match-ups right across the park between a number of the code's most brilliant players, almost all of them internationals or future internationals. This time the Raiders proved far too good, winning 20–4. Laurie Daley was outstanding in attack and defence, Meninga strong throughout and the Raider forwards outgunned their opposing six courtesy of what Steve Roach called Steve Walters' 'genius' around the rucks and front-rowers John Lomax and Paul Osborne never taking a backward step. Artie Beetson was so impressed by the pace and power on show that he thought a forthcoming Raiders–Broncos grand final might require Johnny Tapp, the country's best-known caller of horse racing!

Gus Gould predictably reverted to type when covering the match. Hard-wired to forever undervalue the Raiders' expansive style of football, he felt that Brisbane was better 'for much of the game'. And seemingly oblivious to contradiction, Gus followed up in typical fashion:

> In the difficult conditions, Ricky Stuart and Laurie Daley dominated with their kicking which virtually gave Brisbane no chance . . . Stuart is a great front-runner. It is hard to come from behind and win against the Raiders. Stuart gives you little or no opportunity at their end of the field with his kicking and control.

In round twenty the Raiders visited Cronulla, coached by Artie Beetson, at the Shire's Caltex Field. The re-constituted Raiders' attack had toyed with the Sharks team in round five on the way to a 46–6 thrashing at Bruce. Back in their park, the Sharks were expected to rebound but the Green Machine had other ideas. They went just as well as they had in April, winning 42–12. Not for the first time when his team had been dusted by the marauding Raiders, Artie Beetson felt 'shell-shocked. That's what I am, shell-shocked.'

Going into the season's second-last round, with the Raiders set to face the Parramatta Eels at Bruce, it is fair to say that the majority of league pundits had conceded that the Winfield Cup was once again heading to the nation's capital. Most accepted that the three best teams during the year were the Raiders, Brisbane and St George. The Raiders had recently beaten Brisbane with authority, and in round sixteen they went to Adelaide to play St George (the NSWRL always keen to get Raider football on the road around Australia to promote the code). The Saints were held tryless in an ultra-professional Raiders outing, the final score reading 30–2.

Round 21 in 1993, the Raiders versus Parramatta at Bruce, is firmly stamped in the memory of all Raider fans as one of the most famous—or infamous—in the club's history. It was a day when everything, *everything*, clicked in a 68–0 demolition of a totally demoralised Eels team. The Raiders scored a dozen tries, with Meninga, Daley, Croker and Hoppe each bagging a brace while Noa produced a 70-metre solo try that had the fans in raptures, chanting his name in unison—as they had done over the years with Chicka.

In the *Canberra Times* report the following day Tim Sheens was quoted: 'We've won the game well and there is not a smile in the shed.' Not a smile in the shed? Why? What could possibly explain the sea of solemn faces after such a stirring exhibition of Raider football? One minute into the second half, Ricky Stuart—until then conducting the Raiders' orchestra as if he was a maestro at the Sydney Opera House—went in to make a routine tackle. Somehow his ankle got twisted awkwardly underneath bodies and the result was a fractured fibula and badly dislocated ankle. He would be on crutches for the next couple of months.

The coach tried to be upbeat when stating that, despite the setback, he felt the team would be 'even more grimly determined' to cover for the loss of Stuart. Ricky himself was sure that 'the boys will win it without me'. However, these standard 'on-message' sentiments were said more in hope than belief. It was Laurie Daley who produced a reality check. Stuart, he said, was 'irreplaceable'.

Daley was right. The team played three more matches: a loss to the Canterbury Bulldogs in the last competition game, 32–8; a loss to St George in the major preliminary semifinal, 31–10; and a loss to Brisbane in the minor semifinal, 30–12. Only weeks earlier, with Stuart running things, both of the 1993 grand finalists, the Broncos and the Saints, were easily accounted for.

This was the premiership that got away.

Despite not playing in the last games of the season, Ricky Stuart won the Rothmans Medal, the Dally M Player of the Year and the NSW Press Writers' Player of the Year award. He received his haul of prizes in Sydney on crutches. He was, of course, the Raiders' Player of the Year.

In his biography, Mal Meninga was disarmingly honest about the effect of Stuart's injury on the team which, he said, 'totally wrecked our year':

> From the first minute of our first game without Ricky, we played like premiership longshots, and disappeared out of the competition ... After Ricky's injury, we rapidly developed a phobia about his absence ... we panicked about what was going to go wrong because he wasn't there. As captain, I should have arrested this negative attitude, but before we realised what was going on, we were out of the competition.

Elite teams and their captains learn from setbacks, from experience. The Raiders spent the last few weeks before Christmas doing their homework for the coming year.

Mal Meninga and the last crusade, 1994

During the last months of the 1993 season the head of the Canberra Region Campaign, David Marshall, began a fresh promotional push to encourage tourist numbers by locating 'the true spirit of Canberra'. Who did he choose to launch the campaign? Why, Brad Clyde and Steve Walters of course. 'The Raiders have given Canberra a human face,' Marshall declared, 'and are recognised and respected everywhere.' When John Stanwell, head of Arts and Special Events within the ACT

Government, was asked to name Canberra's 'significant local cultural symbols to date', he felt there were only two: the Raiders and Floriade in that order.

Stanwell's comments were made in June 1994. The Raiders *were* far more than a football team, and this standing within the community only increased as the 1994 year developed. It was a time to remember, Raider captain Mal Meninga's last majestic crusade.

The omens were good from the start when, on 26 January 1994, Australia Day, Meninga was made a Member of the Order of Australia. Shortly afterwards, he announced that 1994 would be his final year. Goals were set.

In the last few weeks before the start of the footy season there was the usual player movement across the competition. Youngsters coming through the fine-tuned junior Raider ranks to stake their claim for inclusion in first grade included Jason Burnham, Simon Woolford, Luke Davico, Graham Appo, Salesi Finau, Bruce Mamando and David Lomax. The Pacific Islands connection was still providing players as the club's reputation spread for its sensitive and sensible handling of cultural difference. Tim Sheens, getting more adventurous and innovative by the year, ruled out no region of the potential player market as beyond the club's domain. During the year an American, Kelton Alexander, was included in Canberra's squad along with Sierra Leone sprinter, Horace Dove-Edwin. Alexander trained with plenty of enthusiasm but ultimately failed to be offered a contract; Dove-Edwin, promoted as the Raiders' answer to England's Martin 'Chariots' Offiah, looked the more likely of the two, though he was let go as well after a positive drug test resulted in his Commonwealth Games 100-metres silver medal being stripped from him.

Within the camp there was sadness over several key departures. Darren Fritz, after five years and 53 energetic games with the club, was off to play for Illawarra; Sean Hoppe went to North Sydney for a year, let go when it was revealed that he had signed a contract with the Auckland Warriors for 1995; Matthew Wood, who had been such a reliable big-match player for the Raiders since 1989 in two premiership wins and over 70 games, was off to Wests with the blessing of the club (the 24-year-old's reserve-grade coach, Dean Lance, stating the obvious that Matt was 'basically a first-grader playing reserve grade'); and most significant of all, the retirement of Gary Belcher.

'Badge' did not rush into the decision. Injury and CEO Kevin Neil's hard line on salary-cap restrictions really made the decision for him. He was deeply disappointed, feeling there was still some fire in the belly and a few more miles in the legs, but these considerations were outweighed by his desire to leave the game on his own terms, with grace, style and good humour. Knee trouble had slowed him down for quite a while. It was the right call for someone who had been the 'Players' Player' in his first year with the Raiders in 1986, the club's Player of the Year and leading point-scorer in 1987 and in 1988, and top try-scorer in 1989, the year of many miracles. Once picked for Australia, he played fifteen Tests in a row. Badge was a crucial cog in the Raiders' era of dominance.

The first half of the 1994 playing year for the Raiders, the first eleven rounds, were good without being outstanding. Twenty-year-old New Zealander Ruben Wiki was a stand-out. His four tries in a round three game against Newcastle at Bruce in a 34–8 win impressed coaches and fans alike. To go with his good speed and silky ball skills was a tackling technique that gained instant respect across the competition. None of his teammates liked being matched with Ruben in contact drills. For opposition players throughout Wiki's distinguished twelve-year career with the Raiders, he was an opponent they mentally asterisked. Whenever possible, avoid his section of the field.

Two patterns re-emerged as the season progressed. One was the struggle the Raiders had during the 'representative' period of games. Players lost to the City–County match in early May contributed to a tight 8–4 loss to the Gold Coast at Seagulls Stadium and, a few weeks later, the three matches affected by State of Origin football produced two Raider losses, both away, to Penrith and Norths. The other issue was that of the five losses the Raiders suffered in the 22 rounds, every one of them was an away game. The home-field form at Bruce was impeccable, the team unbeaten. Away form, something else again. If the Raiders were going to perform in Sydney at semifinal time (and remember they were a miserable 0–2 in 1993), then their form away from Bruce Stadium had to radically improve.

In rounds 15–19, five games with three of them away, it did. Classic, clinical Raider football resulted in 226 points scored, with only 42 against. The Tigers game at Leichhardt, normally a tough assignment, resulted in a 36–0 scoreline in favour of the in-form visitors. The following week at Bruce the Cronulla side leaked ten tries when conceding nearly 60 points as Mullins, Wiki, Clyde and Stuart ran riot. Jason Croker staked a strong claim for selection on the forthcoming Kangaroo tour. Sharks' coach Johnny Lang summed up the game he had just suffered through: 'Every time they got the ball, they tore us to pieces.'

During this scoring blitz, Raiders' star fullback Brett Mullins scored eleven tries in three games. He was 'untouchable at times'. Compliments about his exquisite talents came from all quarters of the league world, not only from Raiders' fans who could not believe their good fortune in having Mullins as the successor to one of their all-time favourites, Gary Belcher. Legends of the game heaped praise on the incumbent Raider custodian including Balmain's Keith Barnes, who was happy to compare the young Raider to another legend, St George's Graeme Langlands.

So what did 'Mullo' do in the middle of this rich vein of form when being compared to past greats? He signed a new five-year contract with the Raiders sacrificing, according to the *Daily Telegraph Mirror*, a staggering $500,000 in the process. Three cashed-up Sydney clubs were determined to get him but as his father Bill, the outstanding Easts winger of yesteryear put it, the Raiders had 'done right by him so he wanted to stick by them'. Bill knew there was some real substance to his boy's decision: 'A lot of players, not just Brett, have shown loyalty to Canberra. There seems to be a deep feeling within the club. It's like a family . . . The club has nurtured him along. It's nice to see when the crunch comes, he remembers that. It is total loyalty.'

No statement about the culture the Raiders had developed in the club's first decade so eloquently grasps the qualities of character and behaviour that buttressed an era of Raider premierships.

Less than three weeks after the Mullins re-signing, the Western Suburbs team headed down to Canberra for round 21, the second-last competition round. It was no ordinary game. Rather, the final game at Bruce Stadium of Mal Meninga, the Baron of Bruce. The entire region made sure that it would never be forgotten in later years when all the major milestones in the captain's final crusade year were compiled. In all, 25,253 people attended the game, a ground record. The Headon family were there, one of many thousands of others, and nothing during the day disappointed. Well, perhaps the half-time score. The Magpies were in front but that was quickly rectified in the second 40 minutes when the Raiders ran away with the game to win 40–22. Rack up another milestone. This victory was the Raiders' twenty-first in a row at Bruce, aka 'Fortress Canberra'.

Meninga masks were distributed (Headon family members still have theirs). Kids were allowed to sit on the field behind the dead-ball lines, everyone was allowed onto the playing surface at game's end and, perhaps most memorable of all, the announcement was made post-game that the western stand would henceforth be known as the 'Mal Meninga Stand'. The crowd greeted this fitting finale with a roar of approval.

The season's last competition game was yet to be played (a tricky away game against Manly at Brookvale) with the semis to follow, but the Canberra community refused to be contained. They were prepared to be a distraction for the greater good of lionising a champion who was now one of their own. At the formal dinner held in Meninga's honour at the National Convention Centre in the week before the Wests game, political commentator and lobbyist Ken Begg spoke for everyone when he said, 'You have bonded us . . . You have captured the hearts and minds of all people.' Co-master of ceremonies on the gala night, political commentator Paul Lyneham, announced that he'd much rather be paying tribute to Mal Meninga than interviewing Bob Hawke about his recent book. Meanwhile, Pavarotti's version of 'Nessun Dorma' played on in the background. It was a night to remember.

Not content with these displays of public affection, song-writer David Burmingham, having already written a tribute song to Australian Rules' great, Gary Ablett, in the mode of 'Our Don Bradman', penned a new song, 'Mal Meninga—You're the Greatest Player in the Land'. In one section he trumpets:

> They call you The Big Fella and it's easy to see why
> When it comes to League, you're our favourite guy
> Mal Meninga (You're the one that we adore)
> Mal Meninga (You're the one we are cheering for)
> Mal Meninga (You're our hero, you're our man)
> You're the greatest player in the land!

While not the most creative lyrics you'll ever hear, they do represent the heightened emotion of a particular time and place, about a special individual. When Mal was asked to comment on all the fuss by indicating how he'd like to be remembered, he said, 'As a good player, and a good fella.'

The legend grew.

But back to the football. There were games to be won, a third premiership pursued.

Semifinal football, so deflating the previous year, awaited. There are a few interesting similarities between the last games of the triumphant 1989 season and those in 1994. The main parallel, a concern in the Raiders' first premiership year and also five years later, was the team's less than convincing form in the preliminary semis. The 'feeding frenzy' of points scored by the Raiders during the season was not fully on show in the post–regular season's first three matches, against Norths, Canterbury and Norths a second time.

In the first of them, against the Bears, the Raiders won handily 26–12 though no-one in the camp got carried away, especially with the minor premier Bulldogs looming as the next opponent. Neither of the teams was a clear favourite and the intensity of the Major Semifinal action showed why. The scores were locked together, 18–18, at the end of 80 minutes. It came down to the Russian roulette of field goals. The Raiders missed three, two of them hitting the post, and then in the second-last minute of extra-time Daryl Halligan knocked one over from close range for the Bulldogs. Their gruff patriarch, Peter 'Bulldog' Moore, told old Don Furner in the tunnel after the game that he was sure the teams would meet again in a fortnight.

The preliminary final pitted the Raiders once more against the North Sydney Bears. This was another game long remembered, not for the quality of the football (which was of a solid standard) so much as the quality of Greg McCallum's refereeing. Twenty-three minutes into the first half he sent Raiders' front-rower John Lomax from the field for a marginal head-high tackle of the kind that fans saw hundreds of times go unpunished and be forgotten. Lomax was shattered, but four minutes later referee McCallum sent Bears' second-rower Gary Larson off for a spear tackle on Dave Furner. As photographs indicated, it was a spear tackle. It was also a square-up. The teams were now 12 on 12 for the rest of a game that the Raiders handled sensibly to chalk up what the *Canberra Times* called 'a gritty triumph'.

They were into their fifth grand final in eight years. The club tried hard to get Lomax cleared to play but failed. The tackle was reaffirmed as 'misdirected and mistimed'. The one-game suspension would stand.

With its magical links to the Steve Jackson '89 miracle, Tim Sheens sent out an SOS to Paul 'Ossie' Osborne who, after three enjoyable years with the Raiders, in the twilight of his career had already bought tickets for him and his family to head to England, where he intended to finish his playing days with Featherstone Rovers. In the blink of an eye, Ossie was in the Raiders' front row for his first-ever grand final, with the number 46 on his back.

Some things never change. In grand final week discussion among a cross-section of Sydney's league fraternity produced the majority opinion that the Bulldogs would win. It is unlikely that Tim Sheens, now a seasoned veteran of grand final hype, took any notice of the pundits. Yet deep down he must have been hoping that Phil Gould would deliver for him once again. As if on cue he did, not once in the *Daily Telegraph Mirror* the day before the grand final, but twice. In one article, 'Why the Raiders Are Gone', Gould was in vintage form: 'I don't think they can win with Lomax out. Canberra already look tired and jaded. I have felt that Canberra has struggled to go forward all through the final series . . . I don't think Canberra can match Canterbury's forward power.' In his other piece, 'Fresh Dogs may have the Edge', Gould 'weighed up the stats, worked out the cat-and-mouse games, looked into his crystal ball' and concluded—again—that the Green Machine was soft in the middle. The man who the *Tele* informed us 'knows what it takes to win Grand Finals' fearlessly tipped the Bulldogs by eight points. Groundhog day.

The Raiders' build-up was measured, orderly, focused. Mal had made it clear in his entry for the 1994 NSWRL Yearbook that he hoped for a couple more 'fabulous memories' to reflect on in retirement, ideally another premiership for his Raiders team and a fourth Kangaroo tour, preferably as captain. The Raiders were thus united in a common cause, a brotherhood. This one *was* for Mal, and Laurie Daley was convinced that in the build-up an often misused motivation was handled in 'the right spirit'. Some of the players were asked to provide a pre-match tribute to their captain and all of them reverted to much the same notion: how much 'George' had taught them. Meninga's personal goal never altered. It was 'to lead by example'.

Running an eye over the statistical output of the two 1994 Winfield Cup combatants, a keen student of Rugby League's facts and figures might have been a little surprised. The Green Machine had left the NSWRL's point-scoring record in its wake before the grand final, outscoring the Canterbury team, for example, by almost 200 points and more than 50 tries. Canterbury's prospects, according to the experts, were based on their consistency and defence, yet the Raiders had conceded fewer tries as well.

But in the last analysis, stats don't win you games. Attitude is everything, and here the Raiders approached their date with destiny on 25 September with a singularity of purpose. It was evident to every person in the green dressing room before running out. The captain later said that, really, there was no need for much talk. Dave Furner noted the room's 'sense and calm' and so did the Kiwi Quentin Pongia. 'Q' admitted to being taken by surprise. The bigger games he had experienced across the ditch in the past were conspicuous for their pre-match intensity. Not here. The players knew their jobs. It was a case of going out there and clocking on.

Tim Sheens, 'the Professor', was his usual composed self. This was something the older players were used to. He had done everything possible in what he felt was the side's 'best-ever' preparation. Sure, there were niggling injuries though nothing to worry about. And the last-minute setback with the loss of hard man John Lomax represented a challenge, but this only brought out the best in the bearded philosopher coach. Ossie Osborne was brought into the fold with a first instruction to go as hard as he could for as long as he could. His second instruction, a masterstroke—another in a long line of Tim's inspired manoeuvres—was to get Ossie to exploit the short side early and often. This was playing to Ossie's strength and, potentially, a Bulldog weakness. With any luck, hefty Canterbury prop Martin Bella would be exposed. Ossie knew he himself was slow, but not as slow as Marty.

There was one other ploy mentioned by Laurie Daley, 'to test out their inexperienced players by putting pressure on them right from the kick-off. The plan worked to perfection.' It certainly did, and quite literally from the kick-off. Let former ABC football broadcaster and star of Australian film and TV Lex Marinos explain the unforgettable start to the 1994 grand final:

> Now the kick-off in rugby league is a pretty straightforward, simple ritual. One team kicks the ball deep into opposition territory; the in-goal area

> is ideal. The other team has a catcher ready to receive the ball and hand it on to one of his big beefy teammates who hurtles back into the stampeding opposition who are preparing to belt him, and the game is under way. And so it should have been on this occasion. Canberra kicked off. Marty [Bella] had taken up his position in his own in-goal area ready to receive the ball from his catcher and start his work for the day—that is, prepare to be belted. The only problem is, the Canterbury catchers are out of position, and the ball bounces in front of Marty. Now he has twelve teammates, none of whom are better equipped to run the ball back and get belted than Marty, but all of whom are better equipped than Marty to catch or pick up a rolling ball.
>
> In the way that a traffic accident seems to happen in slow motion, the panic set in. The ball is bouncing and rolling drunkenly and inexorably towards Marty. He has to make the rapid mental adjustment from being prepared to run into a brick wall, to having to bend down and control the ball. Inevitably he fumbles it. Canberra gets the ball. Soon they scored a try, and then some more tries.

This was a terrible moment for Marty and Canterbury, a turning point seconds into the game. They never recovered. The extravagant expression of Raider football went unconstrained for the full 80 minutes. Warren Ryan was heard to remark after the game that the Dogs were right in it 'until the kick-off'.

The match, like 1989, had its many moments to savour. The main difference in 1994 was the sense of inevitability about the result. Laurie Daley later said that the Green Machine on this sunny September afternoon in Sydney in front of a crowd of 42,234 fans was 'unstoppable'. What were the keys?

Within 15 minutes of the start, Ossie Osborne explored the short right side, dummied, and then fed Dave Furner to score with a brilliant ball that Artie Beetson would have been proud of. Shortly after, on the left side and just as good, he attracted Bulldog winger Daryl Halligan, only to pop a pass to Kyogle speedster Kenny Nagas, who glided

70 metres to score. Canterbury's Scott Wilson was left grasping thin air as Nagas slid past him, barely acknowledging the fullback's presence. Ossie had given his team what Laurie Daley later called 'twenty minutes of gold'. Solid gold.

The opening quarter of an hour featured another big moment in the game when Terry Lamb was tackled by Meninga just as he received a 'hospital' pass. He was monstered, in Disneyland when he should probably have been shipped off to St Vincent's, and for the rest of the game he was not his usual feisty self running the show. This mattered.

Noa Nadruku, who had not had the best semifinal series, was back to his best when it counted with several long, powerful runs and a fine try when he steamrolled the Dogs' replacement fullback Matthew Ryan. Add to this the fact that every Raider player, including reserves David Westley and Brett Hetherington, had season-best games. A superb exhibition of open, exciting Rugby League had its fitting climax when, with seventeen minutes to go, the Dogs were forced to gamble and throw a long pass out wide. Who sensed opportunity? Who else? Mal Meninga ran onto the intercept as if it had been intended for him. He casually 'don't argued' Jarrod McCracken and ran 35 metres to score. The team erupted as one, knowing they had the result for the skipper all had vowed to achieve. Steve Crawley in *The Australian* said the big Raider and Australian centre accepted the intercept 'with all the dignity of a large Santa Gertrudis bull'. Laurie Daley ran nearly half the length of the field to embrace him. Nine-year-old Terry Campese, watching on television in Queanbeyan, knew then that he wanted to pull on the lime-green jersey like captain Meninga when he got older.

Second-rower Dave Furner had in the past occasionally been the subject of whispers that he had only got to where he was because of his father Don, and he could not resist a virtuoso response to this utter nonsense in the grand final. He had his usual workaholic-plus game in defence, ran strongly throughout, kicked goals and in the second half made a brilliant break in the middle of the ruck about 30 metres from the Dogs' line (courtesy of a left-foot step that always left defenders nonplussed), looked in, only to find the ever-present Jason Croker backing up and he raced away to score. Awarded the Clive Churchill Medal for his day's work, Furner was surely on the plane to England for the Kangaroo tour. It was a case of how many Raider stars would join him.

The final score of 36–12 flattered the losers. One of Canterbury's two tries was an intercept by Jason Williams gratefully accepted fifteen metres out from his own line and the second resulted from a Darren Britt shepherd that allowed Jason Hetherington to score a try everyone in the stadium knew was illegal, except referee McCallum.

The 36 points scored by the Green Machine, the highest number in a grand final since Graeme 'Changa' Langlands' white-shoe 38–0 debacle against Easts almost twenty years before, was an adequate representation of the Raiders on the day and a public statement about a year in which the team re-wrote the NSWRL record books. With the grand final concluded, the Raiders had scored 779 points in 26 matches, bettering the previous record jointly held by Parramatta and Manly in 1983 by 64 points, even though the Eels and Sea Eagles had played two more games. The seven tries the Raiders scored in the grand final meant they beat the famed 1935 Eastern Suburbs side's 1935 try-scoring record by six. It was a phenomenal scoring performance in the season's last game, a fitting conclusion to a year when seemingly unbreakable records were broken. Smashed.

There were a number of stories behind the scenes, none better than the one surrounding the props, John Lomax and Ossie Osborne. Lomax, the Raiders' deserving Player of the Year, missed only two games in the entire season. Laurie Daley guaranteed his unlucky teammate that, whatever happened, the Kiwi was getting Loz's grand final medal. The offer wasn't required. When the full-time hooter sounded, Lomax raced onto the field to congratulate his teammates, saying afterwards that 'wild horses would not have held me back'. Later, and proudly sporting his number ten jersey, Lomax strode onto the stage at the urging of

Daley and others to receive the medal he had genuinely earned with a year's worth of blood, sweat and toil.

Ossie, as exhausted as he was ecstatic, struggled to comprehend what had just happened in the last two hours and in the last two days. He had not played football for a month and hadn't been in first grade for eight weeks. Despite maintaining that he had played his best football under Tim Sheens at Canberra, the fact is that he joined the Raiders in 1992, the year of re-development when the team finished twelfth—the same year his previous team St George made the grand final (and lost). Saints coach Brian Smith did not let Ossie forget it. How did he respond to his former coach? 'I just told him that one day I'd send him a photo of myself holding the Winfield Cup.' Ossie, the 'King of Tuggeranong', had plenty of pictures to choose from on a day when he firmly believed he was the beneficiary of divine intervention: 'Anyone who doesn't believe in miracles should look at me today. I am one. God has worked a miracle.' Amen.

A number of publications over the years have talked about the 1994 year as a 'fairytale finish' to Mal Meninga's remarkable career. Mal was having none of it: 'Fairytales are about winning in the dying seconds. When you win comfortably without pressure, that's not what fairytales are all about . . . Out of all the Grand Finals I played in, 1994 was the most comprehensive. Each member of the team played to their potential that day, and that's why we won so well.' His even more revealing observation about his last-ever Winfield Cup match was contained in the Raider club's 1994 annual report, *The Champions: The Ultimate Dream*:

> The feeling was so good I thought we might just blow them away. And the satisfying thing about the result was that we won playing football the way we believe it should be played.

Raider football received official endorsement when seven members of the side—the 'Magnificent Seven'—were chosen for the forthcoming

The 1987 Canberra Raiders, the first Raiders squad to make a grand final at first-grade level. They were defeated by the Manly Sea Eagles 18–8 at the SCG. *(NRL Imagery)*

The 1989 Canberra Raiders celebrate with the J.J. Giltinan Shield after defeating the Balmain Tigers 19–14 in the 1989 NSWRL Grand Final, widely recognised as the greatest grand final ever. *(NRL Imagery)*

The Raiders celebrate their back-to-back premierships after the 1990 Grand Final. They defeated the Penrith Panthers 18–14 at the Sydney Football Stadium. *(NRL Imagery)*

The club's third premiership win in 1994 was a dominant 36–12 victory over the Canterbury–Bankstown Bulldogs at the Sydney Football Stadium. *(NRL Imagery)*

Mal Meninga (Raider #76) celebrating a try in his final appearance as a Raider in the 1994 Grand Final win. This iconic image was the basis for his statue at Canberra Stadium and the Meninga Medal—awarded to the Raiders Player of the Year. *(Canberra Raiders)*

Steve Walters (Raider #78), a three-time premiership winner with the Raiders, revolutionised the hooker position. He is a member of both the Raiders and NRL Halls of Fame. *(NRL Imagery)*

Laurie Daley (Raider #88) won three premierships with the club and also captained the team from 1998–2000. He is a member of both the Raiders and NRL Halls of Fame. *(NRL Imagery)*

Glenn Lazarus (Raider #90) is a two-time premiership winner for the Raiders and a member of both the Raiders and NRL Halls of Fame. *(NRL Imagery)*

Ricky Stuart (Raider #98) is a three-time premiership winner and a Clive Churchill Medal winner (1990). He is a member of both the Raiders and NRL Halls of Fame. He captained the club from 1995 to 1997. *(NRL Imagery)*

Bradley Clyde (Raider #97) is a three-time premiership winner and two-time Clive Churchill Medallist (1989 and 1991). He is also a member of both the Raiders and NRL Halls of Fame. *(NRL Imagery)*

Three-time premiership winning Raiders coach Tim Sheens brought innovation and meticulous preparation to the head coaching role. He's pictured here at Seiffert Oval with a number of his elite players. *(Canberra Times)*

Tim Sheens on the sideline during a game in 1990. Sheens is a member of the Canberra Raiders Hall of Fame. *(Canberra Times)*

One of the club's key signings before the 1986 season, Gary Belcher (Raider #73) is a two-time premiership winning player and a member of the Raiders Hall of Fame. *(Canberra Raiders)*

A New Zealand international, Brent Todd (Raider #85) is a two-time premiership winning player and a member of the Raiders Hall of Fame. *(NRL Imagery)*

Dean Lance (Raider #51), seen here demolishing Souths' Ian Roberts, is a two-time premiership winning player and a member of the Raiders Hall of Fame. Lance captained the club between 1985 and 1989. *(Canberra Raiders)*

John 'Chicka' Ferguson (Raider #75) is a two-time premiership winning player and member of the Canberra Raiders Hall of Fame. *(NRL Imagery)*

Dean Lance, carried around the Sydney Football Stadium by Ashley Gilbert and Craig Bellamy after the historic 1989 Grand Final win over the Balmain Tigers. *(NRL Imagery)*

Above: Chris O'Sullivan and Gary Coyne (Raider #74) celebrating with the Winfield Cup after the club's 1990 Grand Final win against the Penrith Panthers. *(Canberra Times)*

Left: John Ferguson spending a special moment with his son Adam as he celebrates the 1989 premiership win over Balmain. *(NRL Imagery)*

Nicknamed 'the Brick with Eyes', Glenn Lazarus kicks back in the sheds after the 1990 Grand Final to contemplate the team's achievement of back-to-back premierships. *(NRL Imagery)*

Captain Mal Meninga and Clive Churchill Medal winner Bradley Clyde hoist the Winfield Cup in 1989 as Prime Minister and Raiders fan Bob Hawke looks on. *(NRL Imagery)*

Grand final warriors Dean Lance and Gary Coyne celebrate the 1989 premiership after the Raiders defeated Balmain in extra time. *(NRL Imagery)*

One of the driving forces in the Raiders' bid to enter the NSWRL competition was Labor politican Ros Kelly, pictured here with Mal Meninga after a match in 1990. *(Ros Kelly)*

Fan favourite Chicka Ferguson enjoying a Raiders lime milk in the changeroom with Prime Minister Bob Hawke. *(NRL Imagery)*

The representative class of 1993 in their playing kits: Sean Hoppe (NZ), Brett Mullins (NSW), Gary Belcher (QLD), Jason Croker (NSW), Quentin Pongia (NZ), Laurie Daley (Australia), Steve Walters (QLD), John Lomax (NZ), Mal Meninga (QLD), Bradley Clyde (Australia), Ricky Stuart (NSW). *(Canberra Raiders)*

1994 New Zealand representatives Ruben Wiki (Raider #153), John Lomax (Raider #148) and Quentin Pongia (#149). Hard men all. Tim Sheens targeted New Zealand for recruitment in the early 1990s. *(Canberra Raiders)*

The Raiders went scouting in Queensland in the mid-1980s to recruit big name talent. In 1987 the club boasted eight Queenslanders. Back Row (L–R): Sam Backo, Rowan Brennan, Peter Jackson, Gary Coyne, Mal Meninga. Front Row: Steve Walters, Kevin Walters and Gary Belcher. *(Canberra Raiders)*

The 1993 season was derailed when Ricky Stuart broke his leg in the side's round 21 win over the Parramatta Eels. The Raiders did not win another game that season. *(Canberra Times)*

Despite breaking his leg, Ricky Stuart went on to win the Dally M Player of the Year in 1993. Stuart also won the Rothmans Medal as Player of the Year. *(NRL Imagery)*

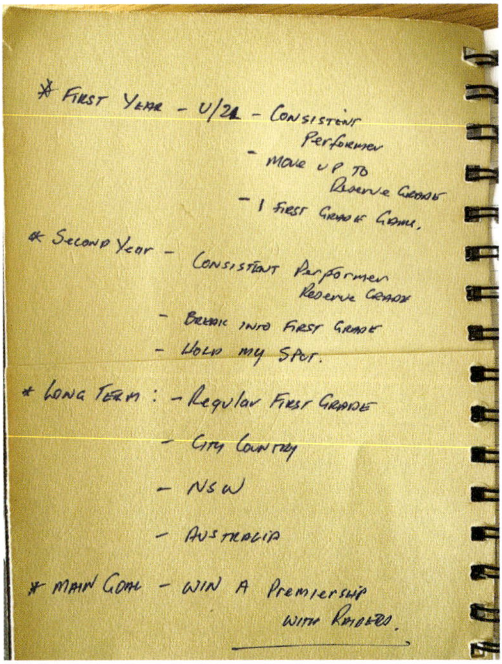

A page from David Furner's sport diary. He would go on to achieve everything he set out to, including his main goal of a Raiders premiership. *(Canberra Raiders)*

David Furner (Raider #135) announced as the Clubman of the Year in 1994. Presenting the award are club stalwarts Ros Kelly and Fred Daly. Furner also collected the Clive Churchill medal that season as best player in the Raiders' Grand Final win over the Bulldogs. *(Canberra Raiders)*

Fijian Flyer Noa Nadruku (Raider #151) makes another dazzling break down the sideline in the 1994 Grand Final. Nadruku scored 73 tries in 92 appearances for the Green Machine. *(Canberra Times)*

Ken Nagas (Raider #146) played 142 matches for the Raiders between 1992 and 2002. A gifted athlete, he possessed natural speed. Nagas won a premiership with the club in 1994, scoring two tries in the grand final. *(Canberra Raiders)*

Brett Mullins (Raider #118) scored some of the most memorable tries in club history and was an instrumental part of the club's 1994 premiership win. He scored 22 tries in 24 matches that season. *(Canberra Raiders)*

Ruben Wiki (Raider #153), a 1994 premiership winner, endeared himself to the Raider faithful as someone who gave his all every time he pulled on the green jumper. He went on to play 225 matches for the club. *(Canberra Times)*

Mal Meninga broke his arm four times during his career, but perservered and went on to win three premierships. He has been rightly judged a rugby league Immortal. *(Canberra Times)*

A wonderful moment for Mal Meninga as he bids farewell to a huge Bruce Stadium crowd for the final time as a player in 1994. The Western Grandstand was renamed the Mal Meninga Stand in his honour that memorable day. *(Canberra Times)*

Kangaroo tour: Meninga as captain, Ricky Stuart, Laurie Daley, Brad Clyde, Steve Walters, Dave Furner and Brett Mullins. They would all share in the spoils of what *A Centenary of Rugby League* depicts as Mal Meninga's 'Last Crusade' in England and France. The Australian selectors did make one error, leaving out brilliant utility Jason Croker, who had played superbly in the grand final, a standard he had maintained the whole year no matter what position his coach played him in. John Hogan in *The Australian* rightly observed that Croker was 'the unluckiest man to miss selection'. Fortunately the selectors of the national team would in time see the errors of their ways.

How good was the 1994 Green Machine? Brad Clyde is in no doubt they were the best team he ever played in. One thing is certain. It will take a powerful case to surpass the Raiders of 1994 in any 'best of' assessment for they were a champion team *and* a team of champions.

Surviving Super League, 1995–96

In the months of August and September 1994 the Canberra community enjoyed itself like it never had before. The farewell game for Mal Meninga at Bruce Stadium and then the command performance in the grand final produced such an emotional reaction that when the team had another civic reception in the middle of town to celebrate a third NSWRL competition win, 'Canberra's hysteria for its premier Raiders overflowed'. Flimsy barricades threatened to give way when the crowd attempted to get closer to their heroes. The portents for the future looked as bright as ever.

But if the years from 1987 to 1994 had contained the various episodes of a fairytale, the next few years were about to resemble a Shakespearean tragedy, Acts IV and V. For the Raiders club and Rugby League itself, a dramatic fall from grace was close—and no-one, not in Canberra or anywhere else, had an inkling about the depth of the fall. On the day that Canberra celebrated the final game at Bruce of the Raiders' greatest captain, word came through that the Raiders' first inspirational captain, David Grant, had died at the young age of 38. Was this the talisman of a looming change in fortune? A convulsion about to happen?

In November 1993, the Brisbane Broncos negotiated a deal with Rupert Murdoch's international media company News Limited (News Corp's Australian arm), making them Australia's first privately owned Rugby League club. The Broncos' point of difference, as *A Centenary of Rugby League* states, 'put them on a collision course with the code's hierarchy'. It impacted on the entire 1995 season and for a number of years afterwards.

There were some clues to the calamity about to happen during the Raiders' triumphant 1994 season. In the 2 March edition of *Rugby League Week*, for example, the magazine's Queensland editor wrote that a 'breakaway rugby league competition, similar to World Series Cricket ... has been mooted as relations between the NSW Rugby League and Broncos deteriorate'. A meeting apparently took place mid-year between ARL Chief Executive Ken Arthurson and Ken Cowley, the chief executive of News Ltd, concerning the code's future direction. Who would be in charge, and of what? The tense meeting ended in stalemate, though Arthurson must have walked away knowing that Cowley, through the Trojan horse of the Broncos, would not accept anything other than News Ltd having a voice in decisions around issues such as Rugby League's sponsorship, ground signage, the judiciary and competition logistics.

With the benefit of hindsight, Laurie Daley got it right in his book when he restricted himself to a summary statement: 'The arrival of Super League turned the game on its ear in 1995 ...' How significant was it for him? It is enough to say that twenty per cent of the book, *Laurie: Always a Winner* (2000), written with David Middleton, is devoted to 'The War'. How significant was it for the leading sport journalists of the era? With the story breaking, respected Fairfax journalist Greg Growden told his colleagues that 'this is the biggest story any of us will ever cover'. The only precedent was the great schism of 1908 when the breakaway rugby league code began.

The battlelines were drawn up by the rival parties in the first months of 1995, with the generals and chief strategists of the News Ltd–Broncos army better prepared for the opening engagements because they wanted to escalate hostilities as soon as possible. From 31 March to 5 April, News Ltd envoys signed up as many players as possible for their breakaway competition. About 100 players were contracted in a single, mad weekend. With shock and awe tactics, their leaders intended the war to be won before it had really started. The core Raider players by common consent all signed with Super League during a frantic few days.

The first Super–'Star' League concept consisted of twelve fully professional teams promoted and funded by News Ltd, which would retain a financial share in each team. Super League aimed to be an international competition promoted to a global audience. The ARL would administer the game, have oversight of the various competitions that fed into Super League and look after the Test program. News Ltd was in it to run the business of Rugby League.

The first mistake News Ltd made was that in the first week of April its representatives failed to pursue all the players initially targeted. The ARL had just enough time to counter-attack and, once backed by Kerry Packer (with his formidable background in the business of sport) and pay-television operator Optus Vision, they did. Leading coaches Bob Fulton and Phil Gould were assigned to negotiate immediately with the many players who had not yet signed with News Ltd. Within days, the ARL had secured a mass of agreements worth tens of millions of dollars. The football players were, as Ray Chesterton observed, 'swept up in a financial whirlpool'.

And which team was placed smack in the middle of the publicity because it had more of the code's best players than anyone else? Canberra's Raiders. The Green Machine, the team of the '90s. Their players were, like it or not, pushed to the centre stage of negotiations.

The faces of Ricky Stuart, Laurie Daley and Brad Clyde, in particular, were featured day after day in the newspapers. The accompanying stories, slanted in favour of one side or the other, depended on whether the newspaper or magazine was owned by Rupert Murdoch or Kerry Packer. However, with the dollar numbers being thrown around and the sort of photographs being used, the impact on a typical supporter of Rugby League—whether in Queanbeyan, Canberra or anywhere else—was much the same: disgust with the two media barons involved; disgust with the prominence given to their sons, young Lachlan and young James; disgust with the sudden, destructive impact on the game of Rugby League. And, lastly and unfairly, disgust with the players in the spotlight who were regularly being portrayed as selling out to the highest bidder and selling out the game.

Irrational opinions, prejudice and wilful propaganda aside, the only paper that got a headline exactly right—and that by accident—was Murdoch's *Telegraph*. The words on the front page of its 7 April edition were emblazoned in large type: 'The Day Football Changed Forever'. Raider supporters throughout the region, like everyone else, were vainly trying to make sense out of the bombardment of information. They knew much of it was fake news, but that only made it worse.

The major Rugby League radio stations in Sydney—2UE, 2GB and 2BL—had by the end of June collectively shed 110,000 listeners. They took years to come back. Some never did. As historian Andrew Moore observed at the time, many of league's devoted fans fell out of love with the game: 'People have decided that it's a pox on both their houses.' It was grimly appropriate that Moore should use an allusion to the Shakespeare play *Romeo and Juliet*, with its feuding families and tragic ending.

Raiders' coach Tim Sheens did his best to placate the club's loyal supporters, who were perplexed, depressed or just plain angry. Why did the Raiders decide in a block to align with Super League? Sheens was happy to name names: 'We were about to be pillaged by Phil Gould's Roosters, Stuart and Clyde were being offered huge money from them and were nearly ready to go. The salary cap was non-existent and there were dollars everywhere.' The Raiders had to sign with Super League to avoid a heavy loss of players, or possibly extinction, but that did not mean that either they or their band of supporters were necessarily thrilled with the decision. It came at a high cost in terms of the team's honoured place in the wider community.

Despite the daily, weekly, monthly distractions of the war of attrition taking place around them, the Raiders manufactured a productive season in 1995 that probably should have ended in another premiership. The team finished second in the minor premiership, beaten only twice in 22 rounds. In the process, several milestones were reached which deserve some attention. For good reason, the round eight home game against the Broncos had Raiders fans, battered by weeks of Super League shocks, hoping for a match that might allow them simply to enjoy a day out at the footy. They got it and more. The Broncos were crushed 26–0 at the hands of Raider football at its most clinical, the highlight being a try by Brett Mullins after he twice chipped ahead to score. Years later Mullins said that the try was carried into the realms of perfection not by the degree of difficulty of his four-pointer, but the television call of the deed by Ray Warren on Channel Nine. Remember this? 'Kick and chase by Mullins . . . Kick and chase again by Mullins . . . This'll be a miracle . . . Oh, it *is* a miracle! Oh my goodness!'

It was only fitting that the outstanding win over the Broncos was the Raiders' twenty-fifth in a row at home, a sequence stretching back exactly 25 months to March 1994. Numerologists might enjoy the fact that in their extraordinary run the Raiders won every game by an average of 25 points. Raider tragics have always been proud of the sequence because it embraced the entire undefeated 1994 season. The win over the Broncos was in addition the ninth in succession to start 1995, the Raiders' best-ever start to a season. In the years from Bruce Stadium's first Raider game in 1990 to mid-1995, the Raiders' home record was almost 75 per cent. It had been a golden era.

But perhaps the most significant of all these statistics went unnoticed into history a few games later. When the team easily defeated Newcastle, it broke the 7,000 mark for points scored since entering the competition in 1982, an aggregate placing them first among all NRL clubs for the same period.

The Broncos game was also a termination point. A fortnight later the Raiders suffered one of only two losses in the competition rounds, beaten 16–10 at home by Manly. The stellar run at Bruce had ended. This game was almost as disappointing as the season's third loss, which happened in the post–regular season. Having beaten the Broncos in a first semi 14–8 in front of a huge, parochial Brisbane crowd—a tough win—the Raiders played the Bulldogs in a second semi, producing their worst performance in years to lose 25–6. What Ian Heads termed 'the season from hell' was over.

Despite the loss to the Dogs, there were a number of positives to take out of the year: Steve Walters' two-hundredth game for the club was notched up in round seventeen (and five games later he passed Chris O'Sullivan's club record of 204); Jason Croker achieved his 100-game milestone shortly after; Ken Nagas confirmed himself as an elite NRL winger, four tries scored by 'The Flash' in the last competition round against South Queensland further evidence of a deceptive, loping running style that defenders found impossible to read; the magnificent season put in by Laurie Daley, despite numerous distractions, saw him named the club's Player of the Year and, deservedly, the Gold Dally M award winner ahead of Cliff Lyons and Andrew Johns; a number of players, after serving their apprenticeship in the lower grades, emerged as robust top-graders, including Luke Davico, Steve Stone, David Westley, Michael Maguire, David Boyle, Jason Death, Graham Appo and Albert Fulivai; and, as pleasing as any single aspect of the '95 season, the club finished up in second place in the club championship to go with premierships achieved in the President's Cup, S.G. Ball and Harold Matthews competitions. For good measure, the Raiders were Junior Club champions by a long way.

In any other year, multiple achievements of this quality would have been the stimulus for well-earned celebrations. However, in 1995 everything was muted. Slices of unwelcome news later in the year only added to the restrained mood. On 2 August, irreplaceable club patron Fred Daly died peacefully aged 83. His passionate support for his beloved Raiders, starting in the months leading up to the club's entry into the NRL competition, was appreciated by everyone associated with the club. He was popular with the players, staff and fans alike due to an infectious optimism and a fundamental decency. To honour Fred's contribution, player number 83 was named on the Raiders' bench as an official reserve until the end of the season. It was a fine tribute to a true gentleman.

The other news that followed soon after Daly's death was expected by some in the club though that did not make it any easier to digest. Tim Sheens had signed to coach the North Queensland club in the 1997 season. As Tim himself later said in the book, *Masters of the Game*, he was one of the game's luckiest coaches because he had left Penrith (the only other NRL club he had coached) on the same good terms as when he departed the Raiders. 'Most of us go out the back door ... like players ... fighting, kicking, screaming.' By the end of the 1996 year, Tim had put in nine seasons with the Green Machine. It was a tough decision but it was time for a change. He had always believed that coaches have a 'use-by' date at any club and his had been reached. He would go with the best wishes of the entire Raiders organisation.

Early speculation about Sheens' successor had a number of individuals in the frame including Graham Murray, Peter Louis, Wayne Bennett, Peter Sterling, Mal Reilly, and the Raiders' own Dean Lance, Shaun 'Bomber' McRae and Gary Belcher. Mal Meninga initially ruled himself out as a candidate.

Sheens' announced departure was only one reason for the 1996 season being covered in retrospect as one best forgotten. A *Canberra Times* editorial on 27 November 1995 declared that the Raiders had picked the winning side in the Super League war, a statement as premature as it was naive. Destructive conflicts have no winners and this one playing out in the Rugby League community and in the courts was no exception. In February 1996 Justice Burchett in the Federal Court found in favour of the ARL, barring Super League from starting during that year. The behaviour of the Super League executives involved was 'deceptive' and 'secretive', according to Justice Burchett, making 'it plain that News Limited and the Super League companies acted, in the relevant sense, with dishonesty'.

Rugby League remained trapped in a holding pattern until Super League, on 23 May, appealed the Burchett judgement to the full bench of the Federal Court. For months, both warring camps awaited the crucial decision without a clue as to what that judgement might be. On 4 October, after a depressing football season was concluded, Judges John Lockhart, Ronald Sackville and John von Doussa produced their decision—unanimously overturning the Burchett ruling. The ARL camp, taking their turn to be rocked by a game-changing court decision, immediately sought $120 million from Optus Vision to enable them to continue operating independently. Super League's people were relieved. Their competition could start in 1997. According to *A Centenary of Rugby League*, 'the long-feared split in the game would become a reality'.

Rugby League fans prepared for one of their worst nightmares: ten Super League teams were about to play for the Telstra Cup while twelve ARL teams would vie for the Optus Cup. Names, traditions, reputations, salaries and contracts were all cast into doubt.

The two milestone court decisions in 1996, one in favour of each warring side, crippled the 1996 football season. In case you're interested, the Raiders finished sixth, making them a 'quarter-finalist'. The team played one post–regular season game, only to be beaten by St George at the Sydney Football Stadium, 14–6. Laurie Daley was the club's Player of the Year, Noa Nadruku was back to his best as the Players' Player, scoring a competition-best 21 tries, and Ben Kennedy was named Rookie of the Year. Dave Furner made a well-deserved debut in the NSW State of Origin team, which reversed the previous year's 3–0 whitewashing by the Cane Toads to obtain its own 3–0 result. NSW captain Laurie Daley maintained his rich vein of form. In addition to his own club's awards, he was runner-up to Alfie Langer in the Dally M awards, as well as being the Dally M's Five-eighth of the Year, Captain of the Year and Players' Player.

On the other hand, Ricky Stuart spent many weeks during 1996 on the sidelines with a recurring knee problem, Brad Clyde was out for a long period and Steve Walters suffered his worst run of injuries in eleven seasons with the club.

It was a bad year for rugby league, too. Would 1997 be any better, given that for the first time in the 90-year history of the code, there would be two competitions? Opinions were divided. The misery continued.

The changing of the guard, 1997–2001

1997

In one of his best one-liners, witty super-coach Jack Gibson described 1997 as 'the season of the asterisk'. With two competitions to run simultaneously for at least one year, the only way this strange season could be statistically accommodated in Rugby League's historic records into the future was to isolate its point of difference with an asterisk or, for the contemporary record-keeper, perhaps a sad-faced emoji.

The ARL's twelve Optus Cup teams consisted of St George, Sydney City, Wests, Newcastle, Souths, Norths, Parramatta, South Queensland, Gold Coast, Balmain, Illawarra and Manly. The ten Super League teams contesting the Telstra Cup in an abbreviated eighteen-round competition were the Raiders, Broncos, Cronulla, North Queensland, Perth Reds, Hunter Mariners, Penrith, Canterbury, Auckland and Adelaide. It was significant that two of the ARL's strong men, Ken Arthurson and John Quayle, resigned their positions early in the year. Given their combative stance from the earliest days of the troubles, their decisions to quit cleared the way for more fruitful conversations about some kind of merger.

In the meantime, there was some football to be played. Despite at one point saying he was not interested in taking over the coaching reins of the Raiders after Tim Sheens, on 28 May 1996 Mal Meninga did sign to coach his old team for three years, 1997–99. No-one in the club was more aware than Meninga of the lofty expectations of the Green Machine's supporter base, despite the Super League upheaval and the fact that the Raiders' core of superstars was fraying through a mixture of age, retirements, contract pressures, injuries and departures. His long-term coach Tim Sheens had experienced a few awkward moments at the start of his tenure, and Mal expected much the same. On the plus side, he had inherited a quality crop of young players to work with including Todd Payten and Ben Kennedy from the previous year and new blood headed by Luke Priddis, Andrew McFadden, David Atkins and Matt Gafa. All of them helped to lessen the effect of a wave of departures from the club to Super League's new, cashed-up teams. Steve Stone, Michael Maguire, Bruce Mamando and Mark Corvo were all off to the new Adelaide team; Steve Walters (sadly, for all Raider fans), Jason Ferris and John Lomax were headed to North Queensland to once again play under Tim Sheens; and Steve Collins joined Parramatta. While it was not as bad as the great migration of 1992, it was not far off it.

The team felt the impact of the player drain immediately, losing a string of early games. Laurie Daley felt for the new coach. He was adamant that there was no excuse for the players: 'We stay at the nice hotels, we fly everywhere, we get everything spoon fed to us and we go out and play like a bunch of sheilas.' Whatever was said behind closed doors, it worked. A six-game winning streak got everyone energised. In fact, in the last twelve games of the eighteen-round competition, the Raiders lost only twice more, a home loss to Brisbane and a close away loss to newcomer Hunter Mariners. Meninga's initially cautious coaching evolved into something more expansive.

The Raiders went into the semifinals in form but they were not helped at all by the scheduling. Their last two competition games, big wins against new clubs Adelaide and Western Reds, did them no favours in terms of hardening up for the rigours of post–regular season play. Cronulla had the home advantage in the first semi and, despite an inspiring 80-minute performance from Laurie Daley, the Sharks won narrowly 22–18 in front of their loud, partisan fans. It was an exhausting encounter, raising questions as to whether the Raiders could rebound the following week in a home semi against Penrith.

They were easily up to the task. In front of a modest crowd, generating little atmosphere, the Raiders played some of their best football of the season to beat the Panthers 32–8 and book a spot for the following week, once again against Cronulla at Shark Park. As with the first game, the venue was probably the difference between the two teams, who engaged in a torrid struggle in the forwards. Cronulla were always the better side though the Raiders stayed close on the scoreboard. Sharks' coach John Lang was terrified of a Raider moment of brilliance that failed to materialise. The Raiders were not able to move the ball wide with any consistency and went down 10–4. Laurie Daley later said that it was 'a good effort to advance as far as we did', given the season start and ongoing Super League tremors, but that reaction might not have satisfied his newer, younger teammates, who had ambitions of their own to win a first premiership regardless of the chaotic state of the game's administration.

Looking back, the 'asterisk' year was a mixed bag. The ARL's grand final produced an unforgettable Andrew 'Joey' Johns–inspired finish, resulting in Newcastle's first premiership. On the other hand, Super League's grand final between the Sharks and Broncos, ending in a 26–8 Broncos win, was disappointing—an appropriate conclusion to a season of poor crowds which concocted numbers could not disguise. Rule-change problems and embarrassingly inappropriate, well-funded half-time shows parading second-rate imported entertainers at the expense of local junior footy clubs angered fans. There was also a so-called 'World Cup Challenge', a mid-year 'global' competition that cost a heap and was treated by the players, whether or not they were prepared to admit it, as a junket. When Laurie Daley won the Telstra Medal as Super League's Player of the Year, the presenter was a

'Baywatch' girl. Might this rank as the most culturally illiterate decision ever made in sport?

The Raiders' own deflated season finish reflected aspects of their year as well. First and foremost were the deaths of two people from the club's inner sanctum. One was the supremely talented centre three-quarter Peter Jackson, who had played with the club in 1987 and 1988. Jackson, it was revealed, had experienced abuse at a young age and subsequently suffered from depression throughout adulthood. When he took his own life at age 33, the league world mourned.

The other sad loss was Eileen Jamieson, the 'mum' of the so-called 'Taj Mahal'. A staunchly committed member of the Canberra Raiders Supporters' Club, Eileen died of cancer in June. She had looked after countless numbers of young Raider footballers on their arrival in Canberra–Queanbeyan at the home they dubbed the 'Taj'. Eileen had no children of her own and a passion for Rugby League. She spoiled her 'boys', many of whom went on to distinguished football careers. Raiders life member Don Elphick wrote a lovely poem, 'Requiem for Eileen', recalling her dedication, decency and loving kindness.

Players, coaches and supporters were all unhappy late in the season with the handling of the club's first-grade captaincy issue, especially since the individuals involved, both champion footballers and two of the club's favourite sons, were Ricky Stuart and Laurie Daley. Daley felt that he was the best person for the job in the new season, 1998. Stuart had been captain since 1995, appointed by Tim Sheens, and he would go on record stating that he was 'very disappointed to lose the captaincy at the end of 1997'. While not naming names, he was far from happy with new coach and friend Mal Meninga, with his long-time teammate and friend Daley, and especially with Chief Executive Kevin Neil. His disgust with Neil's role in the decision is a sore point to this day.

After a couple of productive years as CEO from late 1991, Neil had become increasingly unpopular within the club for his management style. Laurie Daley was one exception. As he discusses in his book

Laurie: Always a Winner, he was assisted by Kevin Neil on matters of finance even before Neil took on the Raiders job in early 1992. Neil wanted Daley to get the captaincy and he made his sentiments known to the coach. Meninga found himself subject to pressures he was probably unprepared for. How to choose between two greats of the game, mates, both with outstanding credentials? And how to ignore the chatter within the club? He opted to go for Daley in the new season, a decision which inevitably divided the club.

The captaincy debate escalated into a more serious issue in the 1998 season, when salary-cap pressures came into sharp focus. Which players would be kept and who would be released?

1998

On 19 December 1997 new ARL Chief Executive Neil Whittaker announced that a deal between the ARL and Super League power brokers had finally been reached. While it was welcome news, the war had lasted nearly three years and inflicted untold damage on the game and its legion of supporters. There would be a single competition of twenty teams in the new 1998 season under the 'National Rugby League' banner. A program of rationalisation was set to cut the number of clubs to sixteen in 1999 and fourteen in the year 2000. 'Global vision' was gone forever. So too countless friendships lost in years of bitter argument and counter-argument.

Suddenly, the pressure to survive the cull was the pressing consideration for all clubs with the exception of the Brisbane Broncos. The Broncos' 'brand'—with its coffers full, a big stadium and tens of thousands of spectators at every game—appeared untouchable. In the previous season with its divided competition, the Super League Grand Final was still able to draw 58,912 spectators in Brisbane, almost all of them Queenslanders attending what was in effect a home game.

Rival clubs were thus given a taste of what the new world order of Rugby League looked like. A few clubs were going to be well off, able to exert influence, have their games routinely televised and purchase targeted marquee players of other clubs and their talented juniors. The rest would struggle.

The Raiders sought to fortify their position. However, unlike the financial turmoil of 1991–92, this time round the situation was entirely different. The Canberra and regional community did not band together in support. The challenge for the organisation heading into an uncertain future was two-fold: maintain a place in a competition set to reduce its numbers by about a third, and try to win back a disenchanted constituency of fans. In 1996 Kevin Neil had commissioned Price Waterhouse to produce a report detailing the dollar benefit the Raiders added to the ACT economy. Perhaps someone should have pointed out to Neil that validation of the club and its players during the warring Super League years was not a matter of cash. It was all about hearts and minds.

Spare a thought for Mal Meninga, a first-time coach trying to cope with unprecedented times and knowing that his club's ability to contract new players was restricted, even as the resident champion players were negotiating the twilight stage of their careers. A couple of new signings did brighten his day: Mark McLinden, another West Belconnen youngster who had dazzled in his junior football days in the halves, and a stocky 18-year-old winger from De La Salle College, Auckland, Lesley Vainikolo—soon to be dubbed by Peter Sterling as 'the Volcano'. Vainikolo's two heroes growing up were Mal Meninga and Alfie Langer. When Meninga called, Vainikolo signed on the dotted line, spending four successful years at the club before heading to England.

The 1998 season was solid, though with few genuine highlights. Everyone agreed with Andrew McFadden's assessment that the round five clash against Manly at Bruce Stadium on 12 April was one game that stood out. The Raiders were awful in the first part of the match, so bad that at one point the Sea Eagles led 20–2 in front of a small crowd, some dedicated, others grumpy. There might even have been a few boos. Ten minutes into the game, and with Manly already dominating, Laurie Daley left the field with a hamstring injury. Mark McLinden came on to partner McFadden in the halves. When they clicked as the game progressed it was a joy to watch, culminating in McLinden's sprint to score the match-winning try after the bell, giving the Raiders a 26–20 win that equalled their best-ever comeback. Manly's big lead folded in the face of a new-style, new-look Raider attack. For 'Cappy' McFadden (given his nickname by Craig Bellamy during a card game because he was sporting a hat which made him look like the cartoon character, Andy Capp), the match was the 'most memorable' in his five years with the club.

The other milestone game during the season assumed a significance that went far beyond the result. After finishing seventh at the end of the competition rounds, the Raiders again beat Manly at home in a first semifinal 17–4, a result which meant they had to travel to the Olympic Stadium in Melbourne to play the Storm, who had finished third in a stand-out debut season. In this sudden-death semi the Raiders, according to Robert Dillon in the *Canberra Times*, 'self-destructed' to lose 26–10 when confronted by superior ruck speed and go-forward. Walking off the field, Ricky Stuart wiped back tears that he dismissed as a 'bit of sweat'. In all likelihood the display of emotion had little to do with the game's result, as disappointing as it was. Rather, it was a reflection of the intrigues within the club which stretched back to early July when it was first reported, by Dillon again, that the Canberra Raiders had informed the 31-year-old Stuart and 28-year-old Brad Clyde 'to start searching for new clubs'. Despite their lofty status, the club was apparently not prepared to keep them on as 'one-club' players.

Kevin Neil argued that the decision was necessary if the club was to retain a new generation of promising players including Mark McLinden, Leslie Vainikolo and Andrew McFadden, but others felt there was more to it than that. It had been rumoured in the press that Neil and Stuart had not got on for some time. The decision to release the two champions was, it was claimed, a joint decision arrived at by Neil, football manager Robert Finch (whose son Brett signed his first contract with the club at the end of the year) and the coach. Stuart remains convinced to this day that there were other considerations involved that had nothing to do with the NRL's salary cap for the 1999 season.

Injuries and illness made the situation even more difficult at the time. Stuart was finally diagnosed in May with a severe bout of viral encephalitis which impacted on the rest of his year, and Laurie Daley—retained by the club—experienced what he called 'another one of those frustrating seasons punctuated by injury'. Stuart, Daley and Clyde stayed firm friends, though the tensions prevailing in 1998 were obvious to all club insiders.

By late September, *Sports Week* reported that when the 'dust settled' the number of players departing the club went well beyond the 'three or four' Kevin Neil had flagged in June. The latest messy clean-out set to test the Raiders' playing strength comprised Stuart and Clyde (going to the free-spending Bulldogs), Luke Priddis (Adelaide), David Boyle (Gold Coast), Brett Hetherington and Ben Rauter (North Queensland). The incoming tide that had delivered the Raiders so many gifted Queenslanders over many years was now a Gulf tide going out. To make matters worse, Royston Lightning and Albert Fulivai, two players who had promised so much for the Raiders when signed, were given their release.

Were there *any* bright spots in a season the coach described in September as 'traumatic'? A few. There was the emergence of the pairing dubbed the 'Super Macs', 'Cappy' McFadden and Mark McLinden, both about the same diminutive size and both wearing the same headgear. They brought back memories of the 'Heckle and Jeckle' combination of Chris O'Sullivan and Ivan Henjak. When the action was congested, it was almost impossible to tell the Super Macs apart. The Raiders' *25 Years* supplement, published in 2006, was right to state that the two West Belconnen Warriors juniors 'breathed energy' into a troubled 1998.

McLinden's year was so good that he won the Raiders' Rookie of the Year award and, better still, the prestigious Dally M Rookie of the Year. Ken Nagas helped a wobbly season along with a number of excellent games at fullback. Brett Mullins was not very happy with the fact that

Meninga moved him to the wing but there was little he could do about it while Nagas continued to perform so well. There was one other positional switch tried by Meninga which looked so obvious once made that it was only a matter of time until it became permanent. The intimidating backline enforcer, Ruben 'Muss' Wiki, played in the second row against Parramatta in July. When he moved into the forwards for good there were plenty of centres across the competition who slept more soundly at night.

1999

Mal Meninga was relieved to put the '98 season behind him. Like his acting captain, Dave Furner, who had filled in when Laurie Daley was injured during the year, he felt that the side had underachieved for the past two or three seasons since the advent of Super League and he looked for improvement in the new year.

It failed to materialise. If anything, the statistics were worse in a season where the Raiders finished ninth out of seventeen teams, losing about half of their 26 games including a worrying four losses at Bruce. The fortress had been breached. On-field highlights during the year included a convincing win in round one against incumbent premiers Brisbane at home in front of a crowd of 20,122 (as memories of the past came flooding back for stitched-on fans), another come-from-behind 29–16 win against Manly at Brookvale Oval midway through the year, and a typically hard-fought 18–2 victory against arch-rivals the Canterbury Bulldogs (now with Stuart and Clyde in their ranks).

Occasional good form only accentuated the bad. It had also become clear that skipper Laurie Daley, retained with the aim of leading the team into the new millennium, was likely to have his brilliant career cut short by recurring injury. Daley's State of Origin swansong on home soil in Sydney happened in the season's second game when he inspired the Blues to a 12–8 victory in a man of the match performance. However, injury concerns had convinced both the Australian and NSW selectors to appoint Brad Fittler as captain during this time, a decision which did not surprise too many. Daley's knees were on life support. He was now not always taking an active part in Raiders' training in a desperate bid to get on the field at the weekend and prolong his career. It was a temporary measure at best.

Over the next year the club, in consultation with its champion captain, would have to grapple with his retirement. The farewells of both Ricky Stuart and Brad Clyde were not handled well. They deserved much better. Hopefully, Daley would get the send-off he deserved.

2000

When Mal Meninga began to run training sessions at the beginning of the new year, he had plenty on his mind. There were a dozen or so new faces, including players destined to make their presence felt such as Alan Tongue (and what a presence!), Jamahl Lolesi, Lincoln Withers and Terry Martin, though the potential of this new blood was trumped by the implications of a number of unanswered questions. How long did Meninga think his veteran captain would last? Was it a matter of weeks or months? Could he fill the spot left by the departure of Ben Kennedy, the Raiders' Rookie of the year in 1996, who was off to Newcastle? Could Meninga put a halt to the inconsistency of the previous year? Could the Raiders attract one or two top-tier players, something they had struggled to do in the past few years? And lastly, could the coach re-shape a squad that appeared to be on a downward trajectory?

For the Raider true believers, their numbers slowly picking up after the setbacks of the recent past, the year progressed as a welcome surprise. On-field performance improved right from the start when the first three games, all at home, resulted in hard-fought wins. As the season progressed, the Raiders rebuilt Fortress Bruce, losing only two games at home in 26 rounds. Perhaps it was because the club had enticed the retired Glenn Lazarus back into the fold as the forwards' coach.

Home form, however, sharply contrasted with games on the road. For most of the season the team was winless away, finally managing to pick up three games late. The best of them by far took place in round 25 when what was described by the coach as 'a skeleton' of a Raider team headed to Melbourne to play the Storm. The 20–16 Raider victory was so courageous that years later Meninga mentioned it among a few that really stood out for him in his five years at the helm. The form displayed towards the end of the competition rounds was so good that the Green Machine finished in fourth place overall, entitling them to a first semi-final at home against Penrith. It produced a convincing 30–10 win, the coach delighted that the team played 'fantastically well' in front of their most loyal fans.

There was only one hitch. On two occasions in the match, big Panther second-rower Tony Puletua was solidly put on the turf in tackles that were judged to have involved illegal lifting. The culprits in one of them were Simon Woolford and Jason Croker; in the other, Andrew McFadden and Dave Furner. Three of the four—Woolford, Croker and McFadden—were suspended and thus ineligible to play the following week. Furner escaped a match penalty. It is just possible that a family connection played a role in the decision. Furner had played 199 games for the Raiders, a wonderful achievement that would be crowned by the two-hundredth game in the semi against the Roosters the following week. The tribunal, made up of older chaps who had close Kangaroo tour connections with father Don Furner, decided that Donny's son had no case to answer. In later years, Dave has on occasion jokingly referred to his partner-in-crime that day, not as 'Cappy' but 'Patsy'.

The Raiders took a massive hit, their 'spine' for the next game broken by the three suspensions. The charges were contested by the club but to no avail. Thus the Roosters, belted by the Raiders at Bruce 40–12 only five weeks before, won the match 38–10. Meninga had it right when he later said that 'you need your best players on the park to win comps'.

The year had its lasting consolations, memories never to be erased. The first of them occurred in round seventeen when every stereotype that opposition teams had about Canberra was confirmed. It snowed heavily before and during the match, the first and (to date) the only premiership game ever played in the snow. It was 28 May 2000 and the Raiders won the game 24–22 against the Wests Tigers. Newspaper and magazine headlines the next day more or less ignored the football and ran with the obvious theme. 'The Big Chill', 'Winter Magic', 'Ice Fortress Cold Comfort', 'Winter Wonderland', 'Extreme Sport', 'Thrills and Chills' and 'Snowed Under' were a small selection, but you get the idea. For the hardy 7,384—and the Headons were there in balaclavas, parkas and gloves—the many magical scenes remain as the happiest of recollections, another unique slice of the club's history.

That might not hold true for all the players involved. For some of them it was quite literally the first snow they had ever seen in their lives. For others, buckets of warm water were necessary to thaw out frozen fingers. Luke Williamson got the shakes early and couldn't stop. He was not alone. The players survived as best they could; for we fans, the club distributed free pies and coffee. It was a great day out, the kids watching footy and throwing snowballs.

The other day circled on the year 2000 calendar also involved Mother Nature, this time taking on an entirely different appearance. In round 23 on 9 July 2000, Laurie Daley, Dave Furner and Brett Mullins—three champions who had made major contributions to the club's years of dominance—played their final game at Bruce Stadium. On a day when everything they did turned to gold in a 40–12 demolition of the Roosters (payback for the semi the previous year), a rainbow formed as if on cue, providing the retiring Daley with photographs he'll have forever. A retirement game played in miserable conditions gave way to a series of cinematic moments.

Daley richly deserved the extraordinary reception he got from the 23,603 fans. As with Mal in 1994, his last game featured a host of Daley masks, youngsters on the field and an entertaining collection of tries. 'I remember running onto the field,' Daley later recalled, 'with all these little kids lining up in a guard of honour that brought a tear to the eye . . .' He deserved all the plaudits, winning three premierships with the Raiders, touring twice with the Kangaroos, captaining the NSW

Blues to three successive series wins and captaining his country. In his fourteen seasons with the Green Machine, the team of this one-team player missed the semis only twice. The joyful expression of Raider football over all those years had Laurie Daley as one of its principal artists.

Daley's two champion teammates, Dave Furner and Brett Mullins, were off to play in England and they too received an emotional farewell from a grateful, adoring crowd. When Furner, a Raider ball boy as a lad, kicked four goals in the win over Melbourne early in the season, he went past the 40-year-old record set by South Sydney great Bernie Purcell of 1,152 career points, the highest-ever tally by a forward. On the way, Furner smashed a variety of Raider club records.

During the year Brett Mullins had created his own bit of history. His pair of tries in a crushing win over the Auckland Warriors made him the first Raider to score 100 tries in the top grade. He joined his father Bill in elevated Rugby League company, the duo becoming the first-ever father and son combination to achieve the feat. Later in the year Brett went past his dad's record, prompting Bill to say that while his son was 'pretty quick' over 40 metres, he felt he 'could have reeled him in over the length of the field'.

On 6 September 2000, Mal Meninga announced that he would step down from the head coaching position at the end of the 2001 season. While he still had a year on his contract, he was keen to see his successor appointed to an assistant's role for the coming year in order to facilitate a smooth transition. It was a typically selfless gesture. Meninga was not ruling out more coaching further down the track, but he felt it was time for a break after a fifteen-year association with the club.

The search for a new head coach began immediately. In-house candidates Dean Lance and Craig Bellamy were two possibilities in the frame though Kevin Neil emphasised that the club was prepared to search far and wide for the best coach available. The controversial player clean-outs of recent years meant that the Raiders in 2001 and 2002 were going to be young sides. Team leaders, wiser heads, needed to be identified by a coach who felt comfortable as part of a re-build. Raiders football manager

Robert Finch assessed the situation this way: 'We are conscious of the fact that we are undergoing a changing of the guard and it is a chance for us to put in place or reaffirm the kind of culture we want at the club.'

On 29 September former St George player Matthew Elliott, coach of Bradford Bulls in England, was announced as the Raiders' 2002 head coach after it was reported that he had been head-hunted by Kevin Neil. It evidently came down to a choice between Elliott and Craig Bellamy, and Elliott got the nod. When contacted about the announcement, Mal Meninga was a little surprised, seemingly caught off-guard: 'I expected that would happen but I have had no confirmation. I haven't even met Matthew Elliott, so I don't know what's happening there.' According to the *Canberra Times* on the day it reported the story, neither Kevin Neil nor Robert Finch was available for comment.

This was hardly the most auspicious start to a transition year that was bound to have its uneasy moments with an incoming assistant coach and an outgoing head coach.

2001

Doubts about the coaching set-up were soon realised in the 2001 season. Five losses in the first eight games had the Raiders' more forensic supporters going back to Meninga's pre-season plea to have patience: 'They are young, full of talent, enthusiastic and potential champions, but they will make some fundamental mistakes early in the competition.' They did make errors and it remained to be seen whether any champions would be unearthed.

The outgoing coach and his staff had gone looking for additional recruits in the off-season, recognising that with the massive losses of Daley, Furner and Mullins added to the departures at the end of 1998 of Stuart, Clyde, Priddis and Hetherington, the club had lost champions, leaders, play-makers, try-scorers and point-scorers. The search was on for those who might take their place, ideally 'potential champions' in Meninga's optimistic words, but at a bare minimum players of solid first-grade standard.

The recruited class had a number of interesting young players, the likes of Sione Faumuina, Ryan O'Hara, Michael Hodgson, the Monaghan brothers Joel and Michael, Darren Porter, Jarred Lawrence, Michael Robertson and Troy Thompson, and a quality addition, the prolific point-scoring Queenslander Clinton Schifcofske. With Daley's retirement, a new captain had to be found to lead the group, the job going to reliable hooker Simon Woolford in his eighth season with the club, a fitting reward for his contribution over many years. Woolford recognised that he had become a more important cog in a club 'basically starting again'.

The problem that became apparent with the string of losses early in the season was that neither the head coach nor the assistant coach could systematically pursue the course they otherwise might have if left to their own devices. This contributed to an unsatisfactory year. The Raiders won nine games, lost sixteen (a disastrous six of them at Bruce Stadium) with one draw. The team finished eleventh of fourteen teams, and could only point to a small number of games where potential was on show, if only temporarily. The team's most courageous win of the year came in round seventeen against the Roosters at home.

Why courageous? This was another game in Mal Meninga's 'best of' list, and it starred club stalwart Jason Croker. 'His personal effort that day was phenomenal,' Mal recalled with admiration, 'the ultimate sacrifice for his team.' It was 24 June 2001, and the Raiders trailed the Roosters 22–10 at half-time. Because some Raider players unwisely took niggling injuries into the game, and with a diabolical run of bad luck on the day, the team was left with not a single player on the bench and 40 minutes to play. The sheds at the mid-game break resembled a hospital casualty ward. 'Toots' Croker trudged back out for the second term with a torn cruciate ligament in one knee and strained ligaments in the other leg. 'I just knew I didn't want to let my mates or the club down,' he said later on. He did not. The Raiders scored 22 unanswered points after half-time to win 32–22. Croker's contribution was epic, inspiring all his teammates around him. Assistant coach Matt Elliott at first had no words to account for what he had witnessed. He found some: 'It was one of those things that makes the hair stand up on the back of your neck.'

In a year when newcomer Clinton Schifcofske set a club record 245 points for the season, the club staged a first reunion of the 1982 Pioneers to acknowledge its twentieth NRL season. Nearly 30 players attended, including all but one of the first-grade team announced in late February 1982. Memories were shared, a few beers consumed, jokes exchanged and a game of Oztag enjoyed. They all took part, including an enthusiastic John McLeod, who refused to sit on the sideline just because he had lost a leg in an accident. He was in the thick of all the action, just as he always had been two decades earlier.

While the camaraderie of the past was still on show, the departure of Mal Meninga was a deeply worrying sign for the Raiders' immediate future. Outwardly, Green Machine officials were calm as they looked ahead. Privately, every one of them knew that the next few years were going to be marked by uncertainty and survival fatigue.

6

HARDER YARDS

2002–PRESENT

Matt Elliott's stint as head coach of the Raiders, from 2002 to 2006, represents another distinct stage in the club's evolution. While he tried hard to arrest the external forces damaging the club, in the end Elliott succumbed to the fashion for player migration that dogged the Raiders for several years.

Winters of content, winters of discontent, 2002–06

The Raiders signed only five new players in 2002, the best of them Phil Graham, Tyran Smith and James Evans, at best solid acquisitions. The new coach was intent on carefully assessing the line-up he had at his disposal, wanting to commence his own rebuild on a fresh sheet. What he had not counted on was the swift and dramatic series of behind-the-scenes decisions and announcements that radically restructured the club's administrative set-up within a matter of a few hectic days in late April. It was only seven games into the coach's first season.

Some brief background information is required here. During the 2001 season *Big League* magazine reported that, yet again, some NRL clubs were cash strapped. In desperation they had approached News Ltd for 'sponsorship' support while the ridiculous player payments that had begun in 1995 were slowly reduced to manageable levels. Most of the Sydney clubs put the bite on their respective leagues' clubs for help. With a line that would come back to haunt him and his club, Bulldogs CEO Bob Hagan stated it in plain English: 'The game still can't afford itself.' News Ltd continued to bleed money and, given the company's ambition six years earlier to run the 'business' of Rugby League, their investment had soured.

The hand-outs by News and Optus to a range of clubs, including the Raiders, were always going to come to a halt. It was only a matter of time. In November 2001 John McIntyre, Chairman of the Queanbeyan Leagues Club (QLC) group and a key member of the Raiders finance committee, commenced discussions with Peter Jourdain, News Ltd's business development manager, about a possible sale of the News share in the Raiders to the Canberra and District Rugby League. Discussions continued through January–February 2002.

Karl de Kroo in the *Canberra Times* reported on 22 April 2002 that:

> . . . a deal to sign over full ownership of the Canberra District Rugby League (CDRL) is thought to be all but finalised, but the power-brokers behind the takeover bid continued to play their cards close to their chests yesterday . . . News Ltd, which has held a 50% share in the Raiders since 1996 and has funded the club's football operations, is expected to sign over its stake to the CDRL tomorrow.

This article appeared together with an intriguing photo of former Raiders Secretary and CEO John McIntyre and current CEO Kevin Neil, both watching a Queanbeyan Blues–Valley Dragons match. McIntyre is captured looking purposefully ahead—into the future? Neil is looking sideways, somewhat puzzled. Inadvertently or not, the picture anticipated the dramatic events about to occur.

The next day the takeover story was front page again, this time with a bigger headline, the full story told and a photo of a confident-looking John McIntyre standing outside the large Mawson Club development.

The headline read: 'Raiders upheaval as News pulls out'. News Ltd had agreed to hand over its 50 per cent stake to the CDRL, lock, stock and barrel at no cost, not even a peppercorn. The Queanbeyan Leagues Club group, in time to be called the Raiders Group (the primary financial backer of the CDRL), assumed full ownership of the football club. The Raiders were back in local hands. A new board was announced with John McIntyre at its head, after the resignation of the existing board under former Defence Department Secretary Tony Ayers. The *Canberra Times* suggested that the jobs of Neil, football manager Robert Finch and development manager Peter Sollis were under scrutiny.

In a bizarre twist, on the sport backpage of the *Canberra Times* on the same 23 April, Karl de Kroo provided the details of a story that had been circulating for a week or two. The Raiders' poor start to the season (more on that shortly) had prompted Kevin Neil to propose that he would 'withhold payment to players who under-perform', a suggestion that drew a hostile response from the Rugby League Players Association, among others. Neil said that he had received legal advice indicating that, on the basis of a clause existing in the Raider players' contracts, he could hold back the wages of those who failed to 'perform to the best of their ability and skill'. Neil's brain explosion threatened to embed the club in expensive legal proceedings, not to mention the damage inflicted on the playing group itself. Most insiders thought that Neil was fiddling as his Rome burned.

On 24 April the *Daily Telegraph* reported that Neil 'had resigned' and that the letter about to be sent to under-achieving players had been torn up. The latter was true; the resignation, however, came in the form of a sword to be fallen on. On 25 April, the *Canberra Times* dedicated almost a whole broadsheet page to the story, including a piece on the 'Life and Times of Kevin Neil'. His most capable work for the club had occurred in his first few years as chief executive when his hard-nosed decisions helped Tim Sheens to re-establish the platform for a premiership bid in 1993 (that with luck would have succeeded) followed by the stunning achievement of 1994.

To Neil's subsequent detriment, he aligned himself too tightly with News Ltd and Super League, a connection increasingly difficult to justify. His public pronouncements became more erratic. On one Monty Pythonesque occasion, after I had been critical on ABC Radio of aspects of the News Ltd program for Rugby League, Neil insisted on being allowed to respond, the next day 'banning' me from Bruce Stadium. He was not the only participant in the sorry saga of the 'war' who spoke erratically under pressure and came to regret it.

The Raiders' new general manager and CEO was 39-year-old Simon Hawkins, since 1995 the general manager of the Queanbeyan Leagues Club. All the newspapers, including the *Canberra Times,* alluded to his self-made business background and the fact that, as Chris Wilson pointed out in the *Times*, he 'began his career as a waiter and he hasn't laced a football boot in his life'. Hawkins and his family, like so many from the Queanbeyan–Canberra region, started going to Raider games in 1989 and got hooked on their uplifting brand of football entertainment. In his new positions, and situated to be an objective voice, Hawkins was acutely conscious that his job was to confirm a structure that enabled the coach and footballers to go about their work unhindered, in search of improved results. His chief finance officer, Yvonne Gillett, went on to conscientiously attend to the books for the next fifteen years, driven by the need to never give the NRL a chance to question the viability of the Raiders' financial situation. Run a tight ship and stay in the black.

The Canberra community responded fairly favourably to the new arrangements after the exhaustion of Super League, the *Canberra Times* noting that the Raider Group's recreation clubs (at Queanbeyan, Mawson, Gungahlin and Logan City in Queensland) provided the football club with its 'only genuine chance of survival'. Some observers expressed reservations about John McIntyre's close involvement in what had just transpired, given his forced resignation as CEO in 1991 when the Raiders were on the verge of collapse, but there was also sympathy for the grey areas that surrounded the sequence of events at that time and the question of who would take the fall to appease the NRL.

In the present, the Raiders were struggling on and off the field, and losing $100,000–$200,000 a month. McIntyre pointed to the profitable trading of the licenced clubs that had seen them reach a position of zero debt on a number of occasions. The group was ready and able to take on what he called 'this type of venture':

> In the end, necessity is the mother of invention. News Ltd decided to call it a day. We were the only interested buyer. Our aim is to bring some heart and soul and passion back to the Raiders.

It was a noble and welcome goal. Super League's green jersey was banished forever. For many stitched-on Raider fans, it was a case of good riddance.

In late April, Matt Elliott was beset with his own immediate problems and they had nothing to do with the recent back-room dramas. On the same weekend that the *Canberra Times* covered the full CDRL–News Ltd story in detail under the heading 'Sale takes Raiders into whole new ball game', the footballers travelled to Parramatta for a round seven clash with the Eels. Elliott hoped that his 'heart to heart' meeting with the players during the week might turn their fortunes around but it was not to be. The pain continued, the team returning home, tail between its legs, thrashed 38–0 in a match where even internationals Jason Croker and Ruben Wiki made uncharacteristic errors.

Seven games, seven defeats for the new coach. In an attempt to alter things he moved a contingent of young, hard-working players further up the pecking order, including Alan Tongue, the definitive hard-worker, Darren Mapp, Troy Thompson, Michael Monaghan and Rod Jensen. This splash of new chemistry worked. Slowly results improved as the season progressed. The Raiders were overwhelmed by the Bulldogs, 46–6, a few weeks before the Sydney team was stripped of nearly all its points, but for most of the games in the second half of the year the team was far more competitive, winning eight of the last sixteen to squeeze into the semis in eighth place, good enough for a quarter-final in New Zealand and ironically made available to the Raiders because of the

Dogs' demotion from first to last place. The Warriors accounted for the plucky Raiders with relative ease, a result expected by the Sydney scribes.

Matt Elliott was no fool. It did not take him too long in the top job, especially after suffering through the early defeats, to get his head around the full extent of the challenge in front of him. His background had him better equipped than most to deal with the task. Born on Thursday Island to a ship's pilot father and a nurse, he balanced a street fighter's application with dry if at times impenetrable humour, whether talking to his young group of players or doing media interviews. He had, as they say, the gift of the gab. The footy journalists were never quite sure whether he was serious when answering their questions or tongue-in-cheek. The same was true for Raider fans. Many did not know what to make of his highly individual, often peculiar post-game assessments or his prose when he strayed into official club publications.

The Raiders' promotional membership booklet for the start of the 2003 season, for example, included a few choice words from the coach under the title, 'Harvesting Success'. The punctuation and eccentricity are his:

> I hope you will allow me to take an agricultural approach. Last season represented the planting process: the ground needed to be turned over, a new crop had to be decided on and the right fertilizer needed to be selected.
>
> Now it's time for us to Grow; as an Organisation, Club, Team and individually . . . While the yield will, on occasion, fall short of these targets, we must always expect the very best . . . The premium harvest we all seek for this great Club will be a result of hard work, skill, execution and believing in what we are doing.

According to one of his ripest vegetables, captain Clinton Schifcofske, Matt was always taking 'the piss out of himself'. He constantly used a classic First and Second World War phrase, 'shitter's ditch', to describe a grim predicament, as in 'we're in shitter's ditch'. The team often was. At the press conference following a dour victory by the Raiders—but a win nonetheless—Elliott commented that his side had pulled itself out of 'a deep and dark ravine' to win, a win he described as 'worse than ugly . . . a bit like the girl I used to date'. These were not comments that would be acceptable today in light of the 'Me Too' movement, but in the early 2000s the young male footy reporters could not get enough of it. They loved his brand of humour. But could he back it up with improved results?

Going into the 2003 season, the club and its coach had to absorb further setbacks. The year before, the competition was won by a very good Roosters side under the guidance of a first-year coach, Raider great Ricky Stuart. Never short of cash and able to finesse the salary cap, the Roosters signed up two of the best Raider youngsters coming through the system: Brett Finch and Todd Payten. In all likelihood the Finch departure was explained by the sacking of his father Robert at the same time Kevin Neil 'resigned'. Whatever the reasons, the reality was that both players were offered the opportunity to go to a club at the top of its game and both took it.

Warning bells at the Raiders club were starting to ring. Having difficulty attracting quality players to Canberra was one thing; having your emerging young stars pinched from under your nose was quite another. Little wonder that the club was battling constantly to attract and keep a major sponsor.

After the stresses and strains of 2002, Elliott brought some innovation to the table. He had become aware of Michael Lewis's book *Moneyball* (later turned into a successful Hollywood film), a non-fiction account of Billy Beane, the manager of the Oakland Athletics baseball team. Recognising that he could not compete with the dollars offered for free agents by teams like the New York Yankees, Beane targeted top-quality, second-tier players who met certain mathematical criteria. These would be the individuals with whom Beane would try to win a championship.

Matt Elliott imagined something similar happening at the Raiders.

Parramatta, in particular, had some good players on the market. While not having a lot to spend, like Beane in Oakland, but coaching a team with a similar lack of appeal, Elliott and General Manager Don Furner (Junior) managed to sign a worthy intake of new players including underrated Eels forward Ian Hindmarsh, young Eels centre Adam Mogg and Eels half and hooker Brad Drew, together with former Australian Schoolboys' captain, Moruya's Michael Weyman (a bright prospect), hard-man Ben Cross and promising back Jason Bulgarelli. It was, to use the coach's favourite metaphor, a good crop. Could he make it work? Could he pull off a Billy Beane in the nation's capital?

In season 2003, to the delight of Raiders fans beginning to head back to Bruce Stadium in better numbers, the answer seemed at first to be a resounding 'yes'. Ignoring for the time being five disconcerting losses at home, the year was full of pleasant surprises and good, sometimes outstanding results. The coach put it on the line at the outset in the *NRL Season Guide*: 'You can't go on saying we've got a young team forever and that we're building. It's time for us to grow, to step up and play some consistent footy.' And that is exactly what happened. Tipped to come last by the Sydney 'experts' headed as usual by Phil Gould, and what do you know? The Green Machine won their first eight games in a row to lead the competition, including a stirring 40–28 win against Penrith at Penrith Park when the team trailed by sixteen points at one stage.

The Raiders' true believers had never wavered, but the football Elliott's side was starting to play enticed back more of those fans repelled by Super League. The round seven game against the Bulldogs, a terrific game won 26–22 by the men in green, drew 19,372 fans. When the number of wins grew, Sydney journalist Jacquelin Magnay wrote an article in the *Sydney Morning Herald* called 'Raiders of the lost spark' in which she maintained that Matt Elliott's approach had made 'the no-frills Raiders the surprise packets of the NRL'. In a typical press interview, Elliott gave credit for his sporting genes to his dad, 'a crooner who once cut a record and played lower-grade for Easts'.

The 2003 NRL surprise packets pummelled the Parramatta Eels 50–14 in round thirteen, Cronulla 40–12 in round twenty and thrashed

Manly at Brookvale, 51–16, in round 22. At various points as the year progressed the Raiders led the competition outright—and as late as round twenty. But for a few close and untidy losses mid-season the Raiders could have been minor premiers. As it was, the team finished a creditable fourth (equal third on points with the Bulldogs) and entered the semifinals with confidence. The coach felt that the best was yet to come.

In the first semi the Raiders drew a short straw when hosting a team that had definitely had the wood on them for a few years, a star-studded Melbourne Storm side boasting the likes of Billy Slater, Cameron Smith, Matt Orford, Stephen Kearney, Matt Geyer and Robbie Kearns. It was a quality team with a quality coach, former Raider Pioneer Craig Bellamy, and once again the Storm was too strong, winning convincingly 30–18. The Raiders then went to Aussie Stadium to play the Auckland Warriors. Win it, and they were a game away from the grand final. Older Raider fans will remember this one vividly. It had a shattering climax. With the Warriors ahead 16–10 well into the second half, Luke Davico scored. After the Schifcofske conversion, it was 16-all. The Raiders dominated from that point for the rest of the game, bombing one try when Joel Monaghan failed to hold on to the crumb of a Mark McLinden bomb, and then Jason Bulgarelli somehow managed to spill a McLinden grubber bouncing end-over-end into the in-goal. He only needed to fall on it. The Warriors re-grouped, Stacey Jones managing to steer over a field goal minutes before the end against the run of play.

The emptiness felt throughout the club in response to this result was eased a fortnight later when the Raiders Premier League side ended their excellent season with a big grand final win, 31–6, over St Mary's-Penrith. There was so much to like about the victory beyond the six tries to one margin. A number of players put their hands up to play first grade the following year, among them Matt Gafa, Ben Cross, Michael Monaghan, Josh Miller, Phil Graham, Terry Campese and Michael Weyman. Some showed they had the ability to play representative football.

A buoyant year ended on an upbeat note. In the 2004 year ahead, was the club about to embark on another era of prolonged success?

Matt Elliott and his coaching staff thought so. In a personally signed letter that went out to Raiders' season ticket holders at the end of September the coach asked all the green believers out there to 'reflect on 2003 as a year that was the start of something special'. Captain Simon Woolford supported the comments, his message ticking off 'a great year for the Raiders', one in which the young team unearthed 'some great emerging stars'. The Raiders' fan day in early March 2004 reflected the exuberant mood. It was a festive occasion. The Raiderettes were all energy, the crowd of kids star struck, their parents all smiles, the players sported grins as wide as Lake Burley Griffin and Victor the Viking made it clear to everyone within earshot that this was going to be the year of the Raider, the return of the club to the competition's top echelon.

General Manager Don Furner proudly stated that the Raiders were at heart 'local'. The aim was to restore the practices that had worked years earlier—whenever possible signing bush kids and Queenslanders. So the new intake included Terry Campese (a Queanbeyan Blue), Josh Miller (a Forbes Magpie), Todd Carney (a Goulburn Stockman), Alan Rothery (from Norths, Rockhampton) and Kris Kahler (Gympie).

But smart recruitment, cultural and behavioural benchmarks and an abundance of optimism about the future do not necessarily win you football games. Elliott regarded 2003 and the forthcoming 2004 season as integral parts of the club's 'evolution'. He looked to further improvement in his team's results. He expected more wins.

Twenty rounds into the new competition year the Raiders stood at ten wins and ten losses, good enough to be clinging on to eighth position yet hardly convincing as an indicator of a team on the rise and rise. The season buckled badly after that, with five losses in the final six games. Somehow, the Raiders remained in eighth spot with an 11–13 record, just enough to get them a game against Ricky Stuart's Roosters in week one of the semis. It was not a contest. Final score: Roosters 38, Raiders 12. Sadly, it was also Raider great Ruben Wiki's final game with the club. He had been playing hurt for some time. Barely able to walk the week before his farewell game, he insisted on taking the field with his left ankle supported by a plaster cast, making 25 tackles and ten hit-ups. His gutsy, inspirational performances were going to be missed. The man who had introduced his teammates to the mysteries of the kava post-game recovery ritual had spent virtually his entire playing career in the green jersey. Ruben was heading back home to New Zealand to play out his last years with the Warriors and, while everyone in Canberra and Queanbeyan wished him well, the circumstances in which the Warriors secured his services (a salary cap rort for which the club was later fined) stuck in the craw of Raider officials.

Wiki was not the only notable departure. The Raiders also lost Luke Davico (off to English club, Wigan), Brad Drew (Huddersfield), Mark McLinden (London Broncos) and Joel Monaghan (Roosters). Taken as a group, this represented a substantial loss of talent, speed, experience and leadership.

There was no disguising it now. No amount of sugar coating from the coach, staff or Raider officials could escape the fact that the club had started to shed, annually, some of its best players. Worrying patterns were emerging: the Raiders each year were picked by most league journalists to come last; bookmakers routinely had them at the longest price to win the competition (125–1 at the start of 2005, odds which blew out further as the season progressed); Raider appearances on free-to-air television were almost non-existent; the club's inability to attract top-quality players meant that it had to venture into the player market prepared to pay more money, 'overs', for either players of average ability, players whose best years were behind them or players who had shown just enough ability to make them a calculated gamble; and, perhaps worst of all, the club's junior talent was now apparently fair game for the richer clubs with bottomless pockets. The promise of *Moneyball* miracles had disappeared.

In the March 2005 *NRL Guide*, published by the *Canberra Times*, Peter Fitzgerald lamented the previous year's 'mass exodus' of players, as he labelled it: 'Gone went the heart and soul of the club in Wiki, the workhorse Davico, the try-scoring machine Monaghan and the halves combination of Drew and McLinden.'

Fitzgerald, like many others, withheld judgement on the club's new buys, while noting that arguably the best two of them were in the veteran category. Matt Adamson, a 32-year-old former international, came to the Raiders from the Leeds Rhinos in England after his best nine years were spent at Penrith, and 32-year-old Jason Smith, another former international, came to Canberra from Hull in England after his best eleven years were spent at the Bulldogs and Parramatta Eels. It remained to be seen if they were a positive answer to existing problems. The decision to go with Jason Smith evidently came down to a choice between two players, involving value judgements: either Smith's experience and ability to mentor a new crop of halves or Jonathan Thurston's youth and obvious gifts. Smith got the nod. In hindsight, that hurts.

To be fair to the personnel in 2005 who did their best in a disastrous year for injuries, the side started with four wins on the trot, two of them impressive home wins over Newcastle and St George. Things deteriorated from there. The next nine games produced only two victories, both of them away, and the season ended with seven consecutive losses, three at Bruce Stadium in front of dwindling gatherings of fans who were increasingly frustrated, angry or demoralised. The club finished second last, fourteenth of fifteen teams, it had the competition's worst completion rate and the men in green had to make the most tackles in the league. Contemplating what he called a 'pretty scary' year, captain Clinton Schifcofske rued the fact that injuries had played a big part. When the team ran out to play Manly at Bruce in the season's last round, going down 36–18, there were fourteen first-graders on the sideline nursing a variety of ailments.

At the start of the year the coach said he wanted competition for positions. This did not happen. He also said he had access to 'the greatest depth of talent that I've had'. If so, it diluted over the winter months. There were few bright spots, though front-rower Troy Thompson, a West Belconnen Warrior in his junior days, former Forbes Magpie second-rower and prop Josh Miller and the ever-improving Todd Carney were three of them. Thompson and Miller deserved to share the club's Player of the Year award, while up-and-comer David Milne, playing the first of his seven years with the club, was also a popular pick as Rookie of the Year. He was a sound investment.

It was an ominous sign of the immediate future when local publications (and a couple in Sydney which at least took an interest) began resorting to the tired clichés used to defend and exonerate a lowly position on the competition ladder: that the Raiders were relishing their role as underdogs; that the underdog tag was one thing in the team's favour; that the team was underrated; that the team loomed as a dark horse; or that the team was ready to surprise a few people. These were sentiments recalling the famous sporting line from American football coach Vince Lombardi: 'Show me a good loser, and I'll show you a loser.' The danger inherent in such platitudes is that they can firm up as the dominant narrative, accepted by the players and the public.

Fortunately, club management refused to abandon the search in difficult years for points of advantage that might assist the club. They tried new things. Some worked, some didn't. During a long 2005 season, the Raiders hired a new marketing manager, Jason Amos, who spruiked that he wanted the club to have 'a new look, trendy and corporate'. Amos wanted more 'cocktail-style functions'. In his words, and it would be impossible to paraphrase them to better effect:

> It's all about our new look. There'll be a lot more trendy stuff in a less football-orientated evening. It's all about presenting the new image of the Canberra Raiders organisation. We'll be much more corporate this year and this is the way the club is headed as a whole.

Mercifully, Jason Amos had the briefest of tenures. His New Age approach was tried and failed.

On the positive side of the ledger, the club welcomed onto its coaching staff two Old Boys, champion Dave Furner and the first holder of the Meningans' university scholarship in the late 1990s, Andrew 'Cappy' McFadden.

In the 2006 season the Raiders finished a respectable seventh and qualified for post-season action. How the players managed this, despite the onset of another debilitating coaching situation and the distracting chatter of Sydney journalists consigning them to the depths of the NRL or possible extinction beggars belief. It was a year when the team defied the odds. It simply refused to fold.

What happened to unleash the dire media predictions, and how did the team respond? To start with, the exodus of players continued to such an extent that Peter Fitzgerald wrote in the *Canberra Times*' 2006 *NRL Season Guide* in early March that 'only a fool would say the Raiders fared well in the trading period'. It was hard to disagree. Gone were four regular first-graders—Ian Hindmarsh, Matt Adamson (a failed experiment), Ryan O'Hara and Ben Cross—together with a few fringe players who seemed ready to develop such as slightly built, elusive winger Michael Robertson (a local Valley Dragon off to join the Manly Sea Eagles) and Kiwi international Tyran Smith. Collectively, this was a loss of untapped potential and a bigger loss of engine-room grunt, forward power. Incoming were three inexperienced forwards: Tom Learoyd-Lahrs, Newcastle's Dane Tilse, the son of '82 Pioneer Michael, and the Bulldog's Trevor Thurling (a Queanbeyan junior who had played only one NRL game for his Sydney team). Put clinically, that was almost 700 games of first-grade experience heading out the door and thirteen games coming in. Before a ball had been kicked in the new season it was reported that league odds-makers had 'written off' the Raiders' chances. Again.

The new combination of players would have been just starting to get to know one another in the first couple of months after Christmas when, on 19 February 2006, Raiders coach Matt Elliott dropped a bombshell. He announced that he would be leaving the club at the end of the season to coach the Penrith Panthers. The next day he and CEO Simon Hawkins had to face what was described as one of the biggest 'media scrums assembled at Raider headquarters'. There was 'a barrage of questions'. Hawkins tried valiantly to keep matters in some kind of measured administrative perspective; the coach, on the other hand, inexplicably decided to 'shut up shop'. His interrogators were not too pleased. Asked if he accepted that the mass of Raider fans out there would at least expect to be given some reasons for his decision, Elliott snapped, 'They're private'. It was a retort that smacked of arrogance or indifference. Either way, it was not a good look.

Common sense soon prevailed. I suspect that either Simon Hawkins or Board Chairman John McIntyre had a private word with the coach to point out that he had an obligation to say why he was departing—which he did in a 1,200-word statement in the *Canberra Times* on 26 February. As an explanation it failed the pub test. Money, Elliott said, was not involved; he regretted having 'made a commitment to Simon Hawkins' that he could not keep; his family was 'obviously one of the biggest factors'; and 'the beach was always a big part of my life growing up and I want it to be a big part of my children's lives too'. Cynics advanced the opinion that unless Elliott took up residence in Sydney a long way east of the location of his new club, then his 16-year-old daughter, mentioned by her father, was facing a long commute to get anywhere near sea and sand.

Elliott added as an afterthought that he was also motivated by 'security and commercial reasons'. Whatever that meant.

During a strained few weeks for all, and with the start of the competition imminent, Elliott resorted to the clichés that every coach coming off a poor season uses. They had a particularly hollow ring this time round. In 'five years of hard work' he had assembled 'a block of young players' whom he believed to be 'the equal of any in the competition'. This was delusional. Then he added that if 'the club can hold them together, the Raiders could be a top-five club for a long time to come'. Now if he was alluding to the short-term future of the club, then this too stretched credibility. If he was considering the long-term future, then while 'top-five' was possible, it would be an end result on which the 2007 Penrith coach would have no influence whatsoever.

To their credit, the players went looking for their own set of motivations and goals. It was hard yakka at the start. In the first few games of the season Sydney predictions of a Green Machine wooden spoon looked likely. Round two saw Andrew 'Joey' Johns' Newcastle Knights put 70 points on the Raiders at Bruce Stadium, the most points the team had ever conceded, and the following week the Roosters inflicted another walloping, 56–20, in Sydney.

League commentators were quick to react to the lop-sided results, led by Roy Masters in the *Sydney Morning Herald* and Fox Sports' Warren Smith in his weekly column in *Big League* magazine, appropriately called 'The Rant'. Masters' harsh assessment had a narrow Sydney-centric agenda:

> The Raiders' competitive advantage has declined to a point the NRL has serious concerns about the Canberra club's capacity to attract top talent and continue as a viable member of the league.
>
> Full-time professionalism and national/trans/Tasman expansion together with the migration of players to the coast, have meant a steady erosion of the Raiders' appeal. Recent blow outs against the Knights and the Roosters suggest the club is returning to its debut year, when it was known as the 'the Faders' . . . the Raiders' long-term future is the real issue.

Imagine if Sydney teams over the decades had been subjected to the same criterion: that a couple of bad results in a row meant your credentials to exist were brought into question. The competition would have ceased years ago, given that every single club of ten years' standing or more had experienced straitened times at one point or another, some of them for prolonged periods. Think South Sydney. Masters' argument was as shallow as it was ill-conceived.

This was the context for a round four game in 2006 when the Raiders hosted the Penrith Panthers at home in front of a crowd limited to the hard core of true believers. The Headon family was there, surrounded by familiar faces, and what we all witnessed was another game to store away in the memory bank. The Panthers led 20–14 with seconds on the clock when the Raiders' new recruit from 2005, Thirroul centre David

Howell, scored in the corner. Clinton 'Golden Point' Schifcofske had a sideline kick to take the game into familiar territory. It never looked like missing, nor did his field goal in the eighth minute of extra time to deliver the faithful a clutch 21–20 victory. The result instilled belief into a playing group badly in need of it.

Elliott's replacement as coach needed to be found as soon as possible as a show of faith for the team and its fans. With a diligence and efficiency that recalled the smart coaching adjustments of 1986–87, the Raiders announced on 11 April 2006 that 1982 Pioneer Raider Neil Henry (North Queensland Cowboys' assistant coach at that time) had signed to become the Green Machine's head coach in 2007. It was another timely boost for an improving squad of footballers. They soldiered on, producing three successive wins in the State of Origin weeks—by one point over the Cowboys, two points over the Rabbitohs and two points over the Bulldogs. In all, they won six games during the year by margins of one or two points. There were no representative players among them, only a refreshing camaraderie amidst adversity and a devotion to the task. Their sleeves-up work ethic attracted a number of admirers. 'What we lack in class,' Raiders Chairman John McIntyre said, 'we make up for in character.'

Big League was sufficiently impressed by the 'over-achieving' Raiders that it featured the Green Machine in its round sixteen edition, a week when the Raiders met the Roosters, whom they belted 42–10 in their season's best result. According to Ben Blaschke in an article entitled 'What a Nuisance', the Raiders are:

> . . . the quintessential enigma of the NRL. They boast one of the least recognisable playing rosters in the Telstra Premiership. Their stats read like a runaway train heading straight for a rickety bridge—12th for line breaks, 14th for metres gained, 14th for offloads and 14th for tackle breaks. Yet the Canberra Raiders are equal with eighth-placed North Queensland and are quickly proving themselves more than just the nuisance side of this year's competition.

They were determined to stay in the semifinal mix.

The Raiders faced the Melbourne Storm in the last home game of the season. Once again, a day of farewells was a bitter-sweet experience. The crowd got the chance to be a part of another emotional goodbye to the last two remaining players in the present side, Jason Croker and Simon Woolford, to have been involved in the club's glory days in the early 1990s. Croker was an integral part of the 1994 premiership team. With 318 games for the Raiders behind him, he was off to France to play out his career, while Woolford had been signed by St George. Joining them on the departing train were Adam Mogg (going to Les Catalans in France), Michael Hodgson (Titans), Jason Smith (North Queensland) and Clinton Schifcofske, about to try his hand in more lucrative rugby pastures. Matt Elliott and Schifcofske, it is worth mentioning, shared the same agent, Steve Gillis. The clients probably received the same advice.

This latest exodus represented a watershed moment for the national capital's team. Some clubs, and the Raiders were one, could no longer afford to ignore Rugby League's new realities: the widening gap between rich and poor clubs; the favoured treatment given by Channel Nine to a select group of clubs with respect to free-to-air television games (the Broncos and a few others); junior players nurtured by the poorer clubs being pilfered by the richer clubs; and player managers intent on placing their clients in Sydney, Melbourne and Brisbane clubs. These individuals, many of them loyalty-free zones, had started to wield disproportionate power.

In his contribution to *25 Years in the Limelight* (the *Canberra Times* supplement celebrating the Raider club's twenty-fifth anniversary), Raiders Chairman John McIntyre expressed his relief that the football club had put 'the turmoil and drama of past years' behind it. Always the optimist, he flagged 'a new direction, which will see us soon return to the glory days of the late '80s and early '90s'. McIntyre wrote these words in June. While the team battled out the rest of the year to deservedly qualify for the play-offs, few Raiders fans were under the illusion that another era of success beckoned. The Raiders were knocked out of the premiership in week one of the finals, beaten soundly by the Bulldogs, 30–16.

The challenge for the club in more perilous times was to map out with insight and vision the elements of a successful future in circumstances totally different to the early 1990s. Incoming coach Neil Henry appealed as someone capable of taking the club in a new direction.

Leave your ego at the door, 2007–08

When Matt Elliott began his sixth and last season in Canberra, he put a sign above the entrance to the club's Bruce headquarters which read: 'Leave your ego at the door and step into our team'. The Penrith-bound coach, while never really coming to grips with the fundamental elements of Raider culture, to his credit promoted the importance of a catchphrase which helped to sustain the Green Machine through the testing years ahead. Elliott admitted that he pinched the words from NFL battlers, the Kansas City Chiefs. As with the Chiefs, respectability and spurts of high achievement would only happen through the resolute application of a team ethic.

New coach Neil Henry was a deliberate choice to assume the reins. According to General Manager Don Furner the club did not interview anyone else. 'We just talked about his philosophy,' Furner stated, and where he wanted to take the club. Henry's family had moved to Canberra when he was eleven, he played his early footy with the West Belconnen Warriors, he was a 1982 Pioneer, he coached the Raider lower grades between 1999 and 2002—and his parents still lived in Canberra. With the club intent on putting its focus back on the resources of the region as a means of regenerating, these were background credentials that mattered. Henry wanted staff around him with 'a sense of club tradition' in addition to their football know-how.

It was a sound base that promised to be even better when the coach appointed Alan Tongue as team captain. Back in 2001, his last year coaching the Raiders, Mal Meninga was asked about those players with 'the right stuff' on and off the field. He mentioned a young red-headed footballer the Raiders had recently acquired named Alan Tongue. The young man, Mal said, was 'a pleasure to coach'. Throughout Tongue's twelve years with the Green Machine, that attribute never altered. Even in his first years in the top grade Tonguey's gut-busting efforts made him an unofficial team leader. Each year he seemed to take on a bigger workload, topping the NRL's tackle count in 2006 with 1,042, an astonishing aggregate that made him the most prolific tackler in any NRL season. Ever. His unofficial 57 tackles against Cronulla took him past Melbourne hooker Richard Swain's 2001 mark of 1,004. In the same record-breaking year, Tonguey's eleven tries represented the best four-point output of all the NRL's forwards. He was the right stuff as new captain. He had no ego, never stopped putting in and led from the front.

Henry was keen to commence his first assignment as a head coach. Those who had worked with him knew that he matched technical and tactical nous with no-nonsense, disciplinarian practices. Some of the players called him 'the Principal'. He was dealing with a young and largely inexperienced squad, a fact which prompted the usual forecast from the Sydney media. The Raiders would be the 2007 wooden spooners, they bleated in unison, led by head sheep Phil Gould, who wrote that Neil Henry had 'been given a ticket to the Titanic'. He meant 'on' the Titanic but we get the idea.

The club was not fazed, feeling that this year it had a number of 'exciting young guns', a solid core enhanced by thirteen newly recruited players—the likes of Colin Best, Michael Dobson, Glenn Turner, Neville Costigan, Scott Logan, Joe Picker, Ryan Hinchcliffe and 'Lord' Ted Goodwin's son, Bronx. Nigel Plum was picked up from the Roosters mid-season. No big names, true, but loads of promise.

With the first game approaching and the players keen to get going, a few Sydney journalists could not resist another round of 'Canberra bashing', one commenting that the Raiders were 'up shit creek without a paddle'. They managed to get NRL Chief Executive David Gallop on the record saying that the Raiders' retention and recruitment policies were not up to scratch. However, the *Canberra Times*' Chris Wilson decided to go to the source for clarification of the remarks, conducting an interview with David Gallop that appeared in the paper on 17 March—the Saturday of the competition's opening weekend. Gallop doused the Sydney flames, stating that the Raiders were in no danger of having to relocate and that the club's junior talent was 'the envy of a lot of clubs'.

Don Furner was furious at the timing of the latest unfair criticism directed at his team, and he cited a few facts: Canberra's financial position was 'probably the best it's ever been', far better than many NRL clubs because of its responsible fiscal management; three major sponsors had recently been locked in for three years; the emergence of lucrative, unvetted third-party sponsorships in the big clubs threatened to widen the gap between the rich and the others; and, of genuine significance, the Canberra Raiders were the NRL's second-most southern team, 'towards the border of AFL-ville' as Furner shrewdly observed, and as such it was a vital, strategic outpost for Rugby League in the 'Game of Thrones' being aggressively contested by the various football codes in Australia.

And yet the Sydney 'knives' were still out for Canberra, to use Furner's word again, just as they had been on several occasions in the past stretching right back to 1983. Nothing had changed. The players were for a short time distracted and this probably factored into the results of the first two competition round, two losses to top-drawer opponents, the Sea Eagles and the Storm. The third game, at home to the Newcastle Knights, showed the side that when playing to their ability they were not only capable of winning, but winning in style. In front of a hefty crowd of over 13,000 and utilising the predictable pun of the *Canberra Times*' headline, the Raiders put the 'Knights to the sword', defeating an Andrew Johns–led Newcastle 48–18. This was a 68-point turnaround on the previous year's record-breaking loss to Newcastle in the corresponding game at Bruce in 2006. A year on, with Johns getting closer to the end of a wonderful career, he and his teammates were run ragged by youth and enthusiasm seamlessly interwoven. Three 20-year-olds in green stole the show: fullback William

Zillman and the halves combination of Michael Dobson and Todd Carney. Zillman scored three tries in an exhilarating display.

In getting to the halfway point of the year at six wins and six losses, good for eighth place, the Raiders had already consigned the pre-season prediction of the Sydney pundits to the rubbish bin. Confidence was on the increase when quality recruit Nigel Plum played his first game in Raider colours in round thirteen—another thumping win, 38–10, this time over the Eels, reversing almost exactly the 38–6 defeat the Eels had inflicted on the Raiders at Parramatta in round four. These two sharply contrasting results epitomised a season of 'what might have been'.

The young Raiders blew hot and cold all year. 'Cold' was easily identified in defeats such as the one at Manly in round eight when the Raiders at one stage led by twelve, only to concede 40 points in the second half to lose 46–30. The Green Machine could score points; the problem was stopping them. Inexperience, injuries and 'saloon-door' defence all played their part in a spate of second-half fade-outs. A likely top-eight finish collapsed into an unrepresentative fourteenth place, one win out of eleventh but not enough to eradicate the jibes coming out of Sydney. At year's end, ABC Radio's Tim Gavel was of the opinion that the team had 'made us proud', given they started as wooden-spoon favourites. However, there is no way that such a soft, albeit well-intentioned assessment would have satisfied either the coach, players or staff. There had been moments of brilliance, games of brilliance, yet promise had not been converted into a credible number of season wins.

Hot and cold performances aside, there were two other matters in the 2007 season that sent shivers through the Raiders camp and they were separated by barely a week in May. The first was a short, cautionary column in the *Canberra Times*, a warning to Raiders management 'to keep the vultures away and maintain this team for the next two to three years. Big clubs will come calling with big dollars but they must keep the faith.' Retention of the 'young guns' was essential. The second matter concerned one of the best of the younger Raider players, a target already identified by the birds of prey in other clubs.

Twenty-one-year-old halfback Todd Carney was proving to be a disciplinarian's worst nightmare. The Raiders had done an excellent job rescuing the career of Queenslander Neville Costigan after he had been sacked by the Broncos for alcohol-related incidents—so successful that Costigan played State of Origin in 2007—but Carney was proving to be a far more complex proposition. In late May he was suspended indefinitely by the Raiders when he and teammate Steve Irwin were involved in a police pursuit on a drunken Friday night. Carney already had drink-driving and reckless driving convictions in 2006.

There was no doubt in anyone's mind that Carney was a gifted individual capable of playing representative football in the future—he was possibly a champion in the making—but he presented the club with a major problem. His behaviour had to be censured. The question was how severe the punishment should be.

Raiders Chairman John McIntyre went public on the matter, supported by ACT Chief Minister Jon Stanhope. He indicated that the club's preference was to try to help the player, try to 'redeem' him rather than condemn him and move him on. The motivation was sound enough, and in June Carney said all the right things in a *Canberra Times* article. He did not 'want to be the person that sits at the end of a pub saying "I could have been . . ."'. Carney's innocent school-boy looks belied a troubled individual. His behaviour would soon be called into question again. Worse than that, his unsteady presence de-stabilised the playing group.

How the new season, 2008, might unfold was anyone's guess. There were numerous 'what ifs'. The one irrefutable fact was that a young side of demonstrated ability was now a year older, a year more experienced. It had been strengthened with useful buys in the off-season including Glenn Buttriss and 2007 junior Kangaroo Joel Thompson, while Joel Monaghan was back in the club after a stint at the Roosters. He had returned with a better understanding of his strengths as a footballer and was ready to produce his best season so far.

In the years that had followed the rupture of Super League, as the Raiders adjusted to life without an array of superstars, the last competitive rounds of each season's competition lapsed too often into poor form and bad results. Enthusiasm and a 'them versus us' mentality could only get you so far. The most realistic and achievable aim was a middle-of-the-table, respectable finish. At the halfway point of thirteen rounds, the 2008 year looked to be headed in the same direction. The team had managed four wins to go with seven losses and a couple of byes.

Any prospect of a better performance than that in the first part of the year was subverted by yet another coaching drama.

In an interview he had with the *Canberra Times* shortly before round one of the 2008 premiership, Neil Henry spoke of wanting more consistency from his squad and, when asked about his name being mentioned as a successor to Wayne Bennett at the Broncos, he replied: 'The fact is I've got a job to do here.' It seemed straightforward. However, on 31 March, a bare three weeks after the interview, during the round three weekend of the new season, Henry announced he would quit the Raiders at the end of the year and return to North Queensland as head coach for 2009. The incensed reaction of Raider Chairman John McIntyre, unaware of the exact details of Henry's contract, was that the board would not allow the coach to renege until the last year of his contract, the 2010 season. Henry then cited a get-out clause he had apparently negotiated in his agreement, which he intended to exercise. The board had no choice but to accede to his wishes.

General Manager Don Furner tried to look at the 'positive side . . . we know that we picked the right guy because he is in demand' but this response failed to placate the club's chairman, and it was no consolation at all for the fans. Worse still, a number of the Raider players were also caught by surprise so that when Henry stated that he had been 'honest and up-front with the club here', he was being less than forthright. The captain and players had cause for complaint, especially Todd Carney, who on 14 March sought Henry's assurance that he would remain in Canberra for the next two seasons before he went ahead and signed a new contract with the club. When Carney found out about Henry's suddenly altered plans, he said it was 'a kick in the face'.

A special moment for Jason Croker (Raider #124) as he departs Canberra Stadium for the final time as a player in 2006 with his two children, Lily and Jesse. Croker is the first Raider to play 300 matches, retiring after 318 appearances. *(Canberra Times)*

A pointscoring machine! Jarrod Croker (Raider #284) holds the club records for the most points, goals and tries. *(Canberra Times)*

Luke Davico (Raider #163) played 176 matches for the club, spanning 1994–2004. *(NRL Imagery)*

Simon Woolford (Raider #165) played 233 matches for the Raiders and captained the club between 2001 and 2005. *(NRL Imagery)*

Lesley Vainikolo (Raider #196) scored 35 tries in 69 matches for the Raiders. 'The Volcano' also represented New Zealand during his time with the club. *(NRL Imagery)*

Alan Tongue (Raider #211) played 220 NRL matches for the club and captained the side from 2007 to 2011. *(NRL Imagery)*

Simon Woolford passes a ball during the first-ever premiership match to be played in snow—against the Wests Tigers in 2000. Naturally, the classic shot was the club's Christmas card that year. *(NRL Imagery)*

David Furner carries the ball in 'the Snow Game' at Bruce Stadium against the Wests Tigers in 2000. *(NRL Imagery)*

Local junior Joel Monaghan (Raider #224) played 129 matches, scoring 69 tries for the club in two stints between 2001 and 2010. *(NRL Imagery)*

Queanbeyan product Terry Campese (Raider #242) played 139 matches for the Raiders. He also captained the club between 2012 and 2014. *(NRL Imagery)*

Canberra junior Troy Thompson (Raider #229) played 156 matches for the Raiders over ten seasons. *(NRL Imagery)*

Clinton Schifcofske (Raider #219) played 139 matches for the club and scored 1054 points. He also captained the team in 2006 in his final season with the Raiders. *(NRL Imagery)*

The *Canberra Times* special poster ahead of the 1989 Grand Final against the Balmain Tigers. It is now a true collector's item. *(Canberra Times)*

Mal Meninga featured in the *Canberra Times* poster ahead of his last match for the club, the 1994 Grand Final against the Canterbury–Bankstown Bulldogs. *(Canberra Times)*

'Catch a Tiger' by the tail. The *Canberra Times*' David Pope cartoon confidently (if incorrectly!) anticipates the Raiders' 2010 semifinal against the Wests Tigers. *(Canberra Times)*

Surf's up! Victor the Viking riding a shark as a surfboard, featured in the David Pope cartoon in the *Canberra Times* ahead of the Raiders' 2012 home final against the Cronulla–Sutherland Sharks. *(Canberra Times)*

One of the earliest incarnations of Victor the Viking. The man behind the mask,Tony Wood, is a life member of the Raiders. *(Canberra Times)*

During the late 1990s Victor the Viking went through a series of transformations which saw him in several new outfits and designs. The wonderful onfield performances never varied. *(NRL Imagery)*

Today's Victor the Viking alongside his sister Velda, who was introduced to Raider fans in the 2018 season. *(Canberra Raiders)*

Matt Elliott coached the Raiders from 2000 to 2006. He was always on the lookout for new techniques. *(NRL Imagery)*

Neil Henry coached the Raiders from 2007 to 2008. He valued hard work and discipline and was the Dally M Coach of the Year in 2008. *(NRL Imagery)*

David Furner coached the Raiders between 2009 and 2013. A club legend, Furner was a coach who paid attention to detail and worked hard to get the best out of his players. *(NRL Imagery)*

Ricky Stuart has coached the Raiders from 2014 to the present. A passionate clubman, he strives to instil club values into the playing group. For Stuart, what has gone before matters. *(NRL Imagery)*

A tearful Ruben Wiki farewells the Canberra fans in 2005. After playing 225 matches for the Raiders, Wiki joined the Auckland Warriors, where he eventually became a 300-game player. *(NRL Imagery)*

Alan Tongue with some of his legion of fans after his 200th NRL match in 2010 at Canberra Stadium. *(NRL Imagery)*

Josh Miller (Raider #243) played 113 matches for the Raiders. A passionate clubman, he always gave his best. Miller is a two-time winner of the Meninga Medal. *(NRL Imagery)*

Dane Tilse (Raider #263) played 201 matches for the club. Tilse's father, Michael Tilse (Raider #16), was one of the 1982 Pioneer Raiders. *(NRL Imagery)*

David Shillington (Raider #282) played 131 matches for the club and would go on to represent Queensland and Australia during his time in green. Shillington won the Meninga Medal in 2010. *(NRL Imagery)*

Jarrod Croker (Raider #284) has captained the Raiders since 2015. He was awarded the Meninga Medal in 2014. *(NRL Imagery)*

Shaun Fensom (Raider #287) played 139 matches for the club. He is a two-time Meninga Medal winner and also captained the 2008 Toyota Cup (under-20s) team to a grand final win. *(NRL Imagery)*

Josh Papalii (Raider #300) is a two-time Meninga Medal winner who has represented Queensland and Australia during his career with the Raiders. *(NRL Imagery)*

Sia Soliola (Raider #326) won the Meninga Medal in 2015 and Clubman of the Year in 2016. He is also an active community ambassador for the club. *(NRL Imagery)*

Jack Wighton (Raider #303), a product of the Raiders junior representative system, has represented New South Wales during his time at the club. *(NRL Imagery)*

The 'Super Macs', Andrew McFadden (Raider #190) and Mark McLinden (Raider #195), were the Raiders' dynamic duo during the late 1990s and early 2000s. *(Canberra Times)*

The Fab Four: the Raiders' English recruits, John Bateman (Raider #354), Elliott Whitehead (Raider #333), Josh Hodgson (Raider #325) and Ryan Sutton (Raider #358) re-create the famous Beatles *Abbey Road* album cover for the *Canberra Times* ahead of the 2019 season. *(Canberra Times)*

The Raiders' own 'Superman', Shaun Fensom, poses for a photo for the *Canberra Times* football guide ahead of the 2016 season. *(Canberra Times)*

Terry Campese surrounded by young fans in a bathtub full of Raiders Lime Milk as the club helps promote the relaunch of the Canberra Milk favourite in 2013. *(Canberra Times)*

The Canberra Raiders' victorious 2005 S.G. Ball team. The Raiders have a proud history of developing junior talent. *(Canberra Raiders)*

The Raiders celebrating the 2003 Premier League title. The team defeated St Mary's–Penrith 31–6 in the grand final at ANZ Stadium. *(NRL Imagery)*

The Raiders celebrate after winning the inaugural Toyota Cup (under-20s) competition in 2008. A number of players went on to play in the NRL. *(NRL Imagery)*

The Raiders have looked to the future by entering a team in the Tarsha Gale Cup (girls under-18s) competition. Krystyana Haridemos in action during the 2019 season. *(Canberra Raiders)*

The Canberra Raiders launched a global sponsorship in 2012 with Chinese telecommunications company Huawei. Raiders players David Shillington, Terry Campese, Tom Learoyd-Lahrs and Brett White with Huawei Australia representatives Lisa Connors, Jeremy Mitchell, John Lord and David Wang. *(Canberra Raiders)*

In 2019, Huawei extended its Raiders sponsorship for a further two seasons to 10 years with the club. Raiders representatives Ricky Stuart, Josh Hodgson, Jarrod Croker, Sam Williams and Don Furner with Huawei representatives John Lord and Hudson Liu. *(Canberra Raiders)*

The first inductees into the Raiders Hall of Fame, named at the 2019 season launch. *(NRL Imagery)*

The Raiders 'Forever Green' program allows past first-grade players to remain connected to the club. Each season the club holds a special match day to honour the players who have worn the green jersey. *(Canberra Raiders)*

Sia Soliola (Raider #326) epitomises what it means to be an active part of the community. Here he signs a junior member's football while promoting the club's charity work through the Cure Angelman Syndrome writing on his arm. *(Canberra Raiders)*

The Raiders' 'Autograph Alley' allows Green Machine fans to get a special behind-the-scenes opportunity before Raiders home matches. Fans are able to get autographs and photos with their favourite players. *(Canberra Raiders)*

Well-versed in setbacks but tired of dealing with them, the club took instant action to fill the breach. Assistant coach and Raider blue-blood Dave Furner, the Kangaroo coach's son and the general manager's brother, was announced as the new head coach in 2009.

If the rest of the team took heart from the Carney signing, they were not able to enjoy the feeling for long. On 20 July, Carney and fullback Bronx Goodwin were the subject of a number of allegations concerning a drunken night, one more drunken night, this time at the All Bar Nun pub in O'Connor. The club had reached its tipping point. Despite Carney's front-page *Canberra Times mea culpa* that began 'Look I am not an angel', the Raiders board sacked him on 7 August. They could no longer justify having someone on their books, no matter how rich his talent, who had become a serial offender.

So there the team stood at the halfway mark in 2008, with a mediocre record below 50 per cent for the year to date, coaching turmoil still thick in the air and Todd Carney's misbehaviour playing out all around them—when, on the field, it was as if a switch got turned on. The season came to life. The thirteen rounds of the second half of the year produced nine wins and four losses, enough to take the team into the semis in sixth place.

The Raiders squad found something special, something galvanising as individuals and as a team, handing out a series of thrashings that electrified their fans, delighted the coaching staff and perplexed their critics. The scale of the wins tells its own story: a 34–16 victory over the Broncos (at home), 58–16 versus Bulldogs (away), 34–12 versus Roosters (home), 46–4 versus Titans (home), 74–12 versus Panthers (home), 38–18 versus Knights (home), 40–25 versus Rabbitohs (away) and 52–33 versus Bulldogs (home). The football was breathtaking Raider football, Rugby League at its entertaining best. It recalled the great Raider teams of the late '80s and '90s in virtually all facets. Tries were scored from all parts of the field.

Media attention increased enormously, week after week scorelines blew out and records were broken. The first win over the Bulldogs was the Raiders' biggest ever against a rival who had always troubled them. In the aftermath of the Roosters game their coach, Brad Fittler, suggested that the Raiders were genuine finals contenders: 'they haven't got the names, they just work really hard'. In August, the team reacted to the Carney sacking by pulverising Penrith in a game that had Sydney journalist Paul Kent full of admiration and Panthers coach Matt Elliott, who had not once beaten his old team in the two years since leaving them, mock-hanging himself with his tie after suffering through the carnage. Terry Campese's 36-point contribution to the club record score was three times that of the entire Penrith team. The Newcastle match that followed produced the headline: 'Too easy Campese—Raiders' young gun blows apart the Knights'.

Nephew of the legendary David Campese, Terry was playing the football of his life, brilliantly supported by the likes of David Milne, Joel Monaghan and Colin Best. The forwards, too, were putting the stops on their better-known opponents led by props Troy Thompson and Dane Tilse, back-rowers Trevor Thurling and Joe Picker, and the indomitable captain Alan Tongue.

Paul Kent in the *Daily Telegraph*, in a mid-August article just after the Penrith game headed 'Capital punishment', opened with the sentence, 'No team does more with so little than the Canberra Raiders'. Describing the men in green as 'the shining hope of the competition', Kent summarised with appropriate flair the latest version of open, attractive Raider football:

> They are the antidote for stale cookie-cutter game plans that are in vogue in the NRL today. Game plans where teams drive out of dummy half one play after the other, forever and ever until they finally grind their way into the opposition's 20m and polish off the set with a kick to the corner. And if they don't score they get to do it all again. Wonderful. These game plans can bore the spots off grandma and are why the Raiders found a new legion of fans with yesterday's 74–12 win over the Penrith Panthers. They are the best team to watch in the NRL.

Matt Johns bought into the hype with his own brand of wry humour:

> Suddenly Canberra's footballers were answering more questions than its politicians. Not since the glory days of the early '90s had the Raiders enjoyed such attention. They were the quiet, nerdy little kid in the corner of the classroom that, all of a sudden, every girl wanted to kiss at the disco.

More thoughtful analyses, and Will Swanton produced one in the *Sun-Herald* entitled 'Culture Club', dug a little deeper, concluding that the Raiders were in the process of embedding a robust culture of core values and beliefs that could last. Egos *had* been left at the door. Assistant coach Dave Furner, about to step into the top job in 2009, was spot on when he praised 'a really tight-knit group'. He understood the club's historic strengths and weaknesses from the inside, and he gave his assessment of the way forward:

> No egos. The feeling at the Raiders has always been one of striving for success, and working hard to get that success. We've got a proud history for a young club. We've had some great players. The other thing I would say is this: it's a mateship club.

The praise and prizes kept coming. On 7 September, the last weekend of the competition rounds, the *Sun-Herald* declared the Raiders to be 'the team of the year' (not too shabby for a team that started as wooden-spoon favourites) and nominated Terry Campese as a star who demanded greater recognition. But then, so did a number of others in the team. This occurred at the prestigious Dally M awards ceremony in Sydney when the Raider contingent headed back to Canberra with four awards in their satchel: Alan Tongue as both Captain and Lock of the Year, Colin Best as Winger of the Year and, with more than a touch of irony, Neil Henry as Coach of the Year. The Raiders were the surprise celebrities of the night, with General Manager Don Furner speaking for all when he said:

'I couldn't believe it when our table was up the front of the room. Normally, we are put down the back.'

The constant highs of the first fortnight in September came to an abrupt halt when the Raiders played the Cronulla Sharks in a first semifinal that many felt was a stepping-stone to bigger games for the Green Machine. A committed Sharks team, always at their best in front of the Shire hordes, had other ideas, winning untroubled by 36–10, the Raiders' seventh consecutive post-season defeat stretching back to the year 2000. And when the New Zealand Warriors upset the Melbourne Storm, a precocious year of apparent over-achievement for the men in green was suddenly over. How did this happen? Was it the side's defensive deficiencies surfacing at the worst possible time? Cronulla's home-field pride? Was it the weight of injuries finally felt at the business end? Perhaps it was a mix of all three that resulted in an unexpectedly lop-sided scoreline.

A few noteworthy consolations did help the deflated Raider camp at this time. Four members of the team—Alan Tongue, Joel Monaghan, Joe Picker and Terry Campese—were selected for a prime minister's side that beat Papua New Guinea 56–30 at the end of September. In addition, and hopefully an omen for the future, the brilliant Raiders' under-20s side claimed the inaugural Toyota Cup with a tense but convincing 28–20 extra-time win over the Broncos. Team members included Josh Dugan, Jarrod Croker, Travis Waddell, Jarrad Kennedy, Joel Thompson and skipper Shaun Fensom (a player with an engine that had him being tipped as the club's next Alan Tongue).

In any normal year the flowering of under-20s talent would have been cause for celebration. Yet even in such a productive year for a club desperate to re-visit the achievements of the past, the scourge of players lost continued unabated. Colin Best was off to South Sydney, Neville Costigan and Mick Weyman to the Dragons, Ryan Hinchcliffe to the high-flying Storm, William Zillman to the Titans, Michael Dobson to English club Hull KR, and Lincoln Withers and Marshall Chalk to Celtic Crusaders. The contracts of Todd Carney and Bronx Goodwin were terminated for disciplinary reasons. While the club did well to pick up Bronson Harrison, Stuart Flanagan, Josh McCrone and David Shillington in the off-season, the annual tidal turn-over was hard for everyone to handle, especially the Raiders' legion of green-eyed fans craving some player stability.

The forces at work in Rugby League, as powerful and as prevalent as ever, continued to make life hard for the less fashionable clubs.

Return of a favourite son, 2009–13

When Neil Henry made the decision to head to Townsville in early 2008, and his assistant coach Dave Furner was appointed within days to take over the Raiders' head coaching position in 2009, the disappointment of Henry's exit was soon overridden by thoughts about the future. For Board Chairman John McIntyre, heir apparent to his father Les's role as venerable patriarch at the club, the appointment was a 'no brainer'.

> He is one of our own. My wife Anita even used to change his nappies. In terms of bloodlines, David Furner is the Danehill of coaching. His father [Don] was the Australian coach in 1986 when the Kangaroos were undefeated on their tour of England.

For the 38-year-old appointee it was 'a dream come true' and, when the 2008 year took flight as the Raiders accelerated into the semifinals, Furner must have felt the stars were lining up nicely for him. Despite being a first-time head coach, he had inked in a four-year contract with the club. In personal and career terms, it surely felt like it was 1994 all over again.

The analogy is not too far-fetched. Just as Super League reared its ugly head for the first time in the year following the Raiders' third premiership, so Dave Furner's world of premiership Rugby League in 2009 was about to be buffeted by events, forces and pressures he would find difficult to harness. As hard as he tried to arrest the pattern of his team's wild inconsistency in his five years at the helm, 2009–13, he finally could not do so.

The inconsistency had started in the middle of the Matt Elliott years as coach. For a full decade, 2004–13, the team had roller-coastered between making the semifinals in the 'even' years and missing out, sometimes badly, in the 'odd' years. By chance, Furner began his head-coaching life in an 'odd' year, 2009.

The pattern of inconsistency suggested a bad season but so too did the bookmakers, who had the Raiders pencilled in at 40–1 to win the comp, equal longest price with the Sharks and Knights. In contrast, Furner felt he had good reason to be excited. After all, he was now part of a proud record as one of eight of the NRL's sixteen first-grade coaches who were either former Raider players or coaches. He would also have known that every representative team coach in the 2008 season had plied his trade for the Green Machine at some stage in the previous twenty years. As the *Canberra Times NRL Guide* pointed out in the pre-season: 'Some of those [coaches] Furner played with, and others he was coached by and still others he watched while he was a teenager dreaming of one day playing for Canberra.'

Noting the tireless effort and long hours Furner was racking up in his first months in the new job, John McIntyre was convinced the club had made the right choice:

> . . . just talking to the fella you can tell he was born to be a leader and a teacher. That's an instinctive thing and those instincts of mine have been pretty accurate over a long period of time . . . His association goes back for virtually the whole life of the Raiders.

Furner strengthened the concerted push to appoint locals that had begun in Matt Elliott's last year or two. The new coach hired Quentin Pongia, his 1994 Kiwi teammate, to be the club's new rehab officer, Cappy McFadden as under-20s coach and Matt Ford, who had also come through the Raiders system, as the club's strength and conditioning expert. Ian Millward, the other assistant coach, was a Wollongong boy who had accumulated extensive experience after coaching stints in England with three Super League clubs.

Furner was contented with the mix of new and old, and the balance of the playing squad he had inherited, with its solid new additions. A number of young bush kids who had played brilliantly for the Green Machine the previous year complemented a few of the older heads. All of them had the utmost respect for the team's 28-year-old captain, Alan Tongue. His reputation as a quality leader on and off the field had spread beyond the nation's capital, a number of Sydney's hardened journalists producing articles on Canberra's skipper full of the highest praise. For one of the scribes, Tonguey's character was 'an asset you just can't buy', while another wrote that 'gutsiness trails Tongue like slime trails a slug'.

The coach was full of expectation for the year in front of him. He knew he had a firm foundation in his resilient captain, he knew he had a squad capable of at least making the play-offs, he knew he had the ear of club legend Mal Meninga (who was about to have his bronze statue built at Bruce Stadium) whenever he needed a chat, he knew he had a generous contract, and he knew he had a front office which would do its utmost to help him achieve his goals. John McIntyre, a family friend from way back, was convinced already; the CEO, his older brother Don, needed no convincing of his drive and commitment. With luck, the sibling relationship would never hinder the contribution made by either of them.

The first year did not go as planned. It was a bruising initiation that started on the wrong foot and never really recovered. In the middle of February, a month before the season's first round, the Raider community got word that the club's founding father, Les McIntyre, had died peacefully in Queanbeyan aged 93. Tributes poured in. For ACT Chief Minister Jon Stanhope he was a lovely fellow. 'The Raiders,' Stanhope observed, 'are an integral part of our everyday life, they are now part and parcel of this city's heritage and we can thank Les McIntyre for that.'

Les's son John knew better than anyone the extraordinary dimensions of his father's legacy: 'Canberra was a city without a soul,' he said, until his father's introduction of an unfashionable team from across the border which captured the imagination of everyone in Canberra and the region, along with their hearts.

Les had been many things in his life—deliverer of newspapers, motor mechanic, projectionist at Queanbeyan's Star Theatre, bus driver and bookmaker. He loved a punt but, according to his son, he had three passions in life: fishing, family and football. He was able to integrate the last two for most of his life. First, with his beloved Queanbeyan Blues and, after that, his Blues and his Canberra Raiders. Near the end, he was still in the habit of watching hours of Rugby League videos, especially the NRL Grand Finals of 1989, 1990 and 1994, matches with a common and compelling theme.

The Monaro region grieved with Les's wife of 69 years, Elsie, and everyone agreed with Mal Meninga's well-chosen words of remembrance: 'He was a man I hugely respected and one of those people who you hung on every word he said because he was a world of wisdom.' In his eulogy at the funeral present-day Chairman of the Raiders Board Allan Hawke stated that Les was 'the doyen of Rugby League administrators in NSW Country Rugby League', recognised by his induction into the ACT Hall of Fame in 1996, his life membership of seven Rugby League organisations, his peerless status as the Raiders' player number one in the club's all-time list of well over 300, and his Order of Australia medal in 2008.

In the year of Les's death, his name was embroidered onto the club jerseys for the entire season. Unfortunately, it did not help the cause. The Raiders lost seven of their first nine games and turned at the season's halfway mark with a meagre four wins against seven losses. There had been one or two promising games—an away win at Shark Park and a decisive 38–12 victory over a beefy Warriors side—but these were the exceptions.

In mid-June when David Jean assessed the first half of the season in the *Canberra Times*, he pointed out that in 2008 the statistics for the team had been identical at the same stage. Could the Raiders again come home with a wet sail on the back of more Terry Campese magic that, early in 2009, had been good enough to get him picked for New South Wales in State of Origin One?

No. Lightning did not strike twice. The side improved, but not enough to finish any better than thirteenth. Glass half-full fans were heartened by the number of youngsters blooded into first-grade football during the year, among them a spiky-haired Jarrod Croker, Travis Waddell and Josh Dugan (minus the tattoos of later years), who was described in one newspaper as 'a revelation'. Fine debuts in the top grade by Shaun Fensom, Josh McCrone and Daniel Vidot reinforced belief in the policy of developing home-grown talent, despite the NRL under David Gallop continuing with its dogmatic insistence on not rewarding clubs that had patiently attended to the development of their in-house lower graders and juniors.

There was some light ahead. Three games in the second half of the season were indicators of a brighter future: a round sixteen win over the Melbourne Storm that broke a seven-year, fourteen-game drought; a huge and surprising 10-try, 56–0 romp against the Broncos at home and, as sweet as both of these, a round 23 game against competition front-runners St George in front of 19,350 screaming, green-eyed fans. The 'enigmatic' Raiders team all showed up to inflict a convincing 24–12 loss on the Dragons. A decade-long stranglehold on the Saints continued. Green Machine supporters at the game recall a really physical encounter dominated by unflinching defence. There were a number of fierce confrontations, none better than Josh Miller's hit of the season on former Raider, Michael Weyman, a (then) legal shoulder charge that, according to the *Canberra Times*, 'knocked Weyman senseless'.

Miller deservedly shared the Mal Meninga medal with Josh Dugan in 2009, having been the inaugural Fred Daly Clubman of the Year in 2004, his rookie year. Throughout the testing eight years that he played for the club (until he moved on in 2012) the unsung Miller gave his all every time he ran out in the green jersey. The fans loved him for it.

They were not so keen on an aspect of Rugby League that was brought to the public's attention in early February 2009 and spread like a contagion as the year progressed: the issue of unacceptable player behaviour off the field. The Raiders were not immune to the problem. Todd Carney's persistent breaches of discipline, which led to his sacking by the club in August 2008, resulted in the Raiders' coaching staff and officials being on constant red alert for any repeat performances. On 2 February, the Melbourne Storm sacked Arana Taumata over a fight. The next day the Raiders stood down their promising second-rower Joel Thompson after he was charged with assaulting his girlfriend, a charge for which he was subsequently acquitted. The rest of the year remained steeped in controversy as club after club had players arrested and charged with a distressing catalogue of serious offences, including a sexual assault charge brought against Manly's Brett Stewart—infuriating the NRL, which had made him the game's face in their expensive 2009 advertising campaign. Stewart, too, was subsequently acquitted.

The exposure of players misbehaving, and often much worse, was brought into clear focus. All sixteen clubs, along with the NRL itself, faced another challenge: how to respond effectively to the problem with an ethical code and policy structure that had clout and would stand up to legal challenge. The Raiders were determined to be one of the leaders in stamping out this blight on the game, pushed along by the *Canberra Times*, which demanded that the NRL 'dump its Neanderthals'.

When Dave Furner contemplated the 2010 year in front of him he had much to think about: the disappointing results of his first year as a head coach, the number of matches lost in close finishes, the lack of consistency from his big pack of forwards, the approach he would adopt towards a squad he knew had ability yet had under-performed, and the pressing issue of player misbehaviour that seemed unlikely to be resolved to anyone's satisfaction.

For his second season in charge, Furner decided basically to stay with the squad he already had, a brave call under the circumstances, picking up only Danny Galea from the Tigers and Reece Robinson from

South Sydney while absorbing the serious losses of Phil Graham, off to the Roosters, and both Adrian Purtell and Nigel Plum, who had joined Matt Elliott's Panthers. Furner committed the club to a youth policy, banking on the fact that in the previous year further invaluable experience had been gained.

In the *Sun-Herald* Phil Gould was his predictable self when he tipped the Raiders to finish fifteenth, yet the feeling in the team's camp was quite different. A stable playing group sharing a common respect for the coach's efforts to achieve better results was probably the reason why the *Canberra Times* in the pre-season noticed 'fresh feelings of optimism and expectation floating around at Raiders HQ. The club has identified the key players it thinks can take it to premiership glory within five years and signed them to long-term deals.'

Steve Jancetic in the *Daily Telegraph* was impressed by the side's maturing 'young brigade', writing an article in mid-April where he talked up 'the Green Machine Mark II'. Six teammates from the 2008 premiership-winning Toyota Cup side were featured: Jarrod Croker, Dan Vidot, Shaun Fensom, Joel Thompson, Travis Waddell and Josh Dugan. CEO Don Furner was happy to be quoted on the approach that he and his coach had adopted towards the club's 'good batch of young kids' who gave the club 'our best shot at winning a grand final'. The trick, he said, was to 'keep them all together and keep them happy'. The 'happy' part was reasonably straightforward. It was holding on to the players that remained the ever-present problem. Jancetic reported that the Roosters were already sniffing about after Josh Dugan, cheque book in hand.

The new season began. While a round one loss away to (of all teams) Matt Elliott's Panthers was far from the ideal start, this result was balanced by the 22–14 win over the Broncos at Bruce in front of more than 14,000 exuberant supporters. Not about to get carried away, the coach continued to search for the right combinations to obtain greater consistency. Like the year before, it was proving to be an elusive commodity. By the end of seven rounds the Raiders had only two wins to show for their efforts, dropping them into second last place, and by the end of seventeen of 26 rounds the picture was only marginally better. Yes, Joel Thompson was making a good fist of the centre position in the absence of an injured Joel Monaghan, and Alan Tongue, the ultimate team man to match all his other personal and playing attributes, had shifted to a strategic, play-making role at hooker to give his team more ruck speed and organisation. This allowed his clone, Shaun Fensom, to play at lock and affect his routine 50-plus tackles a game. Nonetheless, wins were still hard to find.

In getting to the end of seventeen rounds, the Raiders lost four games in a row from round fourteen to round seventeen, two away defeats followed by two at home. Hard-fought games, all of them, but losses. There was no quit in the group. The players kept working hard, united in the belief that with a bit of luck here and there tight losses could turn into wins. They were aware that, in only the second year of his contract, their hard-working coach was coming under increasing pressure for the team's performances. The tide needed to turn, and it did.

Group solidarity and dedication paid off. In the final nine rounds of the year, Green Machine Mark II churned out eight wins, starting with a confidence-boosting 24–22 victory over the Manly Sea Eagles at Brookie Oval, always a difficult away game. Halves Josh McCrone and Terry Campese ran the engine smoothly and, in the aftermath of a game he recognised as a team turning point, Josh Dugan signed a new contract to stay in his home of Canberra. Momentum built, culminating in resounding wins in the final four rounds against formidable opponents: 28–14 over the Bulldogs at ANZ; 32–16 against the high-flying Dragons (again!) at home; a dominant performance against an unhappy North Queensland, 48–14, also at home; and then—arguably best of all, especially with an unlikely spot in the semifinals possible—an 18–16 victory at Suncorp against the Broncos in front of a committed 'Queenslander' crowd of 38,872. The grinding win booked a certain place for the team in post-season play.

Green Machine Mark II had concluded the minor premiership rounds in seventh place after five wins in a row, matching the same feat achieved by the 1989 and 1990 sides (the '94 team produced eight successive wins). Could history repeat itself?

Another timely boost to the team's confidence occurred at this time when exciting Cronulla youngster Blake Ferguson exercised a get-out clause in his contract to sign a two-year contract with the Raiders. The clause stated that he could move on if Ricky Stuart was no longer the Sharks' coach. The Raiders champion had left the Shire club mid-season. Ferguson was widely regarded as one of the best young wingers going around and he was an outstanding addition to a backline already bristling with youth and speed. Asked why he had decided to head to the nation's capital, he replied that he liked the look of the Raiders' pack of forwards and, particularly, the team's free-wheeling style of play, Raider football. As he put it: 'When Campese is on they are virtually unstoppable.'

The considerable number of Raider fans out there who did not regard themselves as rusted on had begun to drift back to Bruce Stadium in bigger numbers as the year progressed. Quality entertainment was again on offer and Super League was dead and buried. An aggressive membership campaign was also producing results, with almost 6,000 signed up late in the year and more expected to get on board in the wake of a revitalised campaign.

The welcome reappearance of a style of play that recalled the past, orchestrated by Terry Campese when fit and aided and abetted by the Toyota Cup graduates of 2008, was a boon for everyone involved. John-Paul Maloney's 'Saturday Serve' page in the *Canberra Times* in late August said it all: it's 'great to be green' again. Dennis Richardson, secretary of the Department of Foreign Affairs and Trade, sent out an email in September to all his staff in Canberra and overseas drawing their attention to the fact that the Raiders flag was about to be flown atop the DFAT building in Barton. He was, as they say, pinning his colours to the mast, and he was not alone.

A real buzz of anticipation preceded the quarter-final against Penrith. Elliott's team had won the right to host the game, which shaped as an attractive encounter. The build-up in Canberra and Queanbeyan brought back old times, with streamers and signs everywhere and the *Canberra Times* producing a green broadsheet page flooded with fan texts, the best of them coming from 'Tuggers Raider', who was obviously impressed by the Raiders' big forwards—hence his observation that the 'Mt Bashmore four will turn the black cats into kittens. Go Raiders!' The game, however, turned out to be much closer than Tuggers Raider thought. The Raiders did lead handily, 18–12, and probably would have won comfortably if a Terry Campese try, disallowed for obstruction, had received the green light. Instead, both sides dug in for the struggle. Penrith scored late and, if the Michael Gordon conversion had been successful, the teams would have gone to golden point. It missed, giving Furner's Raiders the right to host a semifinal against the Wests Tigers the following weekend.

During the second week of post-season play the Canberra and regional community really came alive. The *Canberra Times* got right into the spirit of things, adhering to an established tradition with a special souvenir edition of the paper featuring a full-page poster created by award-winning cartoonist David Pope. Readers were gifted a massive, buffed Victor the Viking tying a knot in the tail of an intimidated tiger. Given the Raiders' opponent, and the indelible memories of 21 years before, it was inevitable that the newspaper revisited the miracles of 1989 and 1990. Mark Webber was on the front page of the Thursday 16 September edition, resplendent in his Red Bull Grand Prix outfit. A self-confessed Raider tragic, the Queanbeyan product was five points clear in the Formula 1 title standings in mid-September. Nonetheless, he declared that he would make the time to get back home if the Raiders reached the grand final. Ball boy for the mighty Green Machine in 1990–91, Webber said that he had 'an extra keen interest' in the present group of players because their coach was 'a close family friend'.

On Friday the *Canberra Times* went looking for more puff pieces to remember, and who better to get people in the mood than the miracle-worker himself, Steve Jackson, always happy to 'dine out on the '89 clincher'. Now living in Mackay, the 44-year-old Jackson simply loved re-visiting the details of a magical year two decades before, though this time he wanted to link it closely to the present, and promote re-visiting the exciting present-day side, 'a team on the rise . . . starting to have self-belief and confidence, and matching it with their potential'. Aware that the Raiders were short-priced match favourites for the game, he warned about 'a Tiger ambush'. It 'scares me', he said, and no-one knew more about historic upsets and unlikely ambushes than Jacko.

Recent history said he was right to be worried. The Raiders had lost the last four games on the trot to the Tigers and, what's more, they had never beaten a Tiger team when Benji Marshall was in it. The Friday evening, semifinal clash proved to be no exception. It was close. There was nothing in it. Inspired by Marshall brilliance, the Tigers got out to a 24–12 lead at the 48-minute mark. Despite the huge setback of losing playmaker Terry Campese twenty minutes from full-time, the Raiders rallied behind a Trevor Thurling try and, with six minutes on the clock, the ever-reliable Alan Tongue swooped on a loose ball to score. Croker converted. A soft Tigers penalty goal a little earlier meant that, with time ticking away, the visitors clung to a 26–24 lead. High drama followed.

Four minutes from the end Joe Picker was hit high by the Tigers' Simon Dwyer and the referee had no hesitation in awarding a penalty to the home team. It was only 30 metres out, in front, and if kicked the teams were off to golden point.

Twenty-year-old Jarrod Croker, whose goal-kicking had made such an invaluable contribution to the team's late premiership bid, lined up a kick that his season 84 per cent record suggested was a gimme. In big footy matches, however, they never are. Sledged mercilessly by the Tiger players nearest to him, Croker missed a kick he would have made 9 times out of 10 with his eyes closed. The *Canberra Times* the next day had the headline, 'The Dream Slips Away', and the photograph of teammate Joel Monaghan consoling his mate etched the finish of this game into the memories of all Raiders supporters.

The narrow miss hushed a disbelieving crowd. Croker was inconsolable, trudging off the field with his head in his hands. He had been one of the Raiders' best all season but this fact, at this time, meant nothing. Club legend Mal Meninga tried to console him, his teammates tried, no-one more so than captain Alan Tongue, but all to no avail. This was one Croker would have to move on from, learn from. The next time he lined up a kick with, as he put it, the 'weight of Canberra' on his shoulders, he was determined to nail it.

It was a measure of the spirit rebuilding within the club that when Croker attended the post-match function at the Dickson 'Tradies' club he was greeted with a standing ovation from teammates and fans alike. Coach Dave Furner, disappointed by the loss naturally, felt the team had set a worthy benchmark for season 2011, one which would inspire his young charges to attain greater heights. He was sure the team had the ability to be a top-four side. They had shown it. The new year could not come soon enough for the coach, his staff and all Raider fans. A return to the halcyon days was so close you could just about touch it.

When Lee Gaskin in the *Canberra Times* produced a pre-season review of the Raiders for the 2011 season, he was understandably smitten by the late-season surge five months before. Like many of his readers, he was quite prepared to go beyond the standard clichés of hope and aspiration, and imagine a larger scenario, one that resembled the media reviews of twenty years before. For Gaskin, there was '. . . a genuine belief that this current crop of Raiders can do something special. Expectations are high on the back of a fantastic finish to the last season . . . On paper the Raiders tick all the boxes of a team which can challenge for the premiership.'

And why not? Coach Dave Furner had been quietly re-signed as coach until 2014; Josh Dugan was being hailed as 'hot property'; the centre pairing of Jarrod Croker and Joel Thompson, 'two emerging superstars' as they were described, was ready to lead the Raiders confidently into the next decade; and the 'Mean Machine', the massive pack, the League's biggest—including the four giants, Tom Learoyd-Lahrs, Dane Tilse, Dave Shillington (last year's Meninga medallist and Dally M Prop of the Year) and new recruit, Cooma-born Brett White—were ready to monster their opponents.

In addition to securing the services of Melbourne Storm's Brett White and Blake Ferguson late the year before, the Raiders had added Matt Orford from the Bradford Bulls to shore up depth in the halves, Mark Ioane (Warriors) and Nathan Massey (Bulldogs). Lee Gaskin's review declared White, Ferguson and Orford to be the Raiders' 'greatest recruiting trio in years'. Even the bookies, when putting up their opening NRL market for the season, cautiously pencilled the Green Machine in as 14–1 shots to win it all. They had the Raiders in the top eight, a legitimate dark horse for the comp.

Key members of the team found it hard to contain their enthusiasm. The skipper, for example, applauded long-overdue club stability that had given the players the opportunity to build combinations; Tommy Learoyd-Lahrs was adamant that 'the days of high-profile players shunning the capital are over'; and new recruit, 32-year-old Matt Orford, steeped in the stable cultures of Manly and Craig Bellamy's Melbourne Storm, looked forward to the Green Machine's 'tight-knit group' becoming 'a real force in the competition in years to come'.

The deficiency in this smorgasbord of optimistic forecasts is that virtually all of them overlooked two defining occurrences in September–October 2010, the implications of which would reverberate throughout the next year and after.

One was an instant of disastrous bad luck; the other a self-confessed 'moment of madness'. With twenty minutes to go in the Tigers semi-final, Terry Campese, the 'unstoppable' Campese, hit the ground in agony, having torn his anterior cruciate ligament. In the whole of the following season he was on the paddock a total of eight minutes. The effect of this blow, personally and for his team, was incalculable—nearly on a par with Ricky Stuart's ankle in 1993, the difference being that Stuart's rehab enabled him to return in 1994.

The moment of madness involved Joel Monaghan. Sometime during the brain deadness of the Raiders' 'Mad Monday' celebrations, a drunk Monaghan was photographed simulating a sex act. It was posted online, much to Monaghan's humiliation and the shame of the individual who sent out the photo. Monaghan hoped that he would not be judged solely on a 'stupid prank' but the issue escalated so quickly that he was soon after released by a deeply embarrassed club. He quit the NRL and left the country to play for an English club. To his credit, he carved out a successful new career, scoring many tries and creating headlines for all the right reasons.

The Mad Monday act was inexcusable. Equally, as Raider great Brett Mullins later commented, those of Monaghan's teammates who were present needed to share some of the blame. Another Raider champion, Brad Clyde, felt the need to respond to the incident more broadly: 'Dave [Furner] has to use it to galvanise the team together . . . But he's going to have to dig pretty deep into the culture to make sure this doesn't unsettle their preparation for 2011.'

As it turned out, the club could not absorb the blow to its evolving culture off the field, nor on it. The team could not compensate for the loss of two of its most important attacking players, both at the peak of their careers with State of Origin and Australian representation behind them. Add to this, the relocation to the Melbourne Storm of stalwart 'heart and soul' player Troy Thompson and the retirements of Scott Logan and Adam Mogg, and you have a situation that unnerved a few of the club's more discerning supporters.

The doomsayers were right. A season of unlimited potential crumbled into a disaster. It started badly with eight losses in the first nine games (the sole win coming in the first round) and it ended just as badly with eight losses in the final nine games. Some of the defeats crushed the spirit of fans and no doubt the coaching staff as well. Two that stood out over the rest were, firstly, the round four loss at home to the Titans when veteran Matt Orford managed to knock on his feed of the scrum, leading almost immediately to a Gold Coast try and conversion that tied the scores, followed by a Greg Bird golden-point field goal that gave the visitors an unlikely 23–22 victory. Matt Orford played six games for the Raiders and lost six. He was released from a two-year contract deal in August. The second game also unravelled in front of the Canberra faithful, a round thirteen clash with North Queensland. After encouraging wins against the Storm and Bulldogs, the Raiders led the Cowboys 22–0 when Terry Campese came off the bench in his return match. He lasted a grand total of 480 seconds before going down with a groin injury. Memories of Ricky Stuart in 1993. The crowd hushed, fearing the worst. They got it, with Campo out for the year, Josh Dugan later limping off injured, and the season on a fast track to confusion and dismay.

After a torturous 26 rounds, Lee Gaskin in his *Canberra Times* 'Year in Review' sifted through the ashes. The Raiders had finished second last, winning six games and losing eighteen, the club's worst result since 1982.

> Only the staunchest of Canberra Raiders fans will look back on 2011 with any fondness. Who can blame them after a season that started with whispers of 'premiership smokey' and turned into one of the darkest campaigns in the NRL club's history. A record-equalling losing streak, winning the fewest games since their inaugural year in 1982, Matt Orford's forgettable stint and the shock retirement of long-serving skipper Alan Tongue culminated in a bummer of a 30th anniversary.

Alan Tongue's retirement came as unwanted news, but as he pointed out in an emotional announcement in August he knew that, multiple broken noses aside, a few nagging injuries were affecting his performance. He was starting to let himself down and 'more importantly let my teammates down, and I don't want to do that'. Tonguey damaged the AC joint in his shoulder in the first-round win over the Sharks and it only added to a list of injuries he had tried to ignore. He didn't want to give it away; his 87-kilogram frame did. The tributes for his leadership, courage and moral example poured in. In tougher times for the club over the previous decade, Alan Tongue stood out like a beacon. He had grown up on the family farm in Tamworth and it showed. Humble, caring, team-oriented, a work ethic second to none, he was going to be sorely missed but his legacy would carry on. Don Furner had to find a place for him in the Raider system as soon as he could.

As if things could not get any worse, about a week after the Tongue press conference 'Raider Army' co-founder Lauren Clayton announced that her fan group, representing some of the Green Machine's most loyal supporters (numbering several hundred at one point), fans who always made their presence felt, had decided to disband. Clayton was adamant that the group, which started in 1993, was not abandoning the club in its hour of need. Rather, personal circumstances had changed. Many members were getting older, starting families and moving on.

Mercifully, the *annus horribilis*, arguably the club's worst-ever year because so much was expected, came to an end. Terry Campese pleaded with fans to keep the faith. This was not going to be easy, Campese.

The failings of 2011 were so visible that management had to act with urgency in order to themselves keep faith with the club's supporters. The highs of 2010 had boosted membership to an unprecedented 9,000-plus and the only way this figure would be maintained was if devoted fans were able to identify a clear pathway they could believe in. The coach knew that. 'We've got to build our reputation back here again in Canberra,' Dave Furner said. 'We've got to earn respect back here at home.'

In the off-season the club undertook what its CEO described as 'the most thorough High Performance Review in our history' to ensure that a 2011 never happened again. There were some sceptics initially, including the *Canberra Times*' John-Paul Maloney, who reported a 'deep cynicism' about the Raiders' review. Was it really independent? Would it deliver a constructive reform plan or just validate the status quo? For Maloney, the jury was out.

The process involved a three-day retreat in Bateman's Bay in September 2011 attended by the players, administrators and board members. It began with an honesty session where everything was laid bare. 'No-one sidestepped the issues,' sports consultant John Waser said. He was one of two people commissioned to conduct the review, along with former NRL coach Michael Hagan. Sixty recommendations were presented to the Raiders board in October 2011. They included the recruitment of an assistant coach whose skills matched the present squad; the positions of under-20s coach and recruitment manager split in two; an additional staff member hired for conditioning and rehab; the appointment of club legend Mal Meninga as ambassador and 'sounding board'; and improved linkages between the football and administrative departments.

Implementation of all the recommendations was not going to be cheap, and this brought the issue of the club not having a major sponsor into the spotlight. By his own admission, CEO Don Furner was someone who 'normally likes to keep things internal' but the universal disappointment with the previous season, he candidly admitted, meant that 'there was no use us hiding'. The actions of coach, board and administrators had to be transparent. The CEO said at the start of the new season that he was confident a major sponsor was close to coming on board and, at the end of March 2012, Chinese technology giant Huawei signed on to a multi-million-dollar sponsorship deal over two years. Negotiations with the telco had begun in July the previous year, and one of the individuals involved in discussions was Raiders board member Dennis Richardson, ASIO's director-general from 1996–2005, former ambassador to the USA, secretary of DFAT and long-time Raiders supporter. The arrangement with the Raiders was Huawei's first with a sporting organisation and, despite continuing controversy surrounding the operations of Chinese companies globally, the relationship has undoubtedly been of mutual benefit.

So the club had secured its major sponsor to help bankroll the review's long list of recommendations. Would this translate into better performance? Dave Furner believed so, and in this opinion he was backed by the club's first roving ambassador, Mal Meninga. Mal recalled his own 'hard times' as Raiders coach and his advice to his former teammate was to 'insulate yourself and the team from criticism' and maintain 'belief in the direction you're heading'.

Coinciding with the round one weekend in 2012, the *Canberra Times* ran a double-page feature on the Raiders' 'rollercoaster' history since 2004. From that year, as discussed earlier in the book, the team went up and down, year by year, bouncing between making the semi-finals in the 'even' years and missing out in the 'odd'. The coach might not have agreed with some of the harsh judgements made by the two journalists who wrote the article, Jon Tuxworth and Lee Gaskin, in their fourteen steps needed for the Raiders to again elevate themselves to premiership contenders, though he must have quietly thanked the football gods that he and his team were about to continue their rocky ride in an evens year, 2012.

Furner had courageously held to his commitment to the young players in the club, with the likes of Sam Williams and Josh Papalii getting a taste of first grade the year before and new under-20s coach Andrew Dunemann very pleased with a group that contained the likes of Jack Wighton (the NYC player of the year in 2011) and captain Mitch Cornish. Furner's two assistant coaches, Justin Morgan and Andrew McFadden, were set to bring additional expertise to the task of moulding a youthful squad. It was needed, for considerable experience and maturity had been lost with both Josh Miller and Dan Vidot off to the Dragons, Danny Galea to Penrith, David Milne and Matt Orford released, and Alan Tongue relaxing into a well-earned retirement.

Due to severe salary cap constraints, Furner was able to make only one off-season acquisition: Shaun Berrigan, a 33-year-old whom the Warriors had moved on. Canberra's signing of veterans in the past decade to mentor a young team had proved to be a mixed bag. It was hoped that the versatile Berrigan would fit into hooker, the halves or centre as required and he brought a background of 205 NRL games, fourteen Tests, two premierships and three seasons in England with him. Growing up, his favourite player was Mal Meninga. Could he be the judicious buy the club needed to link the team's variety of strengths?

The 2012 season unfolded as another puzzling journey. At the halfway mark after thirteen rounds the Raiders were four wins and eight losses (and a bye). Of mounting concern, four of those losses were at home, the ugliest of them a 40–0, seven-try annihilation inflicted by the West Tigers in full view of the one-eyed, green-eyed hordes. Criticism of the coach and players went up another notch. Local papers, magazines, radio, television and social media crackled with complaint. From his first year in the job, Dave Furner had been subjected to bursts of negative commentary. In mid-season 2012, online reaction was as heated as it had been in the depths of 2011.

And how did the coach and his players respond? With a second half of the year performance that produced nine wins in twelve games. In the same impressive manner as a number of seasons past, the team compiled a string of victories, and with them a feast of sizzling tries. The highlight was a final round away game against the Warriors at Mt Smart Stadium when the Raiders scored seven tries to win 42–22. The victory meant the team had once again come from the clouds to finish in a very respectable sixth place in the comp.

History cautioned, however. In the New Zealand game, full of wide-open attack from both sides, the Raiders conceded too many points in defence. This was not the right preparation for semifinal football. As always, Raider football produced points. The problem, as always, was stopping them. A qualifying final saw the Raiders up against an old foe, a Cronulla side that now included Todd Carney in its ranks. This time, fortunately, the Sharks had to travel to the nation's capital to play in front of a capacity crowd, a crowd 'transformed into a sea of lime green' as Don Furner put it. The Sharks were summarily dismissed in a six tries to three, 34–16 win to a Raider team intent on showcasing its attacking best. The following week in the semifinal, against a seasoned South Sydney side on their patch at ANZ Stadium, the Rabbitohs forwards led by Sam Burgess asserted their superiority in the middle third. Souths won 38–16.

For those assessing the merits of the Raiders' performance in 2012, it was a difficult season to mark without resorting to footnotes of clarification. At the start of the year, sixth place would have been accepted with open arms. Making the semis after such a forgettable year in 2011 was a welcome achievement. Questions, however, remained concerning inconsistent performance, lack of squad depth and experience, the issues of player discipline and behaviour, and a pervasive feeling held by some in the club that the present playing group had reached their plateau.

The Furner brothers, in their respective positions of authority in the club, did not share this opinion. Don felt that 2013—the city of Canberra's centenary year—would be a 'monumental' experience, and fitting into twelve months of constant community celebration would be an ambitious Raider club coming of age:

> With our young stars developing at an astonishing rate, coupled with the class and leadership of our senior players, the Raiders are set to embark on an exciting new chapter in the club's history . . .

Coach Dave had a similar message:

> The Centenary of Canberra is a great celebration for the region and what will help that celebration is if the Raiders do well. The best way to celebrate is by winning games and by continuing to strive for improvement. There will be no excuses this year and we'll be constantly working to evolve as a team.

No more excuses. It was all on the line.

This was the backdrop for one of the Raider organisation's most demanding, emotionally exhausting seasons. Big decisions about the club's future would be made, two leading players sacked, a potential champion Raider youngster poached by the permanently cashed-up

Brisbane Broncos, the club's family culture put under the microscope, clandestine meetings held, an interim coach put in place three rounds before the season's end and a new head coach appointed less than a week after the conclusion of the competition rounds. Remarkably, in spite of months of discord and speculation, for seven weeks between 12 May and 4 August (the round 21 weekend) the Raiders were seventh on the ladder for three weeks and in eighth place for four weeks. They were still in ninth spot when Dave Furner was sacked on 20 August with three rounds to go. All three remaining games were lost and the side went backwards to finish thirteenth. It was by any measure an odd and distressing year.

High drama rocked the club on three separate occasions, once early in the year and twice later.

The first two games of the 2013 season were awful. The Raiders went to Penrith in round one only to be well beaten 32–10. The bad start compounded when, a week later, the Gold Coast Titans came to Canberra and won 36–0. The Raiders were thrashed, blanked at home by a team of average talent at best. From this early point in the season, and despite the team reaching the halfway mark with six wins and six losses, pressure for change built across both mainstream and, especially, social media.

Unfairly, some of the heat felt by the coach and team stemmed from a drinking binge by two individuals that took place in the evening of the Penrith game in Sydney. Having admitted himself into hospital with a debilitating virus in early March, Josh Dugan took the field against the Panthers only to come off injured with rib cartilage damage. So he and teammate Blake Ferguson decided to drink heavily with a few friends on the roof of a house in the north Canberra suburb of Nicholls. The police were called in during the early hours of Monday morning. Both had breached the club's strict alcohol policy for injured players and, aggravating an already explosive situation, Dugan posted pictures onto his Instagram account showing the pair on the roof with bottles of alcohol. Both drunk. Both exposed to the world.

On 12 March, ironically the city of Canberra's exact Centenary day, Don Furner took firm action, standing down both Dugan and Ferguson with their punishments to be determined. The next day *The Australian* newspaper stated that some unnamed teammates of the two players involved were thoroughly sick of their antics, which extended well beyond the latest incident. With the issue blowing up, and Dugan's drunken mug published in all the dailies on 14 March, the CEO sacked him for repeated infringements of the club's code of conduct. Ferguson got a suspended $10,000 fine and was stood down indefinitely. Later in the season he went AWOL at State of Origin camp. Dave Furner had sought professional help for his wayward charge, and he also asked the NSW coach, his former teammate Laurie Daley, to place an alcohol ban on him for his own good. This proved impossible to police. Despite the Raider board's reluctance to let another representative player go, Ferguson too was released. Reasons given for his contract termination included being drunk at training and spitting on a patron at a Canberra community festival. Club culture was swaying in the breeze and the coach, CEO and chairman of the board knew it.

Raiders winger Sandor Earl went public with a defence of Dugan and Ferguson but he had few allies. In a matter of a few months the Canberra Raiders club had taken such a resolute stand that it cost them two players of proven ability, players who would go on to wear the green-and-gold for their country. The pragmatist in Dave Furner knew that only too well. As soon as Dugan and Ferguson went back into the player market, despite their rash of serious indiscretions, they were snapped up. Hardly fair on the Raiders, but the world of competitive professional sport is rarely fair.

Who'd be an NRL coach? Insistent on high-behavioural standards, Dave Furner tried hard to help and educate two ill-disciplined, serial offending players of immense talent in order to keep them at the club which had invested so much time and money into them, both on and off the field. For his trouble, the same two players not only trashed the treatment they had received but brought the coach into conflict with a few other Raider players, especially those in the senior ranks. At the time Dugan didn't seem to care. He headed off to the nearest tattoo parlour. Nor did Ferguson, who mumbled a few apologies but soon forgot why he was apologising.

Critical commentary on social media sharply increased, similar to the 'angry crescendo' of tweets in 2011. At that time, Raiders' board member John Mackay was roundly criticised for his off-the-cuff remark that Dave Furner 'would have to lose another 30 games' before his position was in jeopardy.

Two years on, the situation had altered. There was a new wave of concern felt by fans, but this time it was shared by the players and administration. The turning point in the coach's fortunes occurred when the Melbourne Storm came to Canberra for a round 21 clash. Craig Bellamy's team ran in tries at will to win 68–4. It was a humiliating defeat—the Raiders' worst ever—and more losses followed. According to a few of the players in what proved to be a critical few weeks, their brooding coach, desperate to find solutions, became more remote, more distanced from the group. Furner himself had said in an interview at the end of the sparkling 2010 season, when asked how he had personally responded in the past to the pressure of a losing run, said he went

> . . . a bit quiet, but that's just me thinking about everything that's going on. I certainly didn't get on Facebook or any websites or pick up the paper. I found that I was comfortable [in my office]. I'm comfortable here because I know I'm in here doing things to make us better.

Sometime in the weeks of later July and August the coach lost the confidence of the dressing room, a sure point of no return. Three senior players—Terry Campese, Brett White and David Shillington—were set to meet with board members David Thom and Raiders Group CEO Simon Hawkins to express their unease. The meeting did take place, without Shillington. It was later reported that secret meetings among the players had reached the conclusion that as a group they could no longer play under Furner. The situation was deteriorating rapidly, and it was not helped by the fact that some of the players on bigger contracts were not meeting the coach's performance expectations. Destructive rumours were circulating and something needed to be done. In a climate of instability, the coach becomes the readily identifiable scapegoat for poor performance. As the old saying goes, 'coaches are either sacked or about to be'.

The Raiders board met twice in four days. In the second meeting, an extraordinary occasion on a Tuesday afternoon, 20 August 2013, it was unanimously decided to sack the coach immediately. Board Chairman John McIntyre by choice did not attend the meeting. He had been informed that a vote to dismiss would be taken and that all board members, except the chair, had indicated their intention to terminate Furner's contract. McIntyre refused to be a party to it, informing Acting Chairman Allan Hawke that 'if I can't protect a lifelong friend, it's time for me to move on'. For McIntyre, the club's family roots were an integral part of the Raider organisation. His wife Anita, as we have heard, had after all changed Dave's nappies! As always, McIntyre was as good as his word and resigned from the board, though he was destined to remain a powerful force in the organisation as patron.

Another absentee from the extraordinary board meeting who was also aware of the likely outcome was Chief Executive Don Furner. He was not invited to attend the meeting 'for obvious reasons', as he put it. But he knew 'the drums were beating for Dave'.

The vote did pass unanimously, making Dave Furner, favourite son, Raider champion, the first (and only) Raider coach to be sacked in the club's 37-year history. John McIntyre said it was one of the saddest days the club had experienced, and added that it was 'a very sad time for me personally'.

In an attempt to improve the team's fortunes, Dave Furner had taken his players to Batemans Bay on the Tuesday of the board meeting for a bonding session. He wanted to lift the side back into the top eight. Don

Furner, who insisted on being the one to give his coach the bad news, informed the key people around him that he intended to drive to the coast the next morning and inform his brother. McIntyre and Simon Hawkins strongly advised him to head down without delay, fearing a board leak and the prospect of a media story that would probably be splashed all over Wednesday's newspapers. Dave might find out about his sacking from a media report, a prospect to be avoided at all costs. So Don headed off late Tuesday afternoon: 'For it to be my younger brother was gut-wrenching and made it extremely difficult.'

Dave did not see it coming, and conveyed his bitter disappointment to his brother Don, making it crystal clear that he felt he ought to have been given the opportunity to try to make the semis. If he was to be sacked, 'it should have happened at the end of the year'. He was right. The board obviously should have waited. Distraught, he stuffed his gear into his bag, jumped in the car and drove back to Canberra in something of a daze. 'I am on my way home,' he texted. 'Shocked at moment, not up to chat.' Nothing more needed to be said. Don Furner remembers 'sitting alone at Moruya Airport later that evening waiting for an eight-seater plane to take me to Sydney and feeling very empty'. He had already let the players know that assistant coach, Andrew Dunemann, would be the interim coach until the position was formally filled.

The sacking had ramifications. It pushed both Terry Campese and Brett White into the public arena because (with Shillington) they were the instigators of the meeting with Thom and Hawkins. However, both subsequently denied that they were seeking their coach's dismissal. 'We went,' Campese stated, 'with all good intentions of the club in mind. Those issues had been brought up in the past.' His comments failed to clarify recent events and did not absolve the parties involved. When he first heard about the board's vote to sack, Campese said it came as 'a shock'. It should not have been.

There were a number of individuals mentioned as a possible Raider head coach—some old, some new, but all with links in varying degrees to the club. Andrew Dunemann, saddled with a precarious incumbency to promote, was one, along with (according to one newspaper report) Ricky Stuart, Laurie Daley, Mal Meninga, Tim Sheens, Neil Henry, Michael Maguire and Wayne Bennett. It was hardly fair that the last three Raider games of the season, on Dunemann's watch, resulted in their respective opponents—Manly, the Warriors and Sharks—between them piling on 124 points. Dunemann made it known that he had passed on the North Queensland Cowboys' head coaching job to 'send a message' that he wanted the Raiders position. For a short period he was the lukewarm favourite for the job, ahead of a number of high-profile rivals.

The sub-committee hastily formed to recommend a new appointment consisted of Acting Board Chairman Allan Hawke, Don Furner and Mal Meninga. Presumably Meninga had never considered himself part of the very unofficial field of candidates, while Ricky Stuart's situation as the present head coach of the Eels needed clarification. In the fashion of contemporary contracts, apparently he too had a get-out clause based on the continuing administrative instability at the Parramatta club.

On 11 September Stuart was offered the Raiders head coaching position. When accepting, he said that he had made a decision that was 'best for my career and my family . . . I was offered the opportunity. I didn't ask for the opportunity to arrive.' There was bitter disappointment in Parramatta, Chairman Steve Sharp angrily declaring that all future coach and player contracts at his club would be devoid of 'get-out clauses'. NSW State of Origin coach and former teammate, Laurie Daley, someone with a close understanding of Raider culture, commented that it 'doesn't surprise me. [Ricky Stuart] was always the man they wanted. It's a match that everyone wanted to see, being a local boy.'

If Stuart wished to begin with a clean slate at the club which had been his home for so many years, he soon found out otherwise. It had already been determined that Blake Ferguson was off to Sydney and, just as bad, the very day of the Stuart appointment the *Canberra*

Times ran a story suggesting that star youngster Anthony Milford wanted out of the club, citing a clause in his contract which allowed him to return to his hometown of Brisbane because of his father's poor health. Milford, the 2013 Meninga medallist and candidate for the Dally M Rookie of the Year, had been nurtured by the Raiders since he was thirteen years old. Now a name player at age nineteen, he was seeking a release to join Wayne Bennett's Brisbane club on compassionate grounds, his father's heart trouble (a claim later contradicted by Milford's own father, who apparently was reluctant to leave Canberra).

Stuart and Don Furner were not having a bar of Milford departing before the end of the 2014 season. Rumours that Wayne Bennett and the Broncos had their eyes on the young Raider (and Melbourne's Cameron Smith) had started in mid-August and persisted. The Broncos, it was reported, were offering Milford double the Raider contract. Stuart sought an urgent meeting with Milford, aware that his CEO had also spoken at length with Milford's agent Sam Ayoub—an individual described by the *Canberra Times* as 'the agent at war with the Raiders'. It was hardly a good sign. The club dug in, adamant that Milford would appear for the Raiders in 2014 or 'sit out the season'.

A month later, at the beginning of December, Stuart was quoted in the Fairfax media as saying that Sam Ayoub had again given him a 'guarantee' that his client would suit up for the Green Machine the following year. Don Furner chipped in, saying that he had a written guarantee. For Stuart it was a win. 'We've got him for 2014, 100%,' the new coach declared. The net value of the win remained to be seen. It has rarely been advantageous for any side to know in advance that they were going to lose one of their best and brightest the following year.

With justification, Ricky Stuart blasted the Broncos' development strategy, accusing the club of being 'probably one of the worst clubs over the last five years for development', but the new Raider coach could hardly take the high moral ground. He had pulled out of his three-year contract with Parramatta after only one year and, before that, Josh Papalii had done exactly the same thing to the Eels when he opted to remain with the Raiders after putting his signature on a Parramatta contract.

Clearly, the system itself was flawed. The Raiders' embattled 2013 season finished on an unconvincing note, the ball firmly in Ricky Stuart's court to put his stamp on the club he had always dreamed he would one day return to coach.

Forever Green, 2014–19

When the dust of dissension had settled in the first months of 2014, the single-minded Ricky Stuart eased into a job he felt it 'a privilege' to have been offered. The circumstances in which he was hired were far from ideal but the situation would only be relieved with goals set, goals achieved and club culture renewed and refreshed. Chris Wilson, often a harsh critic of the Raiders in the pages of the *Canberra Times*, on 4 March asserted that 'the club's spirit and resolve seemed broken by the end of a tumultuous [2013] year'. This was not true, but it had been severely dented. Falling crowds are a sure sign of discontent and the Raiders' home game average of 10,212 in 2013 was the lowest in the NRL.

Right from the start, Stuart paid attention to matters on and off the field. His declared position for the benefit of those interested in playing for him in the future was simple: 'It'll be all about the club and wanting to play for that jumper.' He expected the experienced players to become role models for 'the nursery of youth coming through' in the same way that he had been mentored by the likes of Mal Meninga, Gary Belcher, Gary Coyne and Dean Lance in the late 1980s. For Stuart, connections between the past and present were important. Indeed, in the midst of the Raiders' wonderful run into the semifinals in 2016, Josh Papalii reflected on the spadework of the previous two seasons: 'The first year [2014] wasn't all about footy with Sticks [Stuart], the second year we started to focus more on the footy. He was trying to bring in everything that was successful in his day. It's good to know the history of the famous club . . . The boys are trying to make our bit of history.'

The advantage Stuart had, when compared with Mal Meninga and Dave Furner, was that both of his former teammates took on the Raiders' job as their first head-coaching position. When Stuart returned to the nation's capital, he was assuming the reins of his fourth club, having won a premiership in his 2002 rookie year with the Roosters, guiding the team to three successive grand finals, and going on to shorter stints at Cronulla and Parramatta—both of them every bit as educational as his successful years at Bondi. By the time he returned to the Raiders, Stuart had accumulated invaluable experience, the highs as well as the lows.

Club ambassador Alan Tongue, one of the permanent keepers of the Raider flame, got it exactly right when he said the former champion halfback's 'personality suits the Raiders' and this was evident in Stuart's own assessment of his strengths: 'The one thing I'm never embarrassed about or fall short in is effort. I give plenty of hours and plenty of heart and soul into every coaching job I've had.' He expected nothing less from those already at the club, and the new arrivals. His standard had to be theirs.

Stuart brought on Dean Pay as his assistant coach. On the losing end of the 1994 grand final when playing for the Bulldogs against the Raiders, Pay subsequently roomed with Stuart on a Kangaroo tour. They became close mates. Pay's shrewd approach to football, his intelligent reading of the game and his hatred of losing were attributes he shared with the coach. Stuart also welcomed a healthy crop of new recruits to enhance the 'promising' squad he already had, among them Shannon Boyd, the 21-year-old son of Cowra farmers (with a liking for pig shooting), Queenslander Brenko Lee, Kurt Baptiste, Jordan Rapana and Mitch Cornish, who had risen through the club's junior ranks. At least as important as the fresh faces was the 'team' behind him, those covering his back.

The new coach, a bush kid at heart, had a group of officials and administrators whom he could count on. His club patron, chairman of the board and CEO, like he himself, had all grown up in Queanbeyan.

Solidarity was essential when engaging with the big city teams and Board Chairman Allan Hawke understood this. A former private secretary to Prime Minister Paul Keating and chancellor of the Australian National University, Hawke launched the new 2014 season at a dinner in late February, stating that his 'riding instructions' from new patron John McIntyre were to do all that he could 'to return the Green Machine to its rightful place in the scheme of things. Pride, tradition and professionalism characterise our club. We are all in this together and if we all do our part, success is certain to follow.' Hawke spoke for everyone present.

But the chairman's positive remarks, addressed to the converted, carefully avoided a few of the club's nagging problems. Figuratively speaking, the NRL's patch was not a level playing field. From the time Super League re-shaped the competition landscape, the smaller clubs had been forced to contend with glaring inequities in the system. To give one example in a long list: in 2013, Dave Furner's last year as coach, his cause was not helped when the Raiders received one solitary free-to-air television game. Compare this to Super League's bosom buddy club, the Broncos, with nineteen games; the West Tigers, thirteen; the Eels and Roosters ten apiece and the Penrith Panthers eight games. As every agent knew, television exposure equals 'performance' clauses, equals bonus payments, equals big dollars in (supplementary, unchecked) third-party payments. Quite simply, it is canny business as a player to pursue a footy career in Sydney, Brisbane or Melbourne.

In the same 2013 year, alongside the NRL's shameless allocation of television games, the official salary cap was $5.85 million, a figure intended to stop the bigger clubs preying on the smaller ones. However, the cap failed, and continues to fail to account for three of its inevitable outcomes: the ease with which Sydney clubs can exchange players without those same players having to relocate to new cities; the bigger media market in Sydney and Brisbane able to supply individual players with maximum opportunity to build their 'brand' and value, thus obtaining lucrative third-party sponsorship deals; and the investment having to be made by smaller clubs in player development as a means of survival.

When he returned home, Ricky Stuart knew only too well that he would have to solve the twin difficulties of holding on to quality juniors developed by the Raiders while also attracting 'marquee' talent to the club. As if these weren't challenging enough, history had only recently underscored the cautionary tale that once a Rugby League club adopted a strong stand on discipline, and proceeded to cancel the contracts of some of its top talent if they offended, those same players would then be picked up without delay by another club, regardless of the severity of their misbehaviour.

Stuart must have felt he was between a rock and a hard place. Once again tipped by most experts to finish out of the eight in 2014, the team did little to contradict the pessimistic forecasts when it turned at the halfway point of the season with only a handful of wins, soaking up 108 points in two successive losses away against the Manly Sea Eagles and the Warriors. The size of the losses prompted journalist Chris Wilson to write an article at the beginning of May with the heading, 'How do you solve a problem like the Raiders?', where he pointed to the team's 'all too frequent' lack of consistency. The problem, he wrote, was that for a long time the Raiders had not been up for the weekly grind. The team needed some quality and depth in order to become legitimately competitive.

In May the club decided to test its appeal in the player market and went after Melbourne's Kevin Proctor, the Panthers' Josh Mansour, the Bulldogs' Michael Ennis and West Tigers' fullback James Tedesco. Within a matter of weeks each one of them had rejected the club's offer, the most worrying being Tedesco's case. Offered a three-year $1.9 million contract reportedly worth $150,000 a season more than the Tigers had on the table, Tedesco accepted the Raiders' terms—only to renege shortly after. The Raiders had not only lost out at the last minute on a crucial 'spine' player you could build a team around, but the decision cruelled their plans of finding a high-quality replacement for Anthony Milford. Proctor also reneged at the last minute. As Chris Wilson summed up with offensive accuracy: 'So right now it leaves the Raiders looking like the NRL's most desperate and dateless, with a bucket load of cash and no-one willing to take it.' Phil Gould had no sympathy at all with the Raiders' plight, blaming the club for 'damaging' the whole NRL market. It was a standard remark typical of his Sydney-centric posturing.

Stuart responded to the Tedesco debacle with dignity. His first priority was to explain the situation to the 'shareholders', the Raiders' hardened and passionate supporters, and ask for patience. The club circulated its coach's 'statement', one in which he reaffirmed that:

> Despite the recent disappointments ... we will continue to push forward with an aggressive recruitment program that's aimed at bringing deserved success to a great football club. These disappointments have only added to our resolve to achieve our goals. We want players at the Raiders who share our vision and who will have pride in our jersey.

On the eve of the Raiders' twentieth anniversary of the 1994 premiership, Stuart allowed himself to reminisce that the club's distant third premiership spelled the end of an era, though he and everyone else involved were unaware of it at the time. The celebration round to remember the '94 triumph occurred mid-season in game fifteen against the Bulldogs on 20 June. The Raiders lost, but it was not hard to sense the mood. The host of former players in attendance wanted new milestones to toast in the present day.

They did not get their wish in 2014. The second half of the season was only marginally better than the first. The most that could be said was that the team did show its best form in the season's last three games, all wins, against the Sharks, Tigers and Eels. Jarrod Croker continued his relentless accumulation of points and was rightly awarded the Mal Meninga medal. He and all his teammates were certain they would improve in the new year on the fifteenth place finish in 2014.

The pundits were not so sure. Milford was heading to the Broncos; the luckless, injury-prone Terry Campese was off to try his luck on more forgiving grounds in England; veteran Brett White had retired (though he was not lost to the club); and Reece Robinson and Tom Learoyd-Lahrs, another player constantly hampered by injuries, were both released. None of the Sydney tipsters had the Raiders in their eight for 2015 and the *Telegraph*'s Boo Bailey had some fun at the Green Machine's expense:

> Ricky Stuart tried to import some quality but the floats kept breaking down on their way to his Canberra stables. He probably has a midweek field horse running in elite company. This is a quality trainer looking to restore the proud green colours to their former glory. Still plenty of work to do.

The new season gave Stuart the chance to introduce the first influx of fresh talent for which he, his CEO and scouts were responsible. By any measure it was a stand-out group: flamboyant five-eighth Blake Austin, picked up from the West Tigers, whose style seemed perfectly attuned to Stuart's plans for the re-introduction of high-energy, highly entertaining Raider football; 'veteran' Sia Soliola, who had played under Stuart at the Roosters, coming to Canberra from the St Helens club, which had made such a huge impression on Mal Meninga when he played there; New Zealand international Frank-Paul Nu'uausala, a big rig from the Roosters, who won a comp there in 2013; experienced Melbourne Storm flanker, Sisa Waqa; two promising youngsters, Queenslander Luke Bateman and Mitch Barnett; powerful Newcastle centre Joey Leilua, potential unlimited; and, soon to show himself as perhaps the best of the bunch, Englishman Josh Hodgson, a hooker acquired to shore up the position who quickly stamped himself as a prize recruit. A superb reader of the game, skilful in all departments and with the intelligence of a future captain, Hodgson was fast-tracked into the team's leadership group. An untapped well of English talent had been located by the Raiders and it would soon prove to be a bonanza.

As Chris Wilson summed up in the *Canberra Times*, Stuart had 'started to re-inject his DNA back into the club' with a creativity reminiscent of his long-time coach, Tim Sheens. He announced prolific point-scorer Jarrod Croker as the team captain, the youngest in Raider history, and he elevated Sia Soliola into his leadership group because, at 28, he was sure to inspire younger teammates with his uncompromising, physical approach. Off the field, you could not ask for a better role model. Soliola was familiar with Stuart's style. On arrival, he acknowledged it as one of the reasons he left England for Canberra: 'Ricky has led the charge with outlining what's acceptable in this squad and creating a really good culture in this club.'

Against the odds, the Raiders had begun to attract some class players to the organisation, individuals of character and ability for whom a club's open cheque book was not the one-and-only motivation for playing footy. For a month or two in 2014 the Raiders had tried throwing money around; it didn't work. Canberra's appeal would have to be more broadly based—more imaginative, more holistic. The club needed to spell out that its self-described claim as a 'family club' was not one to which it only paid lip service.

The team's performance did improve in 2015, much to the relief of fans, coach and players, but the 'reboot' that the *Canberra Times* confidently predicted pre-season was only partly realised. The Raiders finished tenth in a season that produced ten wins and fourteen losses. Statistically, the 569 points scored by the Green Machine was over 100 points more than the previous year, 150-odd better than 2013 and 30 better than the last time the team made the semis in 2012. Defensively, too, Stuart's second year at the helm resulted in an improvement on the last couple of years.

The explanation for the anomaly in not qualifying for post-season play lay in the number of games lost by narrow margins. In 2015, seven games were lost by an aggregate of nineteen points, two of them by a single point and three of them by two. Clubs often resort to lamenting 'what might have been'. This time the claim had validity, though near misses only served to frustrate fans who forked out their hard-earned dollars.

When Board Chairman Allan Hawke produced his end-of-year 'Raiders Year in Review' article, he praised the team's attacking style. It was a 'base to build on'. In late September, the *Canberra Times* conducted a survey of some 1,800 Raider supporters. Essentially, they were fine with the team's progress in the season just finished, though expressing their opinion that Ricky Stuart's third season at the helm would only be assigned a pass mark with a top-eight spot. It was, they agreed, 'the finals or bust'.

The survey also indicated that, despite the fact that the Raiders had inexplicably won only three home games during the season, its stitched-on supporters took solace from a couple of outstanding wins: the 30–2 victory over the Tigers when the Green Machine came back from a 22–0 deficit at Leichhardt in a game highlighted by a crushing Soliola tackle on halfback Luke Brooks that re-shaped the result; and an upset win against Souths when the Bunnies, presumably feeling that the match was two points already banked wherever it was played, opted to take their home game to Cairns. It was a rare televised game for the Raiders—only because their opponent was Russell Crowe's team and last year's premiers—and the team revelled in the publicity to inflict a 30–22 defeat on an arrogant Souths. Ricky Stuart took advantage of the spotlight to let the league world know what he thought of the NRL's so-called level playing field: 'We weren't meant to win, we're just here to make up the numbers, that's the most pleasing part of it . . . There's not a lot of respect there for the club or the players . . . I don't say [this] to be smart, I say it because it's just the honest truth.'

From Belconnen to Tuggeranong, Queanbeyan to the Brindabellas, you could almost hear the Raider fan base cheering—at last, a forthright advocate unafraid to state the Raiders' case.

The combative Sia Soliola was the deserving winner of the Mal Meninga medal in a 2015 season that showed he had more productive years in him. His maturity and, above all, consistency led the way for his teammates, and he received the club's highest season honour despite breaking his cheekbone in round 21. He was surprised, though no-one else in the black-tie room was. Interviewed afterwards, Soliola spoke for his teammates:

> Ricky is really excited for the year ahead. He has given us some really great goals for the year and we think they are quite achievable. We are just knuckling down and focusing on those targets.

For the first time in years there was a sense of expectation in the room. The team was on the rise.

The 2015 premiership was won 17–16 by the North Queensland Cowboys in one of Rugby League's most memorable grand finals, a first-ever golden point finish when the great Johnathan Thurston kicked a field goal to sink the Broncos—after the Cowboys had scored a try in the corner in the dying seconds of regular time and Thurston had missed with his conversion after a ricochet off the posts. It was the Cowboy's first premiership since entering the NRL in 1995. Inevitably, the frenzied excitement of the game's last, heart-stopping minutes drew comparisons with the Raiders' 1989 grand final, not least in a *Canberra Times* editorial that took the opportunity to re-visit a game which, it said, 'witnessed their city come to life'. As good as the Cowboys' win was—discussed earlier in the book—the vast majority of the Rugby League world today acknowledges that the Raiders' win was that much better.

Outstanding talent scout Peter Mulholland joined the Raiders at the end of 2015 as the club's new NRL recruitment and high-performance manager, replacing the respected David Hamilton, who had put in seventeen years of dedicated toil. Mulholland enthused about the timing of his new job since it coincided with an overhaul of the player roster that Stuart and Hamilton had undertaken over the past two years. Mulholland looked forward to his first full year, also the first year that Ricky Stuart would 'have his own team ... I think he has done a marvellous job'.

Stuart had again bought discerningly, getting Aidan Sezer from the Gold Coast, Joseph Tapine from Newcastle, Junior Paulo from Parramatta and enticing a second Pom, the versatile Elliott Whitehead, to head Down Under. Turn-over too was noticeable, except that this time the Raiders coach was carefully vetting outgoing players as he firmed up a list that according to Laurie Daley was 'the strongest squad he's had'.

The 2016 year, like many in the history of the Raiders club (including 1989 and 1994), divided neatly in two. The first thirteen games were nothing special. Seven wins, five losses and a draw. In one of the wins at Bruce (called GIO Stadium in the Stuart era) the Raiders put 60 points on the West Tigers in the inaugural 'Forever Green Reunion' match, but on either side of that victory the team had losses. These were scarcely grounds to get carried away and yet, in the middle of the year, three consecutive wins attracted some attention around the league—defeats of the Warriors, Bulldogs and Sea Eagles in which the Raiders scored at least 30 points in each and flagged themselves as a team rapidly growing in confidence. Round fourteen was a brief pause in momentum, a tight loss against the Broncos at Suncorp. And then a tidal surge began, a spine-tingling run of ten wins to head into post-season play in second spot. The three finals games that followed were all tense affairs, ending with a preliminary final loss to the Melbourne Storm, 14–12, at AAMI Park. The Raiders had fallen one game short of the grand final in a match they could so easily have won, and many felt they deserved to win. For the Raiders' band of supporters, it was three months of pure magic.

The sequence started with high-scoring, if relatively tight, wins. The deeper into the season it got, however, the better the Green Machine performed.

The first bold statement of intent was made in the round 21 fixture against 2014 premiers, South Sydney. On occasion in the recent past Souths had bullied the re-grouping Raiders. Devoted Green Machine fans recoiled in horror each time Greg Inglis strutted his 'goanna' in their direction after scoring another effortless try. In 2016 the worm turned, the goanna hobbled, as the Raiders won 54–4 in a ten-try rout, the biggest win over Souths since Ricky Stuart was wearing the number seven, lime-green jumper. David Polkinghorne greeted the win in the *Canberra Times* with the apt headline, 'Ricky's Raiders turn back clock'. In the game, Jarrod Croker took his personal tally of points past the 200 mark, the competition's leader. He was absolutely wrapped in the team performance, declaring that the coach had

> . . . brought the spirit and the history back into the club. It's something the boys really enjoy doing. We have a lot of functions . . . where we get the old players in. The old boys love it as much as the boys love having them in there. Everyone at the club is proud to pull that jersey on and [Stuart] has brought that back, it's a pleasure to play for him.

Something special was happening once again in the nation's capital.

Next up came the Sharks. Two years before, in Stuart's first Raiders coaching year, his team met Cronulla in a clash the media unkindly dubbed the 'spoon bowl', a game to determine who would finish last in the comp and get the wooden spoon, the trophy no team wanted on its mantelpiece. How things had changed, with both clubs in 2016 ensconced in the top three. Before the match, Sharks' man-of-steel Paul Gallen was happy to comment on Ricky Stuart's four years at Cronulla, years that incensed some of the Shire's loyal fans. Gallen was having none of it: 'He's the best motivator. That's what he did for me. He gave me confidence in myself and he motivated me to want to play my best football every week. He made me want to play for him.' These were meaningful comments coming from one of the game's most uncompromising, honest and opinionated footballers. The Raiders beat Gallen's Sharks 30–14. The run continued.

Craig Bellamy's Melbourne Storm, always the sternest of tests, came to town in round 23. Stuart knew that game would provide a more accurate gauge of whether the Raiders had become a serious contender for the NRL title. ACT Chief Minister Andrew Barr certainly thought so. Caught up in the increasing community hype, and with vivid memories of growing up in Canberra during the Raiders' glory days in the late '80s and '90s, Barr proactively wrote a letter to NRL CEO Todd Greenberg calling for a Raiders' preliminary final at home if the team qualified. The chief minister was well aware, as were all Raider supporters, that the NRL had a rule that if either the Storm or the Broncos earned the right to host a preliminary final, then they got to play it in front of their own fans. If the same happened to the Raiders, the game had to be played in Sydney. The rule was so patently unfair that it needs no further comment. It stayed put in the NRL's books.

The Raiders beat Melbourne 22–8. They were serious contenders and now faced the Parramatta Eels in round 24, the team's final home game of the season. In front of a partisan green crowd of about 19,000, the Eels got out to a 16–0 lead only to be steadily, calmly reeled in by a maturing Raiders team. Paul Crawley in the *Daily Telegraph* began his article on the game: 'The last time Canberra had a team this good, Ricky Stuart wore the no. 7 jumper.' Acknowledging that he had no Thurston, Cooper Cronk or Cameron Smith, Stuart stressed the team spirit on show. 'We don't live off one player,' he said. It was the work ethic across the park that had secured a satisfying win over a committed Eels side.

The good news did not stop there. In the Parramatta game the Raiders' marketing staff, always looking for innovative ways to enhance the footy experience for Raider families, trialled an orchestrated pre-game Viking Clap from the crowd like the one used so hypnotically by Iceland's intrepid soccer fans. As Caden Helmers wrote in appreciation in the *Canberra Times*, it was 'enough to make the hair on the back of your neck stand up'. The Viking Clap has since established its credentials as the most popular spectator experience, beyond the football, offered by any club in the NRL. The players love it, fans love it and the free-to-air television commentators (when the Raiders happen to crack it for a game) lap it up. A solid percentage of the fans of opposition clubs happily drive to Canberra just to experience the awesome clap, standing as one with the locals when called on by the military drummer's boom.

There was plenty of applause after the Eels game when Jarrod Croker's eight points took him to 246 for the year, one point better than Clinton Schifcofske's club record set in 2001. He deserved his own Viking Clap for an outstanding achievement.

Under normal circumstances, the round 25 and round 26 games against Manly at Brookie and West Tigers at Leichhardt would have presented problems. Not so in 2016. Despite the Sea Eagles game being veteran Jamie Lyon's final farewell to his home fans, the Raiders bolted to a 38–16 lead and then took the foot off the accelerator, resulting in a 44–30 scoreline. The team was never out of cruise control. The centre–wing combination of Jordan Rapana and Joey Leilua, going gangbusters, never let up as they scored five tries between them.

The Tigers game the following week threatened to become embarrassing for the home team as it vainly attempted to ward off wave after wave of concerted Raider attack. This was the Green Machine at its best as the team creatively manufactured nine tries, the Rapana–Leilua combination—christened the 'Leipana bromance'—crossing for three of them. Raider football, slick, entertaining, try hungry, was back with a vengeance. Statistically the highest-scoring team in Raider history, the 2016 side also established a club record ten wins in a row; it scored 688 points on the journey, beating the previous record of 677 set in the last premiership-winning year, 1994; and it secured a second-place finish, the best since 1995. 'At the start of the year,' the coach proudly recalled, 'we spoke about creating our own piece of history.' Words had turned into potent substance.

For the first time in four years the Canberra–Queanbeyan community indulged in the joy of footy finals fever; for the first time in twenty years they had a team with the ability to go all the way. The city, as Megan Doherty joyfully reported to her *Canberra Times* readers, was once again a 'capital green with frenzy'. Tony Wood, aka Victor the Viking, was as thrilled as anyone. Thirty-three years and 606 games after sporting his first Victor outfit at Seiffert Oval, Tony loved playing his part. A stroke, a heart attack and a quadruple by-pass operation had failed to stop him.

That's commitment. The longest-serving mascot in the NRL, Tony had a huge wrap on the Viking Clap, and he looked forward to finals football giving it a wider audience. He could hardly wait to host the Sharks.

Nor could Raiders fans spread right across the southern region. An overflowing 25,592 turned up to watch the qualifying final, the second largest home crowd in Raider history. Prior to the game, Ricky Stuart warned his players and the fans that the game was no done deal, and he was proven correct. The plucky, scrappy Sharks got to play the game largely on their terms with James Maloney, Paul Gallen, Michael Ennis and Andrew Fifita able to dictate the pace. A late penalty against Elliott Whitehead was converted by Maloney with fifteen minutes to play. Despite concerted Raider attack, the Sharks defence held on for a 16–14 win. Raiders hooker Josh Hodgson, whose master-class performances in recent weeks had reinforced his blue-chip value, rolled an ankle early in the second half and did not return to the field. His absence probably affected the result.

Fortunately, the Raiders' expansive season meant they had another bite of the cherry, and in their own orchard at GIO Stadium against the Panthers. Only the year before the Raiders had played Penrith at home in front of a crowd numbering a bare 6,717 true-believing fans. Fast-forward a year and the same fixture was about to attract four times that number. The Canberra faithful revelled in the chance to 'turn Canberra green' for a second week in a row, and they took their renewed religious fervour out to the game with them.

The Raiders dominated the first 40 minutes, scoring two tries to lead 12–0 at the break. One of the tries was a 'Leipana bromance' special, where the two emerging stars combined for a Rapana four-pointer that projected him into the club's record books. It was the New Zealand flanker's twenty-second, and this placed him alongside club legends Noa Nadruku, Brett Mullins and Jarrod Croker, another worthy milestone for the Green Machine Mark III.

But let's not forget a fired-up Penrith. A talented outfit, they conspired to get back into the semifinal in spite of robust contributions from an injured Josh Hodgson ('one tough Pom'), an injured Blake Austin, who crossed for a typical try off his big right foot, and an aggressive Raider pack with Soliola, Paulo, Papalii and Whitehead in the front line. Soliola's trademark hits shook the stands. The Panthers withstood the Raider pressure. At one nervous point during the second half the game was delicately poised, setting the scene for Jarrod Croker to bury his demons of the past once and for all. Remember the penalty 30-metres out, straight in front, in the semi against the West Tigers at Bruce in 2010—the kick drifting fractionally wide? The inconsolable Croker with his head buried in his hands? Not this time. Two vital penalty goals the young skipper kicked late in the game were clinically, nervelessly taken, to give the Raiders a hard-fought 22–14 victory.

The crowd went wild at the full-time buzzer, Chris Dutton in the *Canberra Times* capturing the mood of the moment:

> If there was a roof on Canberra Stadium, it would have been blown off with a spine-tingling post-match Viking Clap that sent Raiders fans into delirium. After years and years of heartache and frustration, the Raiders are just one win away from a grand final berth and two wins away from their first premiership since 1994. They will play the Storm in their first preliminary final since 1997 and there's no doubt Canberra has turned green for Ricky Stuart's troops. The biggest cheer was for coach Ricky Stuart as he turned to the crowd and clapped, while captain Jarrod Croker was the hero on the field.

The Raiders were off to Melbourne for the preliminary final. In the week leading up to the game there were a number of backstory articles on members of the team, though none of the players was the subject of as many feature articles as the re-born coach. Before the Sharks game, Fairfax media's Andrew Webster wrote a long piece on Ricky Stuart which largely focused on his resistance to profile pieces. Webster said that he had always received the same response from his chosen subject: 'I don't want it to be about me.'

This time, though, the journalist refused to be put off and he clearly enjoyed expanding on Stuart's 'spits', his notorious verbal explosions when tightly wound with 'something bubbling deep inside'. While initially concentrating on the fragile aspect of Stuart's demeanour in the public eye ('Why wouldn't I be paranoid? . . . I don't give a f. . . if I'm paranoid'!), Webster's more interesting insights came later in the article. The Raider coach's home circumstances for one:

> Those close to Stuart say he's flourishing as a coach because he also has stability at home. Stuart rarely talks about his personal life but it's well documented that his teenage daughter, Emma, is autistic. Being in Canberra around his and wife Kaylie's extended family has eased the pressure at home.

Webster also dwelt on Stuart's tight bond with his players. They could never question his emotional investment in the job, visibly represented often enough in his pre-season and post-match addresses when feelings often got the better of him. What Webster referred to as 'The Bottom Lip' appeared when, tearing up, Stuart struggled to hold it together even in a raucous dressing room full of the team's families and friends. I experienced a couple of these 'bottom lips' after Raider home victories in 2018 and can attest to their spontaneity, their compelling honesty. 'I'm hopeless,' Stuart has confessed in an unguarded moment, 'my old man's the same.' Heart on sleeve. What's not to like.

ABC radio's Tim Gavel, one of Canberra's most respected sporting voices, wrote in 2018 that no-one takes a loss as hard as Stuart, a character trait that has resulted in his refusal to tolerate any injustice or unfairness inflicted on his club, his team or its individual players. The only exception to this applies to one of his best mates, Craig Bellamy, who just happened to be the opposing coach in the 2016 preliminary final. Only a week or two before the game, Cowboys coach Paul Green raised the spectre of the Storm's use of wrestling tactics to slow the ruck down, thus enabling the defence to re-set. It is common knowledge that the Storm are the most proficient in this controversial area of the game and Green was attempting to take a stand like many coaches before him.

Ricky Stuart in 2016? Not interested in tactically stirring the pot. There would be no incendiary attack on his good friend like the one he had launched against Shane Flanagan before the Sharks game. All Stuart would say to the media was that he and Craig would have a beer after the game, with the winner buying and taking it to the other one's shed. 'He's been shouting a lot over the last ten years, so I hope I can take one in to him.'

Alas, the dominant pattern of the past was reinforced in the final, though it was a desperately close-run thing. With twenty minutes to go, the score 8–6 in Melbourne's favour and several Raider players hampered by injury, Jack Wighton was sin-binned for a professional foul of the kind usually ignored in the post-season. In less than a minute, Melbourne exploited the referee's generous gift and scored in the corner. The conversion missed but another Storm penalty got them out to a 14–6 lead. The Raiders would not fold, and indeed they created two clear-cut chances late. The first one was not taken when winger Edrick Lee nervously grabbed at a cut-out pass that he should have caught. The second was. With four minutes to go, Elliott Whitehead touched down in the corner. Aidan Sezer converted under immense pressure after he had assumed the kicking duties for an injured Jarrod Croker. Two points separated the teams and . . . Melbourne held on. Just.

After the game Ricky Stuart had nothing but praise for the effort his team had put in for the entire 80 minutes, typical of a year in which the Green Machine, he rightly said, had 'exceeded everyone's expectations'. Michael Lucas, Raiders tragic from the Canberra suburb of Condor, had zero praise for the referee in his letter to the *Canberra Times*, labelling the Wighton penalty given at such a crucial, game-changing moment as plainly wrong:

> The silence has been deafening over the 'dudding' of the Canberra Raiders in the NRL preliminary final. I expected a deluge of letters to the Canberra

> Times over the referee's decision to hand the game to the Melbourne Storm by enforcing the 10-minute send-off rule on Jack Wighton, at a crucial time in the game. This rule is seldom enforced and this decision proved to be decisive in a close-fought game. It is no coincidence that the Raiders' loss suits the Sydney rugby league fraternity.

Perhaps the community's silence was the result of the confidence brewing in the suburbs and on the farms of the Monaro Plains, the Snowy and the Riverina that the lads had more improvement in them the next year. A premiership perhaps?

When compared to the doldrums of the recent past, objective consideration of the current playing roster was an exercise in unbridled optimism: Jarrod Croker had fallen just two points short of joining an all-time NRL group of three players to have scored 300 points in a season, and he was still only 26; Jordan Rapana's try against Melbourne gave him 23 for the year, a new club record; the Englishmen Josh Hodgson and Elliott Whitehead had been a revelation, both rewarded with selection to play for England in the following months and joined in the international arena by Josh Papalii and Shannon Boyd in the green-and-gold, Joe Tapine and Jordan Rapana playing for New Zealand and Junior Paulo for Samoa; Joey Leilua, by his own admission enjoying football for the first time in his life and tagged as an international of the future, had finally begun to realise his full potential; Blake Austin was now a player ready for representative honours; and then there was the incomparable Sia Soliola, 'Solly'.

One person in a city full of admirers of Soliola, David Polkinghorne provided *Canberra Times* readers with the story behind the Samoan's unorthodox decision to come to Canberra. His devout Christian beliefs were a factor:

> Sia Soliola recalls sitting in his St Helens lounge room with passionate Canberra Raiders coach Ricky Stuart on the other end of the phone trying to lure him to the ACT. He had doubts about coming to the nation's capital.

> So he prayed. And the more he talked with his wife, the more 'it felt right' as he looked to prove to himself he could 'still mix it with the best'. Mix it he has, the 30-year-old not only proving to be a 'warrior' on the field, but a spiritual leader of the Green Machine as well.

Thirty years old? In 2016 Solly played with the enthusiasm of a teenager as he re-booted his second NRL coming. Over time, as he has moved into his thirties while continuing to play with the same youthful zest each year, Polkinghorne has taken to omitting Soliola's surname when referring to him in favour of the more mystical appellation, 'spiritual leader'. Soliola and his family are embedded in the Canberra community. His son Israel plays for the Belconnen Sharks; he works voluntarily for a range of charities and, when possible, he joins Father (now Monsignor) John Woods in a prayer session pre-game with a few of his mostly Pacific Islander teammates. There could be no better role model for the younger Raider players.

The 2016 year had been an unexpected, action-packed journey for the Green Machine, undoubtedly the best season in two decades. The crowds were back, rejuvenated, the Viking Clap resonated across the entire region and Raider membership eclipsed 15,000 for the first time in club history. The icing on the cake came at the prestigious Dally M awards in Sydney. Ricky Stuart beat the grand final's two coaches, Craig Bellamy and the Sharks' Shane Flanagan, to be awarded the NRL's Coach of the Year, and Jarrod Croker was a deserving Captain of the Year. To this honour, Croker added the Provan–Summons People's Choice Award and the prize as the competition's leading point-scorer. Then there was Joey Leilua's selection as the leading NRL centre, named in the Team of the Year, and Josh Hodgson's recognition in the Dally M medal count. He was just pipped by joint winners Cooper Cronk and Jason Taumalolo. It was a great night to end a stellar season.

Could it be bettered? Mal Meninga certainly thought so: 'It's a quality football team and will be an even better footy team further down the track.' Josh Hodgson agreed, eagerly anticipating 'some exciting things to come in the next few years', as did David Polkinghorne in his appraisal in the *Canberra Times*. For the Raider supporters, a premiership win in 2017 seemed the next logical progression. Some dreamt of years of Green domination. Why not? It had happened before.

And yet life and sport rarely follow an ideal script. Both the 2017 and 2018 seasons failed to meet the heightened expectations of the coach, the players and the zealous fans. The club and the community were puzzled and frustrated by what unfolded.

A first setback occurred in mid-January 2017 when Raiders enforcer Josh Papalii was pulled over for drink-driving, a charge that embarrassed the player and his family and resulted in him being stood down from the club's leadership group. A second setback rocked the club a few weeks later when point-scoring machine and captain Jarrod Croker, taking a routine hit-up in the Indigenous versus World All Stars game, badly injured his knee and was out for months. Once back, he took some time to regain his confidence. While the team's preparation for the new season suffered on both counts, they had nothing like the impact on the squad that stemmed, ironically, from the previous year's success. Raider players off-contract forced Ricky Stuart to have to seriously consider the salary cap in terms of the team's prevailing strengths and weaknesses. Who to keep and who to let go? The price on the open market of a number of the Green Machine's less publicised team members had deservedly increased. Some chose to accept a better offer.

No-one could begrudge the departing players for looking to their future but the team's player depth took a significant hit when decisions were made to go elsewhere. The Raiders farewelled Paul Vaughan, who had been superb off the bench in 2016, off to St George as a certain starter in their top thirteen; the fearsomely talented Tevita Pangai junior, enticed to the Brisbane Broncos with a bulging contract that made a mockery of his age and experience; Jarrad Kennedy went to Manly; Brenko Lee to the Bulldogs; the tackling machine and fan favourite Shaun Fensom to North Queensland; and flanker

Edrick Lee headed to a new home in the Shire at Cronulla. Sam Williams, such important insurance in the halves, joined the Wakefield club in England.

The main squad gains bulked up an already league-heaviest pack when Dunamis Lui was picked up from St George and Dave 'Coal Train' Taylor was given another opportunity to make it in the NRL after a stint with French club Catalans. The Raiders wisely placed him on a 'train and trial' contract. On arrival he was as big as a coal train. Strength and conditioning coach Nigel Ashley-Jones had his work cut out to strip some excess kegs off big Dave but the job was just as difficult when applied to Shannon Boyd, fresh off an enjoyable sabbatical on his Cowra farm after playing some excellent football for the Kangaroos on their triumphant Four Nations campaign in England. Junior Paulo and 'Papa' Papalii were known to have a taste for the odd Big Mac or two. In the NRL, however, weight can be a two-edged sword. Big is not necessarily beautiful.

The start to the 2017 season, with expectations high, flat-lined. The opening two games resulted in losses, the first in Townsville when a freakish Cowboys try by Gavin Cooper in the eighty-fourth minute gave North Queensland a 20–16 win. In the second game the Raiders hosted Cronulla at GIO in front of 15,807 fans, the biggest first-up home crowd in fifteen years. The Sharks, always a tricky opponent, this time proved far too good when scoring seven tries in a 42–16 thumping of the home team. Already the Raiders had been given a reality check after the 2016 heroics, and it set the tone for the season.

Poor defence, especially late in games, undermined matches that should have been professionally closed out. So Brisbane eclipsed the Raiders by one point in round four, Manly by two in round eight, the Bulldogs by six in round nine, Manly again by a single (golden) point in round thirteen, and Penrith by four in each of their games after unlikely come-from-behind, razzle-dazzle play splintered the Raider defensive pattern, shattered the coach and his players, and broke the heart—and confidence—of many a Raider fan.

At various points during the year the Raiders rallied back with wins to look a rough chance of making the play-offs, only to then lose a squeaker after being scored on late. The most dispiriting defeat came in round twenty at GIO when, everything considered, the Raiders had the better of a tight game against Melbourne. With the Raiders defending their line well, Sia Soliola took out the Storm's champion fullback Billy Slater in a high and late tackle, a tackle made under fatigue, that knocked Slater out. Outrage followed from a number of media commentators who should have known this sort of thing was not Solly's go at all. The mood of the game changed and the Storm held on for a 20–14 win. It was three tries each, with only goal kicks the difference, and it was another game that got away.

Fittingly for a season full of missed opportunities, missed chances, the Raiders went to Melbourne in round 26 with nothing to play for and lost easily 32–6, the Slater tackle in round twenty still thick in the air because it was Soliola's return game after a five-game suspension.

In 2017 the Raiders scored the third-highest number of points in the NRL, the team had a better points differential than four of the eight teams that made the play-offs and Jordan Rapana exploded for a 21-try season. But there was no escaping the stark facts. The side finished tenth, with eleven wins and thirteen losses. One newspaper tagged them 'the big flops of the year' and it was hard to disagree.

Unfortunately, 2018 played out in much the same way. This time around, however, there were several clear reasons, some self-inflicted, some not, contributing to the under-achieving performance. The team again finished tenth, despite having scored the second-highest number of points during the season of all NRL clubs. Only Souths scored more. Raider attack was visibly alive and well. Raider defence, on the other hand, continued to open up and leak tries at the worst times, usually in the last twenty minutes of the game. The Rabbitohs only exceeded the Raiders points tally when they won their round 26 game by a big margin while the Raiders lost another close one, 20–16, in Auckland. If the Raiders had won well, they would have been in possession of an unwanted record as the first side to score the most points in a season and miss the play-offs. No team had managed that since Rugby League began in 1908.

It could have been so different had Josh Hodgson not torn his anterior cruciate ligament playing for England in the World Cup, thus missing over half the season; it could have been different if Jack Wighton had not been involved in a drunken brawl in Civic before the season began and, later found guilty of five counts of assault, was banned by the NRL for ten games and subsequently sat out a vital part of the season; it could have been different if the Raiders had not lost their opening four games, the first three of them by a total of five points; and it could have been so utterly different if leads in games, sometimes substantial leads, had not been squandered at the death. The Raiders were in all but three games during the year, only 'a bee sting' behind some of the teams near the top of the ladder, to use Sia Soliola's phrase, and yet they finished with an unflattering ten wins and fourteen losses.

Some analysts before the season began asked the unavoidable question: 'Is Canberra's big forward pack too big?' The NRL's reduction in interchanges did expose a few of the big boppers in the last minutes of games, and this was noted by the coaching staff. In their round five game against the Bulldogs, the Raiders broke a four-game losing streak to start the season. The newspapers all ran theatrical photos of a relieved, fist-pumping Ricky Stuart jumping for joy—but that came after the previous week's spray when he described his side's performance as 'soft' ten times in the space of two minutes in a post-match interview. The comments only worked temporarily. In the run-up to the round 22 game against the Tigers, Stuart again went public when he put his forwards on notice to shape up or consider their options.

Defence had been the dominant problem all year long, in fact for a number of seasons, and an improved performance in the last few rounds did nothing to paper over the cracks. Something had to be done to get the team's perennially suspect defence to actively reinforce its perennially potent attacking flair. During the season Blake Austin confirmed that he would like to play in England, and the two giants of a gigantic pack, Junior Paulo and Shannon Boyd, accepted attractive offers to leave, Paulo returning to Parramatta and Boyd off to join the Gold Coast Titans. The Raiders' salary cap then had some relief to enable the club to go shopping in the new year.

In 2017 and 2018 everyone suffered a little. It took Raiders' Board Chairman Allan Hawke to put things into proper perspective in his end-of-year summary. He acknowledged the widespread disappointment. However, he remained confident that the building blocks of success were being conscientiously attended to through the creation of a values-based environment he called 'the Raiders Way'. A mature and resilient culture was being steadily forged through a belief in the important symbolic value of the club's distinguished history. When Ricky Stuart's coaching contract was locked in by the board until the end of 2020, it was a proactive move based in part on his cultural leadership. That he was a 'great ambassador' for the club, as Hawke put it, was self-evident. Stuart's enthusiasm, loyalty, heart-on-sleeve emotion, refusal to let the club be pushed around at NRL level—these were character traits that appealed to the green-eyed masses as well as a board anxious to rediscover long-term winning ways.

Ricky Stuart turned 51 in 2018. A Raider legend, he longs for the day when he is not nostalgically referred to as the Raiders' last premiership halfback. He wants a fourth Raider premiership, and after that, more of the same.

His players know this only too well. The wise Sia Soliola, in-house spiritual leader, refers to it as a Raiders 'movement' that will get its hands on another premiership sometime soon. Perhaps Stuart's most important achievement in his years at the club so far has been his restoration of Canberra as a player's destination of choice. The days of players reneging on agreements, playing in Sydney for less money, are gone. Joey Leilua is on record as saying that at the Raiders he has 'grown into a man ... It was the culture here ... that's what made me stay.

I just love it.' And from Jarrod Croker: 'My number-one goal for the club is premierships and that's why I'm hanging around.' The same is true for a cohort of quality players who have recently re-signed longer contracts—among them Jack Wighton, Nic Cotric, Jordan Rapana, Aidan Sezer, Josh Papalii, Joe Tapine and the two ultra-professional Englishmen, Josh Hodgson and Elliott Whitehead.

The coach has been so impressed by his English imports that, before the start of the 2019 season, he once more revisited the untapped UK market and signed two additional players from the Old Dart—John Bateman, who has already played a number of games for England, and Ryan Sutton, on the shortlist to play for his country. They have integrated seamlessly, appreciating the cool of a Canberra winter and a community atmosphere that all four Englishman have said reminds them of their former clubs back home. When Bateman was interviewed at the Raiders launch of the 2019 season and was asked what his goals were in Australia, he replied with a heavy Yorkshire accent, 'to win stoof [stuff]'. This was music to green ears.

The Stuart era as coach of the Raiders remains unfinished, a work in progress, a book yet to have its later chapters written. He senses something special happening within a playing group where new leaders, respected leaders, are emerging. And he is not alone. While results are critical in professional sport, it is heartening to have one of the Raiders' all-time champion products on the job, confident in his philosophy and relishing the immediate task in front of him:

> This club is bigger than everybody, it's bigger than me, it's bigger than the players, we've just got to work hard and do our best while we're here. That's where the players have really bought in. I've got some great coaches helping me and I believe the culture we're growing and developing is heading in the right direction.

The club is in good hands.

7

TIES THAT BIND

In early March 1982 when the Canberra Raiders were set to begin their inaugural season in the NSWRL, founder and patriarch Les McIntyre counselled enthusiasts of the ambitious venture that they 'should not expect miracles'. It was sage advice. Miracles were few on the ground for the lime-green teams in the first years, though effort and old-fashioned guts were there for all to see. Bonds were formed in adversity among the players, coaching staff, board room and the community that formed the backbone of the club. Created initially through an awkward sporting link between a historic country town in the southern reaches of New South Wales and a young capital city, the Raiders club quickly found its feet. Widely expected to fail, within half a dozen years it had become a model of enterprise and success for the rest of the league.

The experience and smarts of the Raiders' first coach, Don Furner, played a key part in this process. He had already put his winning stamp on local Rugby League through the feats of the Queanbeyan Blues in the 1970s, a dynasty that made Furner an obvious choice to coach the NSWRL's newest team. Inevitably, the first squads he put together relied heavily on the rugby league stocks of the region. Bustling country towns such as Goulburn, Crookwell, Albury, Young, Junee, Holbrook, Yass, Goulburn, Cooma and, of course, Queanbeyan supplied a steady flow of aspirational bush footballers. In 1985–86, Furner and Raiders Secretary John McIntyre went further afield, recruiting some top-drawer talent from Queensland, a football stronghold Furner knew well from his own playing days. After the signing of Mal Meninga, a future Immortal of the game, other players from the northern state followed, keen to play with him, most of them destined to play for their country.

Miracles started to happen. The new team on the block, dubbed the 'Green Machine' for the precision of its attacking football, went on a dazzling run of five grand finals and three premierships in eight years, in the process introducing the Rugby League world to the sheer joy and creativity of Raiders football. Meninga famously said that the Raiders played the game the way it should be played. It has proven to be a seductive product.

During leaner times since, Raider teams have continued to play football based on free-flowing attack rather than dour defence. They are a wonderful team to watch.

But the club's contribution to the game extends beyond the on-field brilliance of the glory years of the late 1980s and 1990s. The Raiders' third coach, Tim Sheens, headed to the nation's capital in 1988 to guide a team on the rise. His nine years in Canberra effectively changed the face of Rugby League. It is widely accepted that master coaches Jack Gibson and Warren Ryan shaped the first defining period of the modern game, influencing the likes of Phil Gould. Sheens refined the techniques of old in his years at the Raiders, giving full expression to a range of innovative ideas on and off the field that a number of his players studiously absorbed and selectively copied.

Jump ahead 25 years. The Canberra Raiders' university of coaching under 'Professor' Sheens has directly or indirectly produced two coaches of the national team, five State of Origin coaches, five NRL premiership-winning coaches, another seven NRL coaches and three assistant coaches. A selection of notable graduates includes Craig Bellamy, Mal Meninga, Ricky Stuart, Laurie Daley, David Furner, Neil Henry, Michael Maguire, Anthony Seibold, Kevin Walters, Dean Lance and Andrew McFadden.

Appearing on Channel Nine's *The Footy Show* a few years ago, Daley said that Tim Sheens 'is a great student of the game . . . If you ask all of the coaches who had anything to do with Tim they would say he's top of the tree.' Craig Bellamy and Ricky Stuart responded to Sheens' thoroughness, his meticulous match preparation that emphasised structured training, video reviewing and canny variations of a broad game plan according to your own team's strengths against a particular opponent. For some Sheens graduates, it was about what they learned in terms of on-field strategies and innovations; others responded to his subtle approach to man-management.

Mal Meninga is the best example of a coach who has mastered the way professional footballers should be handled. Coaching the Raiders in the NRL for six years, week in, week out, did not suit his strengths. Once he began coaching the Queensland State of Origin team he flourished, condensing a mix of the Sheens blueprint with his own mature assessment of what he had to offer players of heightened ability. Meninga's decade as the Queensland coach—a period of maroon domination—and now as Australian coach, speak for themselves. Trevor 'the Axe' Gillmeister said recently that when it came to man-management, Meninga is 'the best I've seen'.

In the same way that the Raiders' coaching network has become entrenched across the league, so the club's best-practice cultural program (fostered in-house by Jason Mathie, Ben Pollack and their communications and marketing team) is an NRL leader of the pack. The 'Forever Green' rounds of recent years, when a home game during the season is used to celebrate a notable event or achievement of the past, has been a runaway success. In the 2018 season it attracted over 80 former players, many of them travelling long distances to participate. Every player, past and present, has his place on the Raiders' egalitarian honour roll: from David Grant, the club's inaugural first-grade captain, Raider number two all-time (with only Les McIntyre, the symbolic number one ahead of him) through to Tom Starling, a promising youngster who came off the bench in 2019, Raider number 362.

Brett Dickson, one of the most popular individuals in the Raider organisation, has looked after the program in his role as 'football assistant'. Known to all as 'The Count' because of his resemblance to the Sesame Street character, Brett continues to instil the club's values into the present-day players, going the extra yards by hosting weekly quizzes on the history of the club and putting together video presentations of ex-players. Bonding initiatives of this kind help to take the players' minds off saturation football activities at the same time as they develop humility, respect and loyalty within the group. It comes as no surprise that one of the Raiders' own, Quentin Pongia, when battling a cancer that would end his life in May 2019, far too early, received several calls daily to check on his wellbeing. Once in the Raider family, always in the Raider family.

The examples of Ricky Stuart and Alan Tongue continue to be sources of inspiration to a playing group that now puts in many hundreds of hours per year working voluntarily for a number of charities. In the coach's case, he has dedicated himself to a cause close to his and his wife Kaylie's hearts—their daughter Emma's autism. Well aware that the facilities for autistic kids in the ACT and across Australia were inadequate, the Stuarts set about helping to address the problem. The result in 2016 was 'Ricky Stuart House', a partnership between the Ricky Stuart Foundation and the ACT government that produced a purpose-built respite centre for children aged between five and twelve who have autism or other disabilities. With the strategic input of Foundation Director John Mackay, a former CEO of ActewAGL and chancellor of the University of Canberra, the foundation in June 2018 opened a second facility, appropriately named 'Emma Ruby Stuart House', to assist the families of young people with autism aged twelve to eighteen.

'We're just getting warmed up,' Mackay commented at the time, and he was right. A third facility is in the works.

Since retiring from football in 2011, Alan Tongue has been the spark for many worthy initiatives, just as he was every weekend on the paddock for the Raiders. The ACT's candidate for Australian of the Year in 2016, Tongue was recognised for his youth intervention and rehabilitation programs with the Bimberi Youth Justice Centre, the Alexander Maconochie Centre and disengaged youth in Canberra's schools. Continuing to work closely with the ACT Government more recently, Tongue has developed the 'STOP.THINK. Say No to Family Violence Program' and 'The Aspire Program' in order to pursue social justice goals. Once a captain, always a captain.

When John Mackay retired as a Raiders board member in February 2019, after almost two decades of invaluable service, he summed up the change he had witnessed: 'I've watched the Raiders go from being a great team to being a great community citizen.' The crowds, too, are back and membership numbers are hitting new highs. In 2018, the magic number of 20,000 members was surpassed, a far cry from the difficulties experienced in the aftermath of Super League, when the club was flat-out reaching a third of that number. The community pact between the club and its supporters, such an exhilarating feature of the years when premierships flowed, has been restored.

At the beginning of 2020 the Raiders will officially open a new Canberra District Rugby League Centre of Excellence in the inner-city suburb of Braddon, a complex that includes an oval with a rich history going back to 1927, the year that the village of Hall dominated local Rugby League and the year that the doors of the Provisional (now Old) Parliament House opened to usher in a new national capital city. The high-performance training facility will occupy one of the region's spiritual homes of early Rugby League. It could not be better chosen or more timely.

When visitors to Canberra walk through the new centre, one of the first things they will see is a Canberra Raiders Hall of Fame, a gathering of some of the code's greatest-ever players to proudly wear the distinctive green jersey, alongside iconic slices of the club's illustrious history. That is as it should be.

The Canberra Raiders have enlightened and invigorated Rugby League's story.

KEY SOURCES

Books

Adams, Tony, *Masters of the Game*, Ironbark, Sydney (1996).

Armstrong, Geoff (compiler), *The Greatest Game: A Celebration of Rugby League*, Ironbark, Sydney (2011).

Beikoff, Katrina, *Rugby League: A Modern History 1966-2008*, Gold Coast (2015).

Canberra Times, *25 Years in the Limelight: Canberra Raiders*, Canberra Times (2006).

Daily Telegraph, *100 Years of Rugby League* (to 2006).

Daley, Laurie and Bradley Clyde (with Daniel Lane), *Laurie and Clyde: Young Guns of Rugby League*, Ironbark, Sydney (1995).

Daley, Laurie (with David Middleton), *Laurie: Always a Winner*, HarperCollins, Sydney (2000).

Dennis, N.A., *Canberra Raiders: The First Three Years*, Canberra District Rugby League (1984).

Downie, Graham, *Living on the Edge: The Life of John Mackay*, Halstead, Canberra (2015).

Gillespie, Lyall L., *Ginninderra, Forerunner to Canberra: A History of the Ginninderra District*, L.L. Gillespie, Canberra (1992).

Gillespie, Lyall L., *Early Verse of the Canberra Region*, L.L. Gillespie, Canberra (1994).

Headon, David and Lex Marinos, *League of a Nation*, ABC Books, Sydney (1996).

Heads, Ian and David Middleton, *A Centenary of Rugby League 1908–2008*, Pan Macmillan, Sydney (2008).

Kelly, Roslyn, *A Passionate Life*, Hardie Grant, Melbourne (2017).

Lea-Scarlett, Errol, *Queanbeyan: District and People*, Queanbeyan Municipal Council (1968).

MacDonald, John, *Big Mal: The Inspiring Story of Mal Meninga*, Lester-Townsend Publishing, Sydney (1990).

MacDonald, John, *Meninga: From Superstar to Super League*, Ironbark, Sydney (1995).

McKernan, Michael, *The Brumbies: The Super Twelve Years*, Allen & Unwin, Sydney (2006).

Meninga, Mal (with Alan Clarkson), *Meninga: My Life in Football*, HarperSports, Sydney (1995).

Moore, Andrew, *The Mighty Bears!* Macmillan, Sydney (1996).
Selth, Don, *More Than a Game: Canberra's Sporting Heritage 1854–1954*, Ginninderra Press, Adelaide (2010).

Newspapers and magazines

- *Arrow*
- *Big League*
- *Canberra Times*
- *Daily Telegraph*
- *Daily Telegraph Mirror*
- *Goulburn Evening Penny Post*
- *Labor Daily*
- *Queanbeyan Age*
- *Queanbeyan Leagues Club Journal*
- *Referee*
- *Rugby League Week*
- *Sun-Herald*
- *Sydney Monitor*
- *Sydney Morning Herald*
- *Sunday Telegraph*
- *The Australian*
- *The Raider*

Note

While footnote references have not been used, throughout the text every effort has been made to indicate the source of quotations.

THE CANBERRA RAIDERS

Raider no.	First name	Surname	Raider no.	First name	Surname
1	Les	McIntyre	25	Wayne	Stonham
2	David	Grant	26	Craig	Bellamy
3	Gerry	De La Cruz	27	Rowan	Brennan
4	Carl	Frommel	28	Gary	Britt
5	Jon	Hardy	29	Peter	Elliott
6	Jay	Hoffman	30	Graham	Waugh
7	Lloyd	Martin	31	Angel	Marina
8	Peter	McGrath	32	Ashley	Gilbert
9	John	McLeod	33	John	Algate
10	Steve	O'Callaghan	34	Lui	Bon
11	Chris	O'Grady	35	Col	Brinkley
12	Frank	Roddy	36	Ray	Blacklock
13	Jeff	Simons	37	Terry	Fahey
14	Sam	Vucago	38	Ron	Giteau
15	Scott	Dudman	39	Percy	Knight
16	Michael	Tilse	40	Allan	McMahon
17	Richard	Cooke	41	Gary	Spears
18	Paul	West	42	Mark	Brennan
19	Ian	Hamilton	43	Sam	Backo
20	Allan	Smith	44	Steve	Keir
21	Terry	Wickey	45	Paul	Elliott
22	David	Reid	46	Gary	Wurth
23	Bruce	Bacchetto	47	Grant	Ellis
24	Chris	O'Sullivan	48	Wayne	Jensen

Raider no.	First name	Surname	Raider no.	First name	Surname
49	Chris	Kinna	92	Brian	Battese
50	David	Newham	93	Wayne	Collins
51	Dean	Lance	94	Dean	Lonergan
52	Bill	Walker	95	Chris	Houghton
53	Jamie	Jones	96	Robbie	Collins
54	Ron	Sigsworth	97	Bradley	Clyde
55	Ivan	Henjak	98	Ricky	Stuart
56	Nigel	Wilson	99	Phil	Hurst
57	Matthew	Corkery	100	Mark	Bell
58	Mick	Aldous	101	Ron	Coskerie
59	Robert	Dunning	102	Craig	Dimond
60	Brett	Atkins	103	Matthew	Wood
61	Phil	Carey	104	Perry	Smith
62	Peter	Davis	105	Mark	Lowry
63	Terry	Regan	106	Darren	Fritz
64	Michael	Blake	107	Paul	Beath
65	Paul	Thompson	108	Michael	Twigg
66	Brad	Williams	109	Nigel	Gaffey
67	Kevin	Beardmore	110	Andrew	Halley
68	Darren	Waters	111	David	Barnhill
69	Mike	Smith	112	Stephen	Mills
70	Les	Morrissey	113	Stuart	Stanton
71	Jamie	McInnes	114	Roger	Kenworthy
72	Gary	Wilson	115	David	Woods
73	Gary	Belcher	116	Steve	Stone
74	Gary	Coyne	117	Craig	Breen
75	John	Ferguson	118	Brett	Mullins
76	Mal	Meninga	119	Scott	Gale
77	Darren	Meredith	120	Glenn	Ryan
78	Steve	Walters	121	Darrell	McDonald
79	Paul	Martin	122	Jason	Death
80	Mitch	Brennan	123	Brett	Boyd
81	Alfie	Walker	124	Jason	Croker
82	Paul	Young	125	David	Boyle
83	Jim	Antonakos	126	Matthew	Baker
84	Peter	Jackson	127	Jason	Gregory
85	Brent	Todd	128	Alex	Corvo
86	Kevin	Walters	129	Paul	Jones
87	David	Paterson	130	Michael	Harrison
88	Laurie	Daley	131	Sean	Hoppe
89	Steve	Jackson	132	Paul	Osborne
90	Glenn	Lazarus	133	Phil	Blake
91	Tim	Wilby	134	Brett	Hetherington

Raider no.	First name	Surname	Raider no.	First name	Surname
135	David	Furner	178	Steve	Collins
136	Shawn	Rubesaame	179	Royston	Lightning
137	Brad	Mansfield	180	Todd	Payten
138	David	Gray	181	Damon	Booby
139	Kris	Tassell	182	Matthew	Gafa
140	James	Hunt	183	Luke	Priddis
141	Glenn	Cannon	184	Geoff	McNamara
142	Brad	Foster	185	Craig	O'Neall
143	Brendan	Norton	186	Barry	Lea
144	Michael	Maguire	187	David	Atkins
145	Ian	Graham	188	Darren	Shaw
146	Ken	Nagas	189	Tim	Van Dalen
147	Michael	Spinks	190	Andrew	McFadden
148	John	Lomax	191	Ben	Rauter
149	Quentin	Pongia	192	Brandon	Costin
150	Mark	Corvo	193	Nathan	Sologinkin
151	Noa	Nadruku	194	Anthony	Seibold
152	Jimmy	Veikoso	195	Mark	McLinden
153	Ruben	Wiki	196	Lesley	Vainikolo
154	Albert	Fulivai	197	Anthony	Brann
155	Trevor	Schodel	198	Danny	Lima
156	David	Westley	199	Rod	Jensen
157	Steve	Trindall	200	Damian	Kennedy
158	Peter	Benson	201	Rod	Maybon
159	Bruce	Mamando	202	Luke	Williamson
160	Ric	Emmanuel	203	Jerome	Guisset
161	David	Lomax	204	David	Schrader
162	Jason	Burnham	205	Brett	Finch
163	Luke	Davico	206	Brad	Kelly
164	Martin-John	Kelly	207	Anthony	Colella
165	Simon	Woolford	208	Anthony	Swann
166	Graham	Appo	209	Nathan	Barnes
167	Salesi	Finau	210	Justin	Morgan
168	David	Cox	211	Alan	Tongue
169	Shaun	Mahony	212	Greg	Wolfgramm
170	Ben	Kennedy	213	Terry	Martin
171	Jamie	Kennedy	214	Lincoln	Withers
172	Jason	Ferris	215	Jamaal	Lolesi
173	Adam	Peters	216	Sean	Rutgerson
174	Bert	Tabuai	217	Shane	Kelly
175	Daniel	Baker	218	Sione	Faumuina
176	Luke	Phillips	219	Clinton	Schifcofske
177	Jeremy	Robinson	220	Darren	Mapp

Raider no.	First name	Surname	Raider no.	First name	Surname
221	Ryan	O'Hara	264	Colin	Best
222	Michael	Hodgson	265	Michael	Dobson
223	Odell	Manuel	266	Glen	Turner
224	Joel	Monaghan	267	Neville	Costigan
225	Darren	Porter	268	Andrew	Dunemann
226	Michael	Monaghan	269	Scott	Logan
227	Jarred	Lawrence	270	Joe	Picker
228	Michael	Robertson	271	Brett	Kelly
229	Troy	Thompson	272	Ryan	Hinchcliffe
230	James	Evans	273	Bronx	Goodwin
231	Tyran	Smith	274	Brad	Cross
232	Phillip	Graham	275	Nigel	Plum
233	Mark	Bryant	276	Matt	Bickerstaff
234	James	Buser	277	Glen	Buttriss
235	Mark	Asbock	278	Justin	Carney
236	Brad	Drew	279	Marc	Herbert
237	Ian	Hindmarsh	280	Joel	Thompson
238	Adam	Mogg	281	Bronson	Harrison
239	Jason	Bulgarelli	282	David	Shillington
240	Michael	Weyman	283	Stuart	Flanagan
241	Ben	Cross	284	Jarrod	Croker
242	Terry	Campese	285	Travis	Waddell
243	Josh	Miller	286	Josh	Dugan
244	Alan	Rothery	287	Shaun	Fensom
245	Kris	Kahler	288	Josh	McCrone
246	Todd	Carney	289	Daniel	Vidot
247	Nathan	Smith	290	Danny	Galea
248	Marshall	Chalk	291	Reece	Robinson
249	Matt	Adamson	292	James	Stuart
250	Craig	Frawley	293	Drury	Low
251	David	Howell	294	Sam	Mataora
252	Jason	Smith	295	Blake	Ferguson
253	Andrew	Lomu	296	Sam	Williams
254	Jermaine	Ale	297	Brett	White
255	Jason	Williams	298	Matt	Orford
256	David	Milne	299	Nathan	Massey
257	Ben	Jones	300	Josh	Papalii
258	Adrian	Purtell	301	Michael	Picker
259	Willie	Raston	302	Shaun	Berrigan
260	Tom	Learoyd-Lahrs	303	Jack	Wighton
261	William	Zillman	304	Jarrad	Kennedy
262	Trevor	Thurling	305	Matt	McIlwrick
263	Dane	Tilse	306	Edrick	Lee

Raider no.	First name	Surname	Raider no.	First name	Surname
307	Dimitri	Pelo	335	Lachlan	Croker
308	Sandor	Earl	336	Joseph	Tapine
309	Mark	Nicholls	337	Clay	Priest
310	Joel	Edwards	338	Junior	Paulo
311	Anthony	Milford	339	Zac	Santo
312	Jake	Foster	340	Adam	Clysdale
313	Paul	Vaughan	341	Nick	Cotric
314	Sami	Sauiluma	342	Dunamis	Lui
315	Bill	Tupou	343	Scott	Sorensen
316	Matt	Allwood	344	Dave	Taylor
317	Shannon	Boyd	345	Royce	Hunt
318	Kyle	O'Donnell	346	Michael	Oldfield
319	Mitch	Cornish	347	Siliva	Havili
320	Brenko	Lee	348	Charlie	Gubb
321	Kurt	Baptiste	349	Liam	Knight
322	Jordan	Rapana	350	Ata	Hingano
323	Jeremy	Hawkins	351	Brad	Abbey
324	Blake	Austin	352	Jack	Murchie
325	Josh	Hodgson	353	Emre	Guler
326	Sia	Soliola	354	John	Bateman
327	Sisa	Waqa	355	Charnze	Nicoll-Klokstad
328	Luke	Bateman	356	Bailey	Simonsson
329	Frank-Paul	Nuuausala	357	Corey	Horsburgh
330	Joey	Leilua	358	Ryan	Sutton
331	Mitch	Barnett	359	Hudson	Young
332	Aidan	Sezer	360	JJ	Collins
333	Elliott	Whitehead	361	Sebastian	Kris
334	Jeff	Lima	362	Tom	Starling

INDEX